ANNA'S WAR

DAVID C. WILLIAMS

Copyright page

Publisher's Name: David C. Williams

ISBN: 978-1-962142-46-5

CONTENTS

Preface

A little over a decade ago, I was so inspired by a science fiction movie that I felt compelled to write a sequel. In only three months, the story virtually "wrote itself." Whether that story will ever see the light of day is up to the movie company involved. I did, however, find that I enjoyed writing and decided to marry two of the great loves in my life: writing and military history.

So, it was somewhat of an irony that the same "A-List" actress who helped inspire my interest in writing in the first place inspired this novel. After doing several "Period" movies in a row, she was asked by a reporter if there was any "Period" that she would especially like to make a movie about. She replied that since her family had emigrated from Romania, she thought it would be interesting to do a movie about that country during the Second World War.

Aha, I thought. I have always had a particular interest in the "Eastern Front", as the Germans referred to it. I could write that story in my sleep. Two years of research later, I was ready to put it on paper. I found that I was very touched by the terrible dilemma that Romania found itself in as war engulfed all of Europe. It had to choose whether to follow the Nazi fascists led by Adolf Hitler or the equally fanatical communists under Stalin. What follows is the story of Romania's participation in that struggle. Question: Which side did Romania fight on in World War II? Answer: Both... it supplied the third-largest Axis army in Europe and the Fourth-largest Allied army.

Many people here in the "West" have heard little or nothing of Romania's participation in World War II, but that doesn't mean that it wasn't a horrible trial for the people involved. Indeed, Romania's "junior partner" status made its trial all the more devastating. Our fictitious protagonist, Anna Tompchin, is a surrogate for the Romanian people as a whole, as she travels through the hell that was the most merciless of battle fronts. The events that she witnesses and participates in are actual events as they would have been seen through her eyes.

If you find yourself sympathizing with young Anna, perhaps you will achieve a similar feeling for the Romanian people who are only now, with the fall of the "Iron Curtain," awakening from the nightmare that began for them in 1941.

CHAPTER I

The adventure begins

Now that my short life is almost over, I feel strangely relieved. It is as if the muzzle of the Luger pistol pressed against the back of my neck is an answer to all the worries that have plagued me for the last three years. No longer will I have to wonder if the soldier whose life I am saving will take the life of another. I will not have to watch as my friends die before my eyes or are maimed for the rest of their lives. The nine-millimeter bullet that will soon smash into my brain will relieve the pain of a dead family and an orphaned little brother whose only hope for the future lies in his becoming a good communist.

The Nazi Colonel's grip on my arm is so tight that my hand is going to sleep as we walk down the center of the boulevard. I am supposed to be his human shield, though my five-foot-two-inch height will do him little good if one of the many weapons aimed our way should be fired. If that happens, the truce will be broken and the battle will begin again. I won't have to worry about that either since I will be dead. It is my word, and life, that guarantee this fragile truce I have negotiated.

As his men advance from cover to cover along the sides of the street, the colonel presses the gun more and more forcefully against my neck until I finally have to say, "Hans…if you are going to kill me use a bullet, don't try breaking my neck with that thing."

"Be quiet, you Jew whore!" he snarls.

"That is no way to talk to someone who is saving your life," I said. "And if I am a whore, I'm one whose pants you never got into." I know

I shouldn't provoke a man with a gun, but I just can't resist. I pay for it when he draws the pistol back a few inches and rams it into the back of my skull.

I don't cry out, but the pain makes my eyes tear so that I almost don't notice the building we are passing. When my eyes clear, I can see that we were in front of the railway passenger station. It was this same station from which my adventure began almost three years ago. I had just turned 18 years old…and I was going to save the world.

***

My two suitcases weighed me down like a pair of anchors on a sinking ship as I struggled along the station platform. Between them, they must have weighed very nearly my own weight of 102 lb. Each one of those starched uniforms and every pair of those shiny nurse's shoes had seemed vital when my mother and I packed them. That early in the war, neither one of us suspected that I would one day be discarding nearly all those crisp and neat clothes for the bloodstained combat uniforms and rugged combat boots no longer needed by the dead and maimed soldiers that I was on my way to help.

As usual, I was running late. Not only that, but I was on the wrong platform. My train was one platform over from where I stood, and I just knew that by the time I could struggle back to the station with my heavy bags and cross over to the correct platform, my train would be pulling out.

Never having been one to let silly rules stand in my way, I ignored the signs posted every few meters and slipped off the edge of the platform. I dropped down next to the first set of tracks, which were thankfully empty, and started across them towards my train. I was already having second thoughts about all the clothes I had packed into my suitcases as I struggled over the two sets of rails towards the other platform. I had to cross the second set of rails just ahead of the engine where it sat, belching smoke and steam from its stack. Steam also rolled out from around the four huge driving wheels, each one taller than I am.

As I passed in front of the engine the whistle screeched loudly causing me to jump the last meter to the side of the platform in spite of my heavy bags. I wasn't sure if the train was about to get under way or if the engineer was just having fun with me. With my heart hammering in my chest, I realized that my usual lack of planning had gotten me in trouble again. How was I going to get up onto the platform? It was almost as high as my shoulders, and I was wearing a cursed full-length nurse's dress with a full slip under that. Using both arms, I swung my bags up one at a time, but there were no steps or ladders anywhere for me to climb.

I did the only thing I could. I climbed up the sloping cowcatcher on the front of the train. From there I stepped onto the cylinder of the front bumper that protruded from the engine. *Thank God, they let us wear flat shoes.* A short leap from the bumper landed me on the platform, although not very gracefully. I only avoided landing on my face by scuffing up both hands on the rough concrete.

Wiping the grit out of the palms of my hands, I retrieved my bags and looked up to find that my antics had been observed by no less than the headmistress of my nursing school, Miss Lovinescu. Behind her, my best friend Maria Banis and the rest of the girls from the school were also staring in my direction.

Ms. Lovinescu's expression was neutral, but her eyes could have melted iron. Maria's puffed-out cheeks, pursed lips, and bulging eyes told me that if Miss Lovinescu hadn't been present, she would be wetting herself with laughter. I carried my bags over to the group, trying to look as nonchalant and innocent as possible. I curtsied slightly and said, in the manner appropriate to the person who controlled nearly every aspect of your life. "Good morning, Miss Lovinescu."

Instead of the rebuke I was expecting, she greeted me with a question that seemed, at first, to be altogether irrelevant. "Anna, do you know why they paint these steam engines black?" When I hesitated to answer due to my confusion Miss Lovinescu answered her own question. "It is because the black doesn't show how dirty they are." With that, her eyes quit drilling holes through my head and dropped to the front of my dress.

I followed her gaze downward to find my white nurse's uniform covered with soot smudges everywhere. Even worse, there were several grease smears as well. I almost began to cry as I thought of the hours and hours that my mother and I had spent hand scrubbing and bleaching my brand-new clothes until they fairly glowed. When I brushed at the soot streaks they only spread into larger and larger stains.

Abruptly losing interest in my sorry state, Miss Lovinescu turned to the other girls and said, "Time to get on the train, girls. Be sure you have all your bags and follow me." She then quickly climbed the steps into the first passenger coach. As the other nursing students followed her up the steps one by one, I couldn't help but picture a duck and her chicks crossing the street. Last in line, Maria finally broke down and laughed out loud, saying, "Anna, you're such a silly fool."

Everyone says that I have a complexion as pale as porcelain, but from the heat I could feel in my cheeks, I am sure I was as red as the numbers on the train's engine. I tried to think of something stinging to say in return, but I could come up with nothing quickly enough, so I just squinted my eyes and stuck out my tongue. This just made Maria laugh that much harder. Once into the coach, we all tried to get seats as far away from Miss Lovinescu as possible so that we could gossip freely. All except Girta, that is. That short, stocky, moon-faced girl was the teacher's pet and sat right next to the tall, dour-looking spinster. When the remaining four of us found two empty seats to one side of the car that were next to each other, I said, "Oh dear, they are all facing in the same direction. It's going to be hard to talk amongst ourselves that way.

Maria immediately adopted her superior tone of voice to enlighten me. "You really are a little fool, aren't you, Anna?" With that, she reached out and flipped the back of one of the seats over so that they were facing each other.

I knew that Maria was more traveled than me, and at age 20, she was a whole two years older. But sometimes, like this one, I would have liked to smack her. The other girls put their bags on the overhead shelf. Maria, who is a head taller than me, took my bags from my hands. With a smirk, she tossed them onto the shelf. *If Maria is my best friend, why do I fantasize about smacking her so often?* We had no sooner taken our seats, then the train lurched and began moving slowly along the platform.

"Well, our great adventure begins," said Maria as she removed her nurse's cap and shook out her long hair.

With my coal-black hair hardly reaching my collar, I couldn't help but feel a brief pang of jealousy at Maria's natural blond color. I suppose it was this jealousy that made me want to attack Maria's optimism when I replied. "This isn't going to be any picnic in the park. They wouldn't be asking for volunteer help if the army's regular medical corps. weren't being over-taxed. That means a lot more casualties than the government is willing to admit."

My negative comments seemed to affect more than just Maria as everyone went silent for a moment. Then Sasha said, "You have to admit that they are offering us a good deal, though. One year of volunteer work in the field will count for both our remaining years of nursing school, and they are even paying us, instead of the other way around."

"That's all well and good," replied Maria. "But I don't know if I like being considered an army auxiliary. That means that we have to take orders just like a soldier."

At this, Elaine broke in. "How hard can that be? After all, we've been taking Miss Lovinescu's orders for two years now." We all chuckled quietly while casting furtive glances at the headmistress.

The train gathered speed as it rattled and rocked over numerous switches and sidings. We all grew silent as we watched the city of Bucharest slide slowly behind us. Even though I had been in that metropolis for two years, I was still impressed with the big city. As the train settled onto a steady northeasterly course towards our first destination of Buza, I had a twinge of homesickness. I realized that we would pass only thirty kilometers from my home in Ploiesti.

That rough and dirty town had been my home for the first sixteen years of my life. I had never lived anywhere else until I started attending nursing school in Bucharest. My father was an oil-field engineer in Ploiesti, where he had settled after fighting the Germans in the First World War. He met and married my mother there. I was born there, in a small company-owned house. I had attended the company-owned primary school and grown up with the smell of company-owned crude oil in my nose.

Despite the industrial nature of our small town, there were many horse-drawn wagons and farm animals in the immediate area. I grew up wanting only to care for these creatures, large and small. It was fortunate that I was not born a boy. If I had been, I would have been expected to follow in my father's footsteps and work for the oil company. As it was, I was allowed to attend the primary school and spend my free time patching up cats, dogs, and birds. Any creature with an injury would just seem to seek me out. Well, maybe I did go looking for them.

When I reached the end of my primary school days, I announced that I wanted to go to the university to become a veterinarian. That is when my father really laid down the law for me. He said that if I were to spend years in secondary schooling, costing him money the whole time, I should learn to care for people, not animals. That was how I came to be at the Bucharest School of Nursing under the stern tutelage of Miss Lovinescu.

I met my friend Maria, who was from Bucharest, at the school. She was used to the theaters and parks of the modern metropolis. As our friendship developed, she took me under her wing and showed me many of the sights of the city. I especially liked to walk down the street of tailors and look at the beautiful clothes, while Maria was more interested in the theaters and nightlife that the city offered.

As the imposing structures of the city fell behind, we began moving out into the green, rolling countryside. Once again, we began to talk amongst ourselves. Sasha, who was only a little taller than me, with brown hair and eyes, asked of no one in particular, "Do you think the war will last long enough for us to get our nursing certificates?"

Elaine, as tall as Maria but thin, with black hair and small gray eyes, answered, "It doesn't sound like it. Our troops are chasing the Russians out of the Ukraine already. The Germans will be in Moscow before winter. I think the Russians are almost done for."

Maria said, "You don't believe everything the radio says, do you? They'll never say anything negative." At this, I jumped in. "Maria is right. My father fought the Germans in the last war. He said that the citizens were never told the whole truth, only what they wanted to hear.

"I remember when I was fifteen; my father took me to the inauguration of the Peace Memorial. It was dedicated to the veterans of that war. He saw many of his army friends there, and they all said how awful war is.

They talked of living in the trenches for years. My father almost lost his leg to Trench-Foot."

Sasha said, "I know that wars are terrible, but sometimes you just have no choice. We've already taken Bessarabia back from those thieving Russians."

"Now we just need to get our new friends, the Germans, to force the Hungarians to give us back the part of Transylvania they took," added Elaine.

We all became quiet once again. We all knew that Elaine's family still lived in Bistrita. That unhappy city was in the part of Romania that the Germans had forced us to cede to Hungary.

How odd it must feel. When she came to nursing school, she was only going to a different city. Now, her family lives in another country.

Maria tried to lighten the mood. "When we've helped the Germans beat the communists, they will have to rethink their decision on Transylvania. And then we will take Dobrogea back from those sneaking Bulgarians."

"Those are all brave words," I said. "But first we have to win the war we're already in."

"Let's talk about something much more interesting than war," said Maria. "Let's talk about men."

"Yes Maria, let's hear about all your men," I said, trying to load as much sarcasm into my voice as possible. To my surprise, she didn't want to talk about any of her several boyfriends.

Instead, she said. "No, I mean your man. How is Peter doing, Anna?"

"Peter?" I asked, stalling for time. I really didn't want to share my memories of Peter with anyone, not even my best friend.

"Yes, Peter," said Maria. "You know. That handsome young intern that makes you act so dopey when he's around."

Trying to sound as matter-of-fact as possible as I felt my cheeks begin to burn, I said. "He was drafted as soon as he became a doctor."

Maria wasn't about to let me off the hook so easily. "I know that, you doe-eyed fool. I mean, have you had any letters from him?"

The other girls were all big-eyed and smiles of anticipation as they waited for my answer. But I was not going to be drawn into a discussion of the man I dearly loved and whom I was going to marry someday. I don't know how it is in the West, but in Romanian society, pre-marital sex is unheard of. Not that it isn't practiced; it's just not talked about.

I can't say that I am ashamed that I slept with Peter. After all, we *are* going to be married and it *was* his last night before getting shipped off to the army. Our lovemaking may have been pretty amateurish. After all, I was a virgin, and I think he was also. But despite the pain and the awkwardness, it was the most wonderful moment of my life.

And I wasn't about to share *that* with these nosy cows, so I just said, "He has written a couple of times and I have answered him once or twice. He can't say much because the censors read all the mail. He is somewhere on the Eastern Front with the Third Army."

Maria interrupted with, "But what does he say about the two of you?"

I finally put my foot down and said, "It's none of your business what he says!"

"That good?" Maria chuckled. "I think that he is really hot for you."

I was about to tell Maria where to put her big nose when Miss Lovinescu appeared beside our seat like a wraith from the dark. "We will be getting into Buzau in a few minutes," she said in her typically dour voice. "You young ladies will have fifteen minutes to stretch your legs before we continue. We will not have supper until we reach

Focsani, another one hundred and twenty kilometers farther north. Woe be unto any of you who are not back on the train when it begins moving." This last instruction was delivered while giving us all what we called the "Evil Eye."

We barely had time to take care of our "necessary business" when the train was on its way once again. As we were climbing the iron steps into our car, Sasha asked, "Did you see all those handsome soldiers in the station? I wonder what they were all doing there?"

This time Maria's sarcasm had a target other than me. "Sasha, where is your brain? Those soldiers have been following us all morning long. Only the first two cars of this train are for civilians like us, the rest are carrying soldiers. Why do you think this train has no luxuries, like a diner or sleeping cars?"

Sasha had no answer for Maria, but you could tell that she didn't care for Maria's air of superiority any more than I did. The fact that I hadn't thought of who else might be on the train either didn't need to be mentioned.

As the afternoon wore on, we watched the countryside pass outside our windows. Eastern Romania is a very fertile land. Since it was September, the farmers were busy getting many of their crops in. Most of the fields were covered with haystacks or corn shucks.

After a while, the "city girl" Maria said, "My God, I never knew there was so much open space in this country. With all those crops, why do we have rationing?"

"Because of the 'Cereals Acts,'" I replied. I could tell by the blank stares that greeted my comment that I would have to explain. "About a year ago... August of 1940, I think, we signed the 'Cereals Act' with Germany. It means that Germany gets first choice of all our cereal crops…even before we do."

"But that's silly," protested Sasha.

"Ha, you think that's silly," I continued. "Only three months before that, we signed all rights to our oil over to the Germans."

"But why would Romania agree to that?" asked Elaine.

I'm afraid that I was getting a little hot under the collar as I answered, "Like we had a choice? Germany had just defeated France and kicked the British off the continent. Who was going to stand up for us, America? I think not! Besides, the Germans are paying us for everything. We get all their old tanks and guns, plus some of what they took from the French. Of course, for that, we are expected to help them with their war against the Bolsheviks."

Elaine asked, "How do you know all this? You've been up to your ears in nurse's training ever since Germany invaded... er, I mean liberated Poland, just like the rest of us."

"My father writes me regularly. He may only be an oil-field worker, but he's no fool. After fighting in the last war, he keeps a pretty close eye on what goes on in the world. My little brother is only nine, so my mother and I are all the audience that my father has.

"Papa is a very opinionated man. He railed against the Communists in '38' when they arrested the Iron Guard. Then he railed against the Iron Guard in '40' when they arrested the Communists."

"But the Iron Guard are true patriots," insisted Sasha. "They are our only political party now."

"Sure," I said. "Since Antonescu forced King Carol to abdicate, only true patriots are allowed to live here."

My sarcasm must have been showing again because Elaine broke in. She whispered, "Quiet, you never know who is listening. Besides, the only real troublemakers in this country are the Jews. They control the banks, sell our secrets to the Russians, and even steal babies!"

"Jesus Christ, Elaine," said Maria hotly. "You are getting your Jew and Gypsy myths mixed up again! You don't really believe that Fascist crap..."

Maria's reply was cut short by my elbow in her ribs. Turning so that Maria was the only one who could see my face, I said. "Let's not talk about such unpleasant things." While I kept my voice light, my face and eyes pleaded with Maria to stop before too much was said.

You see, Maria was the only one at school who knew that my mother was a Hasidic Jew, while my father was a Russian Orthodox Christian. They met in Ploesti when my father settled there after the first war. If my mother had been from a more orthodox Jewish sect, they probably would never have even met.

As it was, they met, fell in love, and were married over the protests of both their families. This all happened during Romania's relatively brief period of official tolerance for all religions that followed the war but ended with the rise of the Iron Guard party. While my father was ostracized by his family, they eventually came to terms with it...more or less.

My mother wasn't so fortunate. Her family shunned her completely. To this day, I am very uncomfortable around anyone who, by their dress, shows themselves to be an orthodox Jew. The result of all this opposition was to cause my parents to say, "A pox on both your houses." Though they each maintain their own personal belief in God, they will have nothing to do with organized religion. They have each taught me the ways of their religions and then allowed me to develop my own beliefs, which I must say are somewhat confused. Because I have never practiced my religion through the organized church, I could see no purpose in bringing grief on myself by announcing my Jewish heritage. It seems that Jews are just not too popular in Europe. Now, with the systematic oppression of Jews by the Nazis spreading to the

Iron Guard here in Romania, I have simply decided to keep my past to myself.

That is why I wanted to avoid any discussion of Jewry. Besides, if Elaine went on with any more of her fairy stories, I would have probably had to either laugh in her face or hit her.

Sometimes I wonder if I am a bad person for having so many violent thoughts.

"All right," said Maria. "Miss Lovinescu is watching us anyway."

The train rolled into Focsani just before dark. We had a one-hour layover during which we had dinner at the station. The station gave the appearance of being very old and musty with its poorly lighted interior and crude wooden furnishings.

We had a very quiet discussion about nothing, since we were all seated at one table in Miss Lovinescu's presence. I thought the meal of sausage, cheese, and small, hard rolls was rather awful. Little did I know that in a matter of months, a meal like this would seem like a holiday feast. Apparently, the soldiers in the other cars were being fed on the train since there was no trace of any of them in the station.

These stops were not entirely for the benefit of the passengers. The train needed to take on water and refill the coal bunkers frequently. Speaking of coal, most of what the engine had burned during the trip had left the smokestack, only to settle on our white uniforms. Perhaps I should say our *formerly* white uniforms. At least I had the satisfaction of knowing that everyone's uniform was as dirty as mine now.

Even with a fresh meal in us, it was a rather weary group that climbed back onto the train for the next leg of our journey. By now it was dark, and all we wanted to do was sleep. Unfortunately, the lack of a sleeping car meant that we would have to do any sleeping we could, sitting up. As I watched Maria trying to get comfortable using the window as her pillow, I could see my reflection next to her in the darkened window glass. Compared to Maria's full lips and sexy bedroom eyes, I have eyes that are too big for my face and a mouth that is so... normal.

While Maria had only the window to rest her head against, I had a much softer pillow... Maria. Though I really did try to lean only on her shoulder, every time I began to drop off to sleep, my head would slide down onto her ample breast. I must say that she was very soft and comfortable. She was much better endowed than me since I was just then beginning to outgrow my "boyish figure" stage.

About the third time I slipped forward onto her chest, I began to chuckle uncontrollably. I suppose it was because I was so tired. Finally, Maria said, "Lean wherever you want, I'll just pretend that you are one of those handsome soldiers and have pleasant dreams. And quit giggling!"

Our train continued moving to the northeast through the night. Progress continued to be as slow as it had been all day because we frequently had to wait on sidings as military priority trains raced past.

After a short rest stop at Husi, our train crossed the Prut River into Bessarabia. This was the part of Romania that the Russians had occupied about a year before. By morning, we were pulling into Chisinau in central Bessarabia.

We hurried through our breakfast of porridge and biscuits so that we could take a brief look at the city before our train was due to pull out again. Even though Chisinau is the capital of Bessarabia, it isn't nearly as big as Bucharest. But it is as large a city as you would find in Bessarabia. As expected, Miss Lovinescu threw cold water on our plans by telling us not to get out of sight of the station under penalty of dire, but unspecified, punishment. Even so, we went out to the streets around the station to see what we could.

I was surprised by the lack of movement on the streets. True, it was still early in the morning, but in Bucharest, the streets would be teeming with pedestrians and traffic by now. A few moments later, I saw what I thought might explain the lack of traffic.

As a horse-drawn milk wagon turned the corner and started up the cobblestone street towards us, two policemen stepped from the curb to stop the wagon. They demanded the driver's papers for inspection. I noticed something odd about them. While one of them was indeed a city policeman, the other was a German soldier.

Once they were satisfied with the wagon driver's papers, he was allowed to go on his way. As the heavy wagon rumbled past us, I could see the policemen headed our way. For some reason, this made me nervous.

Stopping in front of the four of us, the Romanian policeman asked, "Are you ladies lost?" Maria, being the oldest, took it upon herself to answer for us. "No sir, we're just stretching our legs until our train leaves. We're from Bucharest."

The officer seemed impressed as he said, "Ah, Bucharest! And where could a group of lovely young ladies such as you be heading?"

We all smiled at the compliment as Maria answered. "We are going to the front, to join the army there, as nurses."

"Nurses," he repeated. "How very nice, you are beautiful *and* talented."

When we began to giggle at his continued compliments, the soldier beside him asked something in German. The policeman's answer was delivered in a halting German that he was obviously having difficulty with. In a moment, he returned his attention to us, saying. "*This gentleman* was asking me what you are doing here and where you are going." His pronunciation of "this gentleman" left no doubt that he was not happy to have the soldier looking over his shoulder.

Sasha asked, "What business is it of his? He's a German."

"It's his business because the Germans wish to weed out the undesirable elements from Bessarabia," was his reply.

"What undesirable elements?" I asked.

"Communist collaborators, spies, and any Jews that might be Russian sympathizers," was the disturbing answer.

"But the Russians only occupied Bessarabia for a year," I protested. "Surely no one collaborated with the communists while they were here."

"Probably very few did," he said. "But the Germans see this as an opportunity to 'clean house', you see."

As if he could understand Romanian, the German soldier said something sounding very cross to the policeman.

To us, the policeman said, "We must be moving along now. I suggest you ladies go back to your train and stay out of trouble." With that, the two of them resumed their walk down the street.

"Let's get back to the station," said Maria as she began herding us in that direction.

Sasha protested. "They can't tell us what to do. This is our country. They have no business..." "Be quiet, Sasha!" I cut her off, hoping that the soldier wouldn't hear her angry tone. "They have the right because they have the guns."

As we hurried back to the station, I noticed Miss Lovinescu watching us from the window in front of the station. She seemed to have a worried look on her face.

In a few moments, we were on our way once again. Now that it was light, we could watch the countryside roll by again. I could see that there were many unharvested crops in the fields, with very few field hands in sight. I had to wonder what these people would do once winter set in.

Less than an hour out of Chisinau, we crossed the Nistru River. This is where we saw our first overt evidence of the war that had raged across this area only a month before. From the rail bridge over the river, we could see the road bridge next to us. It had been a stone and steel structure before the war. Now, the center span was replaced with a not-very-stout-looking wooden structure. Apparently, the center of the bridge had been destroyed by the retreating Russian Army.

We had already finished crossing the rail bridge before it occurred to me that perhaps the bridge we had just crossed had the same kind of temporary-looking repairs holding it up. I shivered a little at the thought.

It was still only mid-morning when a thought occurred to me. To Maria I said, "Look, we are headed Southeast now, instead of East."

I could tell Maria was tired because her reply was unnecessarily snippy when she said, "How would you know, silly?"

I think I showed great restraint when I answered her in a calm, even voice. "The sun still rises in the East, doesn't it? Well, it's on the left side of the train now. Ergo, we're headed South." I finished my explanation with a pleasant, and hopefully irritating, smile.

I was rewarded with a disgruntled mutter that included something about being a smart something-or-other. Maria then continued in a louder voice. "Why would we be headed South? We haven't even entered the Ukraine yet. What's South of us anyway?"

"Um, I'm not sure. The only thing I can think of might be Odessa."

"Why would we be going to Odessa, silly? Our army captured Odessa at the beginning of the month. By now, they must be moving east into the Crimea," Maria reasoned.

"I'll ask Miss Lovinescu," I said as I rose from my seat. I felt that I needed to stretch my legs anyway. Progress up the aisle was difficult with the swaying of the train over the increasingly uneven tracks. At last, I reached the seat where Miss Lovinescu sat beside Girta. Miss Lovinescu, may I ask you a question?" I said.

"Of course, dear," said Miss Lovinescu with a smile whose warmth would have done credit to a crocodile.

"I... I mean we were just wondering if you know why we are headed South instead of East." "We are on our way to join up with the Fourth Army. They are laying siege to Odessa and are in need of additional medical help, as I understand it."

"But I thought the Army had taken Odessa weeks ago," I protested.

"Our heroic Army *surrounded* Odessa weeks ago," she corrected. "The reports of its capture seem to have been somewhat premature."

Was that a touch of humor from the old battle-ax? Aloud, I said, "But I thought we were supposed to be assigned to the Third Army, not the Fourth."

"We were," she answered. "However, I understand that there is an urgent need for us at Odessa. So as usual, plans change."

"Thank you," was all I could say.

As I turned to return to my seat, Miss Lovinescu said, "I'm sorry about your young man, but don't worry, you'll catch up to him someday."

Pretending ignorance, I said, "Pardon me?"

"That nice young doctor that you like so much, Peter. I understand that he is with the Third Army." *My God, how much does she know about me? She must be a witch. Can she read my mind?* I was sure she could read my every thought. Guilt, or fear, or something must have shown off my face because she added, "Don't look so distressed, dear. I'm sure you'll see him sometime soon."

I mumbled something by way of excusing myself and started back up the aisle. Just as I swung into my seat the train slowed suddenly, causing me to bump Maria. Her humor hadn't improved any. "Hey... watch it, clumsy," she grumbled.

Ignoring her ill humor, I said, "Look, we're stopping."

In a few moments, we were at a complete stop. A conductor entered the car and announced that we must all get our bags and disembark. When he passed our seat, Maria asked what was going on.

He explained that we had to transfer to another train to continue our journey. It seems that the Russians use a wider gage of track than the rest of Europe.

"That means that we are in the Ukraine now, doesn't it?" said Maria.

"Yes miss," he answered. "We are near Rozdyl'na."

Upon leaving the train we were surprised to find that we seemed to be in the middle of nowhere. There was nothing in sight for several kilometers except one peasant's hovel. There was, however, a great deal of activity in front of our train. Immediately ahead of us was a short work train piled high with rails and ties for the track. Ahead of that was an area of ground where the track had been torn up. Military personnel were swarming over this area in an attempt to replace the Russian gage track with the standard European gauge as quickly as possible.

Across a half kilometer of this torn-up ground, we could see another train sitting on the wider-spaced tracks, waiting for us. We had to carry our bags across the intervening gap ourselves. The soldiers from the cars behind us were already forming up into ranks to march to the other train.

As we began struggling across this sandy strip of sun-scorched earth, bags in hand, Maria said, "Look at that peasant's house. I thought the farmhouses in Romania were crude, but that is unbelievable."

She was right. This hovel was hardly more than a hole in the ground with low mud and log walls around it. It was roofed over with sod-covered logs. In the back, it sloped down to ground level. This allowed the stringy-looking cattle to climb onto the roof and graze. The cattle on the roof didn't bother me nearly as much as seeing the pigs and chickens roaming freely in and out of the door right along with the peasant children. The door and two visible windows had nothing that I could see to cover them.

I said, "That must be their barn."

"Oh?" said Maria. "Then where is the house?"

She was right again. There were no other structures in sight. Before long, however, we were too tired and out of breath to care.

At last, we reached the other train. It looked almost as crude as the peasant's hovel. There was only one covered passenger wagon. It looked like a boxcar with crude windows cut into the sides. Once we succeeded in dragging our bags into this car, we discovered that there were only hard wooden benches to sit on and no glazing on the windows.

As we sorted ourselves out, it occurred to me that Miss Lovinescu had made the same crossing that the rest of us had, carrying her two modest-sized bags. She had neither complained nor lagged behind despite her age and apparent frailty. In her position as headmistress, she could have insisted on having us girls carry her bags for her, but she had not. Sweating profusely, I wondered how she continued to look cool and composed.

The soldiers were seated on the open flat-cars behind our car. For their sake, I found myself hoping for good weather. The ancient steam engine coughed unsteadily and began to stagger forward. We were on our way once again.

The train traveled east for a while and then turned south once again. At times, I could see a large lake to our west. Later, the lake became a swamp.

It was getting dark again as our dilapidated train came to a shuddering halt. Miss Lovinescu gathered us all together beside the train car. She instructed us to stay with each other, and not to move. Then she left to find out where we were to go from there.

We all huddled close together…even Girta. Around us, military personnel from the different branches of the service hurried to and fro. I had the uneasy feeling that all this hurrying about seemed more urgent than would be normal.

It was completely dark, and we were all getting very nervous by the time Miss Lovinescu returned. She had a corporal of the Medical Corps in tow.

He explained that we were near Sverdlove, just a little Northwest of Odessa on the coast of the Black Sea. He had a horse-drawn wagon filled with medical supplies, and we were to ride with him to the hospital.

When Girta complained that we had been traveling for two days and should be taken to our quarters to rest, he explained that we would be staying right in the hospital. I thought Girta's complaint sounded rather whiny, but I was certainly ready for a good night's sleep. We didn't know it then, but it would be quite some time before any of us got any rest at all.

The medical wagon that we were to ride in was actually a horse-drawn ambulance, with tall, straight, wooden sides and a flat canvas top.

Miss Lovinescu and Girta, of course, rode in the driver's seat with the Corporal. The rest of us were piled, quite literally, on top of the supplies and our own bags. It was a very bumpy and uncomfortable few kilometers to the hospital. More than once, I considered getting out and walking, but I was *so* tired.

The hospital was actually an old-school building, I think. Our wagon approached the back of the ugly two-story, brick and concrete, structure. All the while we could hear the noise of a great deal of comings and goings at the front of the building as we virtually fell out of the wagon and tried to massage some life back into our limbs.

I dragged my two cursed bags to the back door of the building where we were met by an orderly. He instructed us to drop our bags in a nearby room and change into clean uniforms. When Maria asked if we were expected to dress for dinner, he just gave us a nasty laugh and left.

The room had several extremely hard folding cots in it. Boy, did they look inviting? We all knew that if we ever lay down, there would be no getting back up. Instead, we changed into fresh uniforms and went back into the hall.

Soon the orderly returned with an army doctor. The doctor looked us over briefly and then addressed Miss Lovinescu. "Two days ago, the Russians counter-attacked us at Fontanka. They landed a Marine brigade on the coast behind our lines and drove our troops back over two kilometers. We have stopped them, for now at least, but we have over four thousand new casualties. Many are just now getting to the hospital."

"Since your girls are all inexperienced, we will have them work in teams. Miss Lovinescu, we can use an experienced nurse like you in surgery. You can pick one of these young ladies to help you."

Miss Lovinescu only nodded and motioned for Girta to go with her.

Looking at Sasha and Elaine, he said, "You two will help in the recovery room and with post-surgery care."

"But we are only nursing students," protested Elaine. "We are supposed to change sheets, make up surgery packs, and take care of bed pans!"

The doctor exploded. "Bed pans and surgery packs!" You'll have to do a lot more than that!" He gave one bark of a laugh and turned to Maria and me. "You two will help the orderlies in triage," he said. Sounding as confused as I felt, Maria asked, "What do you mean?"

"Triage! Triage! Don't you know what triage is? You'll help the orderlies sort the incoming wounded into three categories. The first category is the lightly wounded. You and the orderlies will care for them. Category two are those in need of immediate surgery. You will send them on to the surgeons. Category three is for the ones that can't be saved. We don't have the time to waste on them. You separate them from the others and make them as comfortable as possible."

Maria and I both knew what triage was, but we also knew that it was usually handled by some of the most experienced personnel, not nursing assistants. We must have looked as horrified as we felt because the doctor added, "Don't worry; you can leave the decisions to the experienced orderlies for now."

That didn't make me feel a whole lot better.

He took Sasha and Elaine with him and told Maria and me to go with the orderly. To our surprise, he led us all the way through the hospital and out the front door to a wide lawn.

The orderly turned to us and said, "We do the sorting right here as the casualties arrive. The lightly wounded, we treat and find room for them inside. The Category two patients are sent to surgery in the south wing.

The 'threes' go to those tents over there," he said, pointing to several large tents to the side of the hospital.

Maria and I were still looking at the tents with a sense of dread in our minds when another horse-drawn ambulance pulled up in front of the yard. It looked just like the one we had ridden in on, except that this one was actually dripping blood from the floorboards.

"Come on. Let's get this one unloaded," said the orderly. When Maria and I approached the rear of the wagon somewhat hesitantly, he added, "The orderlies will unload and sort them. You two can treat the less seriously wounded."

When the doors of the ambulance were opened, the most God-awful stench of rot and decay hit us like a wall. The first soldier unloaded was already dead. He was set gently, but unceremoniously, beside the wagon. They unloaded the next one. "A three," said the orderly, as a man with no legs was carried towards the tents.

When the third casualty was unloaded, the orderly called to us. "Here, you two treat this man and then find him a place inside." Two orderlies carried his stretcher to a clear place on the lawn and set him down.

We knelt beside him, and I looked at the tag that was tied around his neck. It said, "Arm and leg wounds." A quick look under the bandage on his leg showed that it was a minor wound that was already clotted and only needed to have the fragments of uniform removed from the laceration to prevent infection.

His left arm had a tourniquet tied just below the shoulder. Since the arm was beginning to turn a blue-black, I said to Maria, "My God, how long have they left this tourniquet on him?"

I loosened the tourniquet and immediately blood began to spurt from a wound on the inside of the biceps. "Damn," I said. "Arterial bleeding and this tourniquet has been on way too long already. We need a pressure bandage."

It was only now that I realized that we were out here with no medical supplies. Placing finger pressure over the wound, I said to Maria, "Run into the hospital and get bandages and equipment."

A few seconds later, as I was looking at the wound to determine how to position a bandage, I realized that Maria was still kneeling there. I looked up to find her seemingly frozen in place. Her eyes were like saucers as she stared at the blood seeping between my fingers, with a shocked expression on her face.

"Maria! We need bandages, stat!" My yelling had no effect, so I leaned across the wounded man, and with my free left hand, slapped Maria across the cheek.

With a wince, her eyes focused on my face once again. "Bandages, we need bandages!" I repeated. In an instant, Maria was on her feet and sprinting for the hospital door.

Trying to stop the flow of blood with my fingers made the time seem like an eternity, but I am sure that it was only a few moments before Maria returned with an armload of bandages, disinfectants, and dressing tape.

I applied the pressure bandage to the wound along with some of the disinfectant powder. Maria helped me with the bandaging, but when we were done, she looked rather green. It may have been the effect of the emergency lanterns set around the yard, but I said, "If you are going to be sick, go over behind those trees. Don't do it in front of the wounded. They feel bad enough already."

She didn't say anything, but got up and walked quickly to the trees. To her credit, she was back soon and worked steadily through the rest of the night. At least I think it was the rest of the night. Everything from then on seems to be a blur.

I do remember, at one point, running around to find a cigarette for one of the wounded in the number three group. By the time I got back to him, he was dead. Now I always carry cigarettes and matches with me, even though I don't smoke.

The next thing I remember clearly was Miss Lovinescu standing over me as I opened my eyes. I was lying on a cot in our "nurse's room." She asked, "Have a good sleep, dear?"

I sprang to a sitting position and almost passed out. "Oh my God, I'm sorry. I must have fallen asleep. I'll get right out there! I'm so sorry."

As I tried to rise from the cot, Miss Lovinescu held me down with a hand on my shoulder. "Fallen asleep?" she asked in a strange tone. "That's not the word for it. You passed out so suddenly that the orderlies thought you had been shot."

"I'm sorry," I said again. "I didn't mean to leave you all stranded."

"Leave *us* stranded? Why do you think I had to hear about this from the orderlies? We had all given up and gone to bed hours before you passed out. You worked two days straight, and that was after two days on the train. I'm very proud of you."

"I did? I mean, you are? I don't remember much. How long have I been asleep?"

"Fourteen hours."

"Fourteen hours! I've got to get back out there!" I began looking for my shoes. They were all I needed since I was already wearing a horribly dirty uniform.

"Don't be silly, dear," said Miss Lovinescu. The emergency is over for now. And after all, you need to leave something for the rest of us to do.

And... Oh, yes. Welcome to the war."

That's strange, I thought. Her smile seems quite genuine to me now. I wonder if she has changed somehow.

CHAPTER II

On to the Crimea

Realizing that I was famished I put on my shoes and stepped into the hall wondering which way it was to the kitchen. Funny, I had been here for two days and couldn't remember the way. I asked for directions from a passing orderly. He pointed me in the right direction, all the while eyeing me as if I weren't all there. Or perhaps it was my disheveled condition that drew his odd look. I knew I must be a frightful sight, but I was too hungry to care.

When I arrived at the kitchen, I found Maria, Sasha, and Elaine already there. I quickly collected some porridge and rolls from the chief and joined them at their table.

Maria was the first to greet me. "Well, if it isn't sleepy-head," she said. "We thought you would never wake up."

Don't listen to her, Anna," said Sasha. "We've only been up a short time ourselves."

I sat down and began eating hungrily as Elaine asked, "Have you heard about Girta?"

Around an oversized mouthful of porridge, I muttered, "Heard what? Nothing has happened to her, has it?"

Elaine sounded almost pleased as she said, "She broke down. She just started crying in surgery and couldn't stop. I think she's still crying. They put her in a room by herself, and I hear that they are going to send her home."

"That's awful," I said. "Poor Girta. Where is she?"

"She's on the second floor with Miss Lovinescu," explained Maria. "It serves her right. She's just a little teacher's pet."

"Oh, shut up, Maria," I said crossly "Have any of you checked on her yet?"

My inquiry was met with an embarrassed silence. "That's just great!" I exclaimed. "I'll go see how she's doing." To my discredit, however, I found that I was more concerned with eating than Girta's condition, so I finished my breakfast before I went in search of her.

Thirty minutes later I was walking down the second-floor hallway when I saw Miss Lovinescu coming out of one of the rooms. I approached her and asked if Girta was in the room.

"Yes," she answered. "You can visit her if you wish but let me explain some things first."

I didn't say anything, but I must have had a puzzled look on my face.

"First, let me say, I should have known that you would be the first to come and check on her, just as I should have known that this would be too much for her."

"What do you mean by too much?" I asked.

"Girta was raised in a very sheltered environment. She isn't very strong emotionally and hasn't been exposed to much stress in her life. That's why I was opposed to her coming with us, and why I have stayed so close to her on this trip."

"*You've* been staying close to *her*? If she is so frail emotionally, why did she come at all?"

Miss Lovinescu's answers shocked me. "She came because of you, dear, you and the others, of course. She thinks the world of you all and wants so much to be just like all of you."

"But we thought she was just stuck-up...I mean, didn't like us," I stammered.

Miss Lovinescu smiled more softly than I thought she could as she said, "She's a very shy and introverted person. She was never able to tell you and the others how she felt."

I was feeling very small as I said, "I guess I'm not as good a judge of character as I thought. I owe Girta an apology." After some hesitation, I added, "I owe you an apology also."

Before I could go on, Miss Lovinescu asked, "You mean an apology for thinking me a dried-up old prude? You don't need to apologize for that. Judging people is something that you learn with experience. And besides, that's the image I wish to project.

"You see, as your teacher, I need to maintain a certain amount of...shall we say, distance from the students. That is how I remain the authority figure that I must be to do my job.

"I haven't always been a headmistress, you know. In the last war, I was very much like you. When my young man was killed in that war, I volunteered my services as a nurse in the army. What is going on now is terrible, but it is nothing new to me. That's part of the reason that I hope so whole-heartedly that you catch up to your young man."

"I don't know what to say," was all I *could* say.

"Don't say anything, dear. Just go visit with Girta for a little while. I'm afraid we will have to leave soon to catch he next train to Bucharest."

"You're both leaving then?" I asked.

"Yes. Girta can't travel alone, and I was never supposed to stay here anyway. I have to train more nurses. The lord knows it looks like we'll need them."

The room Girta was in was just a converted storage closet like the one the rest of us were staying in. I noticed Miss Lovinesqu's and her bags on the floor, already packed. Girta, sitting on the edge of her cot had stopped crying, but her eyes were still red and puffy. She was wiping her runny nose as I entered.

I really didn't know what to say, so I started the conversation with a brilliant, "How are you doing?" "I'm all right now," she said. "But I feel like such a fool. Two years of nursing school, and now I find out that I can't stand the sight of real blood."

"But we have trained on cadavers and done minor first aid before. Didn't that bother you?" I asked. "Yes, it bothered me some, but I could handle that. This is the real thing here. These men are in real pain and bleeding real blood. And worst of all, they expect us to save them."

"How did you handle the pressure?"

"I don't know," I said. "Back home, even before nursing school, I used to patch-up any wounded animal I could find, so I guess I was used to the blood. As for the pressure... I just don't think about it. As you said, they are looking to us to help them, so I just don't think about anything but the job."

"I wish I could be like that, but I see the blood and I think of the pain, and I just can't stand it. I guess I've wasted my effort and Miss Lovinesqu's time by going to school."

Girta looked so depressed that I just had to say something to help her. "You didn't waste your time. You could go into the psychiatric field. They need nurses with basic medical training there, but you wouldn't have to be involved with surgery."

She looked skeptical, so I added, "They need people with your kind of empathy in that field. You could really relate to the patients the way you seem to feel their pain."

"Maybe you're right," she said. "I'll talk to Miss Lovinesqu about it."

I don't remember the rest of what Girta and I talked about, but we parted with a hug. Later, as she and Miss Lovinescu were leaving on the wagon, my insides felt hollow, the way they had when I bid farewell to my family for the last time.

As their wagon dwindled to a speck down the road, I had the sudden feeling that I would never see my home again. I had to fight a terrific urge to run after them and throw myself into the wagon. I didn't, of course, but I wondered if the others felt anything like I did. No one said anything for quite some time.

We certainly weren't bored. We did all the little things expected of nurses' aides and much more. After a while, I came to realize that a big part of our duty was simply to *be there* for the wounded soldiers.

Not only did the men seem to bear their wounds more stolidly with us present, but I think we reminded them of the homes and families that they were fighting for. It was at this time that I developed a habit that stayed with me throughout the war.

Part of our duty was to visit with the recovering wounded, to talk to them, and sometimes to write letters for them if their wounds prevented them from writing themselves. Unfortunately, our other duties didn't leave much time for these visits. Since I am one of those people who can get by on less sleep than most, I began visiting the wards at night. Many of the wounded can't sleep on a regular basis, so there was always someone in need of a little conversation or companionship.

On these visits, I discovered something very interesting. The soldiers would talk of almost anything with a nurse; their bravery, their fears, what it was like in combat, what their friends did…almost anything. But when sending letters home, they would almost never write of what the war was really like. I think that they didn't want to worry their families, while they thought of us nurses as comrades-in-arms, and therefore privy to their true feelings and fears.

I was very honored to be considered a comrade by these brave souls. At the same time, I learned a great deal about the fighting and what was really going on.

We didn't stay in the Odessa area very long. After several weeks of attacks and counterattacks, the Russians simply vanished one night. On the morning of October sixteenth, we awoke to find that almost all of the eighty thousand Russian troops had been spirited away in the night by ship. Everyone was happy to have this great victory handed to us, even though we knew that we would face these same troops again someday.

Almost immediately after the occupation of Odessa, it was announced that the bulk of the Fourth Army would be withdrawn to Romania to spend the coming winter refitting. The Army had sustained over one hundred thousand casualties in taking Odessa. That was twenty times the number of causalities suffered in reconquering all of Bessarabia... where we should have stopped.

We nurses barely had time to speculate on what would happen to us when we were told that we would be transferred to the Third Romanian Army.

The Third Army had continued East from Bessarabia in conjunction with the German Eleventh Army. Their intention had been to invade the Crimean Peninsula and capture the important Russian naval base at Sevastopol. Instead, they had been forced to fight for their lives in some place called the Nogai Steppe where the Russians launched a major counter-attack against our Romanian units. Only the intervention of a large part of the German Eleventh Army saved our men from being overrun and completely destroyed.

After their initial successes against our troops, the Russian formations had been defeated in a series of great encirclement battles. Once again, our casualties were terribly high. We were needed by the Third Army.

My feelings were mixed as we boarded a convoy of motor lorries to head East once again. I was glad to be joining Peter's Third Army since it meant that I might actually get to see him, but the reports of heavy causalities had me worried. Was Peter one of them? With all the confusion caused by the continual movement of all units involved, I hadn't received a letter from Peter since before leaving Bucharest. We counted ourselves lucky when we received food and medical supplies on time, let alone mail.

The ride in the lorry was only a little better than our previous experience in the horse-drawn ambulance. At least this time we weren't actually piled on top of our luggage. We added extra layers of clothing as the temperature dropped steadily with our leaving the coastal area of Odessa.

As we bumped and bounced over the dusty track, Maria said, "These roads are terrible."

Through the scarf I had tied over my mouth to keep out the fine, powdery dust, I asked, "What Road? Back in Ploiesti, the goat tracks were smoother than this." It seemed that the lorries would stagger up out of one hole in the road only to drop into the next one that was always deeper. Our bottoms were being constantly pounded by the hard wooden benches while our backs took a working over from the equally hard seat backs. With the dust and the dropping temperature in the unheated, canvas-covered, back of the lorry, I thought that we were as miserable as we could get. I was wrong.

We didn't talk much as we bumped along. It took most of our energy and attention just to hold on to our seats. I did, however, manage to talk a little with one of the orderlies assigned to our unit. He was an older man, probably in his forties. His hair was turning gray, and he wore wire-rimmed spectacles with thick lenses. He said his name was Julius Goga and that he was from a tiny town in Western Romania called Balta. When I asked him why he was in the army, he said that he had made the army his career. He had served during the closing stages of the war against the Germans and had stayed on, thinking that he would retire without ever seeing another war. With that, he raised his hands palm outward and rolled his eyes as if to say, "Oh, well."

Just as he made this gesture, we hit another one of the unending pot-holes and he bounced clear out of his seat and onto the wooden floor of the lorry. We all laughed at this, even Julius. I couldn't help but like this gentle person who had devoted his life to helping others.

Except for the dust, bumps, and cold, our first day on the road was uneventful. We stopped for the night at a small tent city that the army had erected beside the road. We were close to a river, but I had no idea which one or where we were. Juluis said that was a normal state of affairs in the army. When I saw the cots set up in the tents I quit worrying about where I was. I just wanted to get some sleep. We all slept like the dead until five in the morning when the orderlies came around and woke us. We could hardly move. I felt like an eighty-year-old woman who had been beaten with a club. I don't think there was a square inch of my body that didn't feel bruised.

After a hurried breakfast, we were herded back onto the lorries. I was the last one to climb on and therefore closest to the rear of the lorry. Looking out from under the canvas top I could see a small car with German markings approaching. Before it passed out of sight towards the front of the lorry, I glimpsed a German officer riding in the front passenger seat. I didn't get a very long look, but his left arm was in a sling, and he seemed very handsome in his neat and clean gray dress uniform. I even had the impression that he was looking directly at me as he passed out of sight.

Shortly after we resumed moving, it began to rain. We were happy that there would be less dust on the road today. Our happiness lasted about two hours. By eight o'clock the roads were becoming muddy. By noon they were a slippery mess.

Being closest to the back of the lorry, I caught most of the backsplash. There was plenty to go around, however, as it worked its way under the canvas side covers and onto everyone.

About noon the rain stopped. A half-hour later, we stopped also. There was a German Army field-kitchen set up beside the road at this point. Everyone from our convoy eagerly lined up to get a hot meal.

Just as Maria and I got to the cook's wagon, the German officer from the staff car stepped into line just behind us. With his blond hair, blue eyes, and ruggedly handsome face, he could have been the model for a recruiting poster for the SS, but his uniform indicated that he was in the regular army. To my surprise, he addressed us in passable Romanian.

"Good day, ladies," he said. "Are you enjoying our little war so far?"

I looked into his handsome, smiling face, and my mind went blank.

Maria, however, was quick with an answer. "Well, if this is your war, could you arrange to have it in better weather?" With this, Maria stretched out the muddy hem of her uniform skirt to display its sad condition.

"Sorry," he laughed. "The ground and the weather are provided by the enemy, and not our responsibility."

I thought he had a very nice laugh. I also noticed that he had insinuated himself near the head of the line. As a German officer, I suppose it was his right anyway.

After getting our trays filled, we found seats on some nearby fallen logs. Our handsome German followed us and sat down without asking permission. Once again, his prerogative, I suppose.

He introduced himself as Captain Hans Roider of the Armored Corps. He was temporarily attached to our medical unit as a liaison officer because we would be treating both Romanian and German casualties at our destination. It seems that his knowledge of the Romanian language and his temporary disability from taking a bullet in the shoulder had combined to get him this assignment.

Smiling brightly, he said, "I must say, I wasn't very happy with a non-combat assignment, but now that I'm here, I think I may like this job."

My curiosity finally loosened my tongue enough to ask, "Did you say that you are a tank officer?"

"That's right," he said. "I commanded a company from the turret of my own tank."

"Well then," I continued, "if you fight in a tank, how did you get a bullet in your shoulder?"

"That's a very good question," he said. "Most people think that a tank crew spends all their time locked up inside their tank, but we don't. You see, it is very hard to see anything from a tank's viewports and periscopes, so as a tank commander, I usually stand up in the turret hatch to be able to see what is going on. That's where I got this," he said, pointing to his shoulder. "Actually, I was lucky. We have lost a lot of tank commanders that way."

After the brief lunch stop, we had to return to our lorry. As we were walking in that direction, Maria said to me, "I think he likes you, Anna."

"Me?" I blurted. "Don't be silly. I saw the way you were flirting with him...batting your eyes and showing your ankle."

"I'd show him more than my ankle if he wanted to see it."

"Maria! You're incorrigible! And I'm too plain to interest an officer like that. I think he wanted to get close to you. You're much prettier than me."

"I disagree...about who he likes, I mean," said Maria. "He only had eyes for you. You know, for some men, the pathetic doe-eyed innocent look is irresistible."

This time I did smack her, but only lightly on the arm. Then I had to turn away from her to hide my smile.

We finished the day's ride on the outskirts of a fairly large town that we were told was called Cherson. It was too dark to see, but they told us that we were near the mouth of the Dnieper River where it empties into the Black Sea. That night, in order to sleep under a roof to get out of the rain that had resumed falling, we slept in some peasant huts. They were lit only with little paraffin lamps and had virtually no furniture in them. I think I picked up my first fleas there.

The next morning, after a session of trying to rid each other of our fleas, we were headed back to our lorries when Captain Roider pulled up in his car. He jumped out and held open the rear door, saying, "Would you two ladies care to ride with me today? My little Kubelwagen isn't much, but I think you will find the ride better than that Hungarian-made lorry."

"Hungarian-made?" I exclaimed. "No wonder it has been trying to kill us." We wasted no time in taking the good Captain up on his offer. I think we were even giggling a little as we climbed into the rear seat. The little vehicle only had four seats. With the Captain's driver, an older man named Lutz, the Captain, and us, the car was full.

With a roar like a small aircraft, the rear mounted engine propelled us past the waiting line of lorries and to the head of the column. The unpaved road was no smoother than before, but the seats in the little car were much more comfortable. Also, even with the canvas top keeping the occasional showers off our heads, the view was much better than from the rear of a covered lorry.

As we drove along the muddy, rutted road, Captain Roider explained that we would be traveling parallel to the Dnieper River for about forty-five kilometers to a town called Beryslav. It was near that town that our armies had forced a crossing of that great river. The German and Romanian army engineers had worked together to build the longest pontoon bridge in the world at that point.

We had only covered about half the distance to Beryslav when we were forced to come to a halt. The road ahead was blocked by an unending line of vehicles of all sorts, and no one was moving at all. We sat in the car for about ten minutes while Captain Roider fumed to his driver in German. Finally, he climbed out of the car and moved about ten meters off the road. His boots were a muddy mess from the soft, rain-soaked ground when he returned.

Once back in the car, he gave some rapid commands to his driver. Even though I spoke almost no German at the time, I got the impression that he was using some very colorful language.

Lutz gunned the motor and swung the little vehicle onto the side of the road. As we began to pass the stopped vehicles the Captain seemed to remember that we were in the back seat. He turned to us and explained, "This column is backed up as far as I can see. I'm going to see if I can find out what is wrong."

Just then our car swung almost completely sideways in the deep mud. The Captain continued as if nothing were happening, "Lutz is a very good driver, so don't worry your pretty little heads about this." Smiling, he added, "This should be fun, eh?"

Bouncing and sliding, we careened through the thick mud that flew up behind our tires. Several times the mud was so deep that we had to return to the road, not that it was that much better. At these times

Captain Roider would order whatever vehicles were blocking our path to move over. Apparently, a line Captain of the Wehrmacht has considerable authority. Despite much arguing and yelling, he always got his way.

In this manner, we bumped, swayed, and swerved our way forward. In half an hour we had covered about two kilometers. The head of the column came into view where the road passed through a cut in the small hillside that rose on the right side of the road. As we approached the lead vehicle, a Wehrmacht officer ran out and signaled for us to stop.

Captain Roider jumped from the car and hurried over to the other man. After a short conversation the two men climbed the hill that overlooked the road. At the top of the hill, they joined many other men in peering over a low stone wall.

Maria and I were discussing whether we would be in trouble for being out of touch with our unit for so long when the two Captains returned to the roadside. They had a heated conference with Captain Roider gesturing wildly with his good arm. Finally, they seemed to come to some sort of agreement. The other Captain went to a radio signals lorry while Captain Roider returned to our car.

After exchanging a few words with Lutz, he turned to us again. "God save me from supply troops and Golden Pheasants," he said.

When we looked at him blankly, he explained. "The supply troops have no combat experience and the Golden Pheasants are even worse. They are the rear echelon officers who prance around in their fancy uniforms and gold medals, contributing nothing to our war against the Bolsheviks. Most of them are only interested in hunting for spies and deserters.

Curiosity getting the better of me, I interrupted, "But what is the problem with the road?"

"Well, that's just it," he said. "There *is* a problem with the road. There is a big fat Russian tank sitting in the middle of it."

"A Russian tank? We have to get out of here," exclaimed Maria.

"Oh, don't worry Maria," I said as I looked into Captain Roider's eyes. "If it was heading our way, I'm sure the good Captain wouldn't be simply standing here beside the road."

Smiling, he said, "That's right. You're very perceptive. Actually, it's just sitting there making a hash out of our schedule."

"Can we see it?" I asked.

Glancing over his shoulder to look at the hillside, he said, "Certainly if you want to. But I'm afraid that you will get pretty muddy."

"I don't care," I said as I climbed from the car.

"You're crazy," said Maria. "I'm not leaving this car!"

I hadn't taken two steps when the mud pulled the low-cut nurses' shoes from my feet. "Damn," I said as I tossed them back into the car and proceeded barefoot. Captain Roider seemed to be enjoying himself as he helped me climb the hillside with me holding the muddy hem of my dress up around my knees.

At the top of the hill, he had me kneel down behind the low stone wall. That took care of the rest of my skirt. "Damn," I said again.

"You look mad enough to kill those Russians for us with a look," chuckled the Captain.

"These nursing uniforms are ridiculous in the field," I complained. "We should wear boots and pants like everyone else."

"Well," said Captain Roider. "You should if you're going to hunt Russians, anyway.

"Look into this spotter's scope," he said, indicating a two-barreled contraption on a tripod. The eyepieces were below the wall while the larger lenses were well above it.

It was focused on a tank sitting squarely in the middle of the road. It looked huge. It was much larger than any I had seen in either our army or the Germans. The tall, slab-sided turret was as high as a man standing. It sat on an equally large, armored box with wheels and tracks on either side. I noticed that one of the tracks was lying broken on the ground beside it. So that was how Captain Roider could know that it wasn't going to be coming our way, I thought. Even though the gun was not pointed in our direction, I could see that it looked like a short telegraph pole.

The road that the tank sat on passed through a broad area of bogs and swamps stretching for as far as I could see in either direction.

"What is it doing?" I asked.

"Just sitting there, keeping all these supplies from getting to the front," said the Captain with some frustration showing in his voice.

"How long has it been there?"

The answer really surprised me when it came. "Two days, or so I am told."

"But why doesn't someone blow it up?" I asked in amazement.

"That's easier said than done," he answered. "That monster has armor over one hundred millimeters thick and a six-inch howitzer for a gun. It also has machine guns in the front and rear."

"But our tanks could destroy it couldn't they?"

"Yes, not easily, but they could. If they were here, that is. Unfortunately, they passed through this area weeks ago."

"What about your cannons, then?"

"Our artillery, you mean? It's at the front with the tanks."

I was beginning to see the reason for the captain's frustration as I asked with some sarcasm in my voice, "And your vaunted Air Force?"

"The Luftwaffe is busy elsewhere I'm afraid," he answered wearily. "My dear, you must understand that this whole southern front is being run on a shoe-string. The Luftwaffe is greatly outnumbered here. Why do you think we need the help of our allies so badly on this front?"

"Well, if our troops came through this area weeks ago, where did this thing come from?"

"Good question, said the Captain." We think it was hidden in that wooded area that you can just make out about two kilometers behind it. We don't know if it was disabled when our troops passed this area or if it was deliberately hidden for just such an opportunity like this. Personally, I don't think the Slavs are smart enough to plan something like this."

Suppressing a brief surge of anger at this obvious bit of prejudice (after all, my father's family *is* of Russian heritage) I simply asked, "What are you going to do then?"

"I've put a plan in motion. Look to your far left. See those men behind that hillock? What are they doing?"

Straining my eyes through the periscope, I answered. "They seem to be pushing two small cannons towards the top of that hill. Can they destroy that monster with those little guns?"

"Of course not, he laughed. "That's why we call them 'door knockers.' But, at the right moment, they will advance into view of that tank. That should draw those Russian's attention while we deliver the killing stroke."

"And what would that be..." I prompted.

Pointing over my shoulder, he said, Look behind you."

I turned to see the largest half-tracked vehicle I had ever seen, climbing the hill towards us. It looked like a large lorry in the front, but the rear half was on tracks like a tank, and it was towing a gun that even *I* recognized. It was one of the famous "88's," a very powerful anti-aircraft gun.

"If those men with their little pop-guns can draw the Russian's attention for a few minutes," Captain Roider continued, "we'll have time to get this gun into action."

The German reputation for good planning is well deserved. Just before the half-track crashed into, and then over, the wall about fifty meters to our right, the men on the other hill advanced into sight of the metal monster. The Russian machine guns began firing immediately, but they were too far away to be effective. Then the tank's cannon fired. The soldiers hugged the ground as the large high explosive shells gouged huge craters in the ground near them.

Meanwhile, to our right, the crew of the anti-aircraft gun was working frantically to get their gun ready to fire. They didn't take the time to unhook the gun from the towing vehicle but instead, began lowering the supporting legs with the towing wheels still attached. As the crew began bringing shells to the gun the firing from the Russian tank ceased. Through the periscope, I could see only one of the small guns. It was laying on its side with what appeared to be several bodies near it.

I couldn't keep the tone of accusation from my voice when I said, "Those men never had a chance." When Captain Roider answered, his voice was calm but firm. "Those men were soldiers. They followed their orders and did their duty. Now it's our turn to do our duty." He nodded towards the enemy tank, so I swung the periscope around once again.

The monstrous turret was slowly swinging around in our direction like some medieval tower come to life.

"They've seen us," I said as the gun came to point more and more directly towards us. Soon, I could see right into its muzzle. Suddenly, an invisible hand was squeezing my heart with a death grip.

My eyes were glued to the periscope as I said, "My God, it looks like you could drop a watermelon into the mouth of that thing. Tell your men to hurry, they must have us in their sights by now."

Just then I felt, more than heard, a high-pitched 'crack'. It was so powerful that the air was pushed from my lungs for a second. Even so, I kept my eyes glued to the periscopes' eyepiece. From this acute angle, I could actually see the shell, in the form of a silvery blur, streaking towards the enemy. It struck the side of the hull just above the wheels and disappeared.

Nothing happened for several heartbeats. Then, instead of the Russian gun firing, the entire turret lifted from the hull in a blinding flash. The sound of the explosion reached us a couple of seconds later.

"Got him on the first shot!" Captain Roider exclaimed. I'll see that gun crew get a medal for this!

And you, my dear, are very brave."

I found myself sitting with my back against the stone wall as I began to shake all over. "Brave? Me? I didn't do anything."

"That's just the point. You didn't run and you didn't freeze in your first exposure to combat. That's more than many trained soldiers can say."

I tried to smile as I said, "I'm shaking like a leaf, and they didn't even get a shot off in our direction. I think I'll stick to nursing. Now, if you don't mind, I'll go back to the car. I need to find a toilet."

Once back to the car, I had Maria stand guard by some bushes as I emptied my suddenly bursting bladder.

Returning to the car once again, I thought I saw the driver, Lutz, looking at me strangely. I assumed that he thought that I must be crazy to go out of my way to get into trouble.

When the Captain returned to the car, I must have looked depressed because he asked me what was wrong.

"I can't help thinking," I said, "what a terrible way to die. The way they were trapped in that burning metal coffin, I mean." Suddenly, I remembered that Captain Roider was a tank officer himself. I fumbled for something to say. "I mean..."

"I know what you mean. We think of that all the time. Those men were lucky. They died almost instantly. Sometimes it's the ones that live that I pity."

Maria had to hear all of the details of my big adventure, of course. As traffic resumed moving on the road, I tried to tell her how I had felt, but I don't think she was listening to that part of my story. By the time our hospital unit came up to our location, Maria was ready to have me awarded the Iron Cross medal for valor above and beyond the call of duty. Somehow, I thought that our unit commander wouldn't quite agree with her.

Maria and I returned to our lorry when it caught up with us. Captain Roider sped away to file his reports, or whatever it is you have to do after a battle.

Due to the delay caused by the Russian tank, our unit didn't make Beryslav that day. We were doomed to another night in the tents beside the road in the ever-present mud. We resumed our trek at first light the next morning, arriving at the great pontoon bridge by mid-morning, where we promptly waited all day for our turn to cross.

The approaches to the bridge appeared to be a mass of utter confusion. We were camped on a slight rise, and as far as the eye could see, there were vehicles and groups of men and animals scattered about in what appeared to be no order whatsoever. Of course, someone must have been in charge because I could see units forming up and moving slowly across the bridge in a steady procession. Once on the bridge the units maintained a very wide spacing for the slow trip across.

I was just about to ask why everyone doesn't just line up on the road and wait for their turn to cross when my question was answered for me by the enemy. Preceded by a sound like distant thunder, an explosion threw a fountain of muddy earth into the air down amongst the waiting mass. Russian artillery rounds began falling randomly over the entire area of the bridge approaches. Since none of the shells were falling near us, we stood and watched the fall of Russian shells. Amazingly, very few fell near a target. That explained the wide dispersal of units. Just then, Juluis, the orderly, walked up beside me. He said that the artillery fire was just nuisance shelling to help spread confusion. If the enemy had any spotters within sight, he said, their fire would be much more accurate.

We took advantage of our distance from the shelling to have our dinner as we watched the spectacle. Although the fire was random and scattered, the enemy did get lucky once in a while. There were casualties amongst the waiting units and twice the bridge was hit, causing traffic to stop each time.

One shell landed directly on the bridge sinking one of the pontoons and severing the roadway that was laid on top. Fortunately, no one was injured by that explosion. The second time the bridge was hit, a shell severed several of the cables that anchored the pontoons in place. This sent a section of the floating roadway spinning downstream. There was a lorry on that section of the bridge at the time. For a while it looked like the unlucky lorry would just float safely downstream, but it hit a sand bank or something and the bridge surface tilted, dumping the lorry and its crew into the swift current. From where we were we couldn't see if anyone made it out of the river or not.

This scene was fresh in our minds when word arrived, just before sunset, that we were to load up and prepare to cross the river. It was a silent and grim-faced group in our lorry as we moved toward the bridge. We were instructed to roll the canvas cover of our lorry up as high as possible. This was done so that, if we went into the river, we could quickly jump clear. Then we were told to jump out on the downstream side of the lorry so that we would not become entangled with the vehicle as it sank. We were then supposed to swim to the nearest riverbank. All these instructions were silly because if we sank in the middle of that swift-flowing river, it could be as much as a half kilometer to the nearest bank, and we were in full clothing including long skirts. Even this bunch of "silly girls" had no illusions as to what would happen if anything went wrong.

Then, as we approached the bridge, our spirits began to soar. The shelling had stopped! We were all smiles and sighs of relief as we waited for our turn to start across. I noticed that Julius wasn't sharing in our good humor, so I asked him, "What is the matter? You don't look very happy."

He gave me a weak smile and said, "Oh, it's probably just an old man's nerves, but I have found that whenever something in the Army seems too good to be true, it's usually not true."

I didn't have a chance to reply because just then our lorry began lurching over the bulldozed riverbank and up the ramp onto the bridge. The ramp led up onto the first pontoon. It was about that time that I realized that the planking of the bridge's roadway was only a few inches wider than our lorry. All that could be seen below us when we were between pontoons was water.

We crept forward at about five kilometers per hour, keeping at least fifty meters between vehicles, so as not to overload the bridge. As I leaned over the side of the lorry to look ahead, I was treated to a curious sight. We seemed to be driving in a hole in the river. Due to the great weight of our loaded lorry, each pontoon we drove over would sink deeper into the water than the ones on each side of it. This made the bridge surface sag under us, giving the appearance that we were continually driving up a hill.

About halfway across the bridge, Julius' words came back to haunt us. I was surprised to hear the "pop-pop" of the anti-aircraft guns at each end of the bridge as they began to fire. Looking at the riverbank, I could see every gun firing furiously into the air. I was about to ask another silly question when the reason for this display became apparent.

Over the noise of the rushing water, the sound of engines became noticeable. I leaned over the side of the lorry again and could see several aircraft flying down the length of the bridge with bright lights twinkling on their wings. That is when I began hearing the sound of bullets hitting the bridge and seeing little spurts of water all around us.

Julius pulled me back into the lorry and shouted for everyone to get on the floor. Just then, Elaine tried to push past us on her way to the back of the lorry. She was yelling that we were all going to die and that we had to jump off the lorry. Jumping off the lorry and getting into a ditch was what we had been instructed to do in case of an air attack, but not in the middle of a river. I stuck out my foot and tripped her. Then I jumped on her back to prevent her from getting up again. Something heavy then fell on me. It was a few seconds before I realized that it was Julius throwing himself on top of us both.

This is when all hell broke loose. By now I could hear the firing of the aircraft's machine-guns. Then there was the roar of the plane's engine as it passed directly overhead. That was followed seconds later by the explosions of the bombs that felt like they were right under the lorry.

The air was filled with strange whining and moaning sounds as I felt the lorry shaking like a mouse in a cat's teeth. Within seconds we were deluged with river water and even some small fish. As I watched one of these tiny creatures gasping out its last moments less than a meter before my face, I wondered which of us had longer to live.

All this happened faster than I can tell about it, though at the time, it seemed to go on forever. Suddenly it was over. Silence seemed to descend like a blanket over everything, though I think it was mainly because I was partially deafened by the explosions.

I could feel the lorry continuing along the bridge, but when I tried to get up Julius refused to get off of me. He shouted into my ringing ears to stay down until we were off the bridge. At least I knew that Julius was all right. I wasn't so sure about Elaine because I could feel her sobbing under me.

So, it came to be, that I finished my crossing of the great Dnieper River as the center of a human sandwich. When we felt the lorry move off the bridge and onto solid ground, we began to untangle ourselves.

I helped a teary-eyed Elaine up off the floor and looked her over for injuries. She seemed unhurt physically. When I saw that Maria and Sasha were also in one piece, I tried to lean back in my seat to say something witty, but all that came out was, "ouch!" I had leaned against a fragment of bomb-casing that had lodged itself in the back of the seat, right where I had been sitting. It protruded a good six inches from the seat back and was as sharp as a dagger. I sat next to the fragment and leaned back against the seat, comparing the fragment's length to my own width. It would have easily penetrated my heart had I been sitting there when it arrived.

I tried to pull it from the wood for a souvenir and issued my second great witticism...another "ouch!" The metal was very hot. Julius was shaking his head; in disbelief I suppose. I merely pretended not to see him.

The lorry came to a halt a short distance from the bridge, where we all climbed out to give our nerves a rest. This is when I noticed that our lorry had *many* bomb fragments in it. Two of the tires were flat and the canvas that had been directly over our heads was shredded.

I hurried around the vehicle to congratulate the driver for keeping us on the bridge throughout all of this. When I arrived at the driver's door, I thought it odd that he had not climbed out of the lorry yet. When I opened the door, I could see that he was sitting very still as he stared through the badly cracked windscreen. He didn't seem to be injured, but his face was white as a ghost.

I asked, "Are you all right? Have you been injured?"

He turned his face towards me slowly and said, "No, I'm all right, I think." Then, reluctantly, he added, "I was so scared. I knew I couldn't stop on the bridge, but I was so scared." He began to weep quietly. I realized that he was about my age, not even twenty yet. I helped him from the lorry. When he collapsed against one of the wheels, I sat beside him and put my arms around his shoulders. I told him that he had saved all our lives by keeping the lorry moving and that he was a hero to all of us. Then I just continued to hold him as he wept.

The following day, our medical unit headed south, away from that embattled bridgehead. Our destination was Crimea. The German Eleventh Army, along with many Romanian units, had fought its way across the Perekops Isthmus at great cost in lives and materiel. It then pursued the fleeing Soviet Army into three defensive positions along the southern coast of the Crimean Peninsula. With their backs against the Black Sea again, the enemy was fighting with grim determination for every meter of ground. The fighting was often hand-to-hand between the two sides. The casualties were mounting, and we were needed there as soon as possible.

Twice that day, our lorry pulled quickly off the roadway while we all jumped out and ran for cover. Each time, we heard firing and explosions, but never close enough for us to see what was happening. I was just as happy to be able to remain ignorant. Julius said that the enemy must have air superiority in this theater since they seemed to be able to attack whenever they wanted to.

A little past midday, our column rolled through the small town of Caplynka. It was like many other towns that we had seen. It had many bomb-damaged buildings and was blanketed by the ever-present smoke of battle. In this town there was a difference, however. Here, a small but enthusiastic crowd had formed beside the road. They waved and cheered as we rolled past. One old lady held up a religious icon that she had probably been hiding since the Godless communists had come to power two decades before. I felt good that we were liberating these people from a corrupt and evil system. During a short refueling stop just outside of Caplynka, I saw two peasants reverently fingering the swastika on the side of Captain Roiders' Kubelwagen. My Russian wasn't good enough to follow everything they said, but I understood that they thought that the Nazi symbol was a variation of the Christian cross. Apparently, they thought that we were conducting a religious crusade against the ungodly. I wondered what "Der Fuhrer" would have thought of that.

While we all waved and smiled back, I noticed that Elaine didn't join in the happy mood. She sat quietly and looked mostly at the floor of the lorry. She had been quiet ever since the crossing of the Dnieper.

Just before sunset, we passed through the narrowest part of the Perekops Isthmus. It was less than six kilometers wide at this point, and the evidence of the terrible battle fought over this tortured ground was everywhere.

The road itself was one of the few all-weather surfaced roads in the Soviet Union, but it was badly cratered. The gaps had been hastily filled by bulldozing anything handy into the craters and covering everything with dirt. We passed many lines of barbed wire and countless concrete structures that the troops called "pillboxes". Shell craters and debris littered the ground as far as the eye could see. The dry grass-cover had been almost entirely burned off and destroyed vehicles and discarded equipment littered the landscape.

A single rail line paralleled the road for most of the way along the isthmus. It was on this track that I saw an odd sight. At first, I thought I was seeing a group of buildings sitting amidst the desolation. As we drew nearer, however, I came to realize that I was looking at the cars of a train. They weren't normal rail cars, however. They were all boxed in with armor plate and mounted guns of all sorts. There were heavy cannons protruding from slits in the sides of some cars, while others had anti-aircraft guns mounted on top of them. There were even two cars that had the turret and gun from a tank mounted on them. The whole thing looked like an armored wall across the isthmus. I later found out that our forces had had a very difficult time overcoming this obstacle since there were no armored units assigned to the Eleventh Army, and the Luftwaffe was heavily outnumbered in this theater of operations.

It took most of another day to cross the gradually rising plain of the central Crimean Peninsula. It was now almost mid-November and the semi-arid land that we drove across was covered with dried grass and harvested grain fields. The temperature was just above freezing, and the intermittent rains chilled me to the bone.

By mid-afternoon, we could see a low range of mountains rising ahead of us. The road soon wound its way into these heights and led to the administrative center of the Crimea, the city of Simferopol. This was to be our home for some months to come, although no one knew this at the time.

CHAPTER III

Hard lessons

Simferopol was a very typical Russian city. The communists had erected large ugly cement apartment buildings that occupied entire city blocks. Since it was the administrative center for the entire Crimean district, there were also many government buildings. These buildings differed from the apartments only in their entranceways. Here you would find a few columns and usually some patriotic slogan etched into the front of the building. If possible, these were even more ugly than the apartments.

The city had been occupied about two weeks before our arrival. The collapse of resistance throughout the Crimean Peninsula had been so rapid, after the breakthrough at the Perekop Isthmus, that the city had been taken almost without a fight. That meant that most of these ugly buildings had been taken intact. That was a bit of good fortune that would serve us well throughout the coming winter.

The best feature of the city, from our point of view, was the large, if not well-equipped, hospital. The structure was three stories high and made of, what else, reinforced concrete. It even had several operating rooms with tables and surgery lights, although little else. The medical supplies were almost nonexistent. Whether this was because they had few supplies to begin with, or had taken the supplies with them, we didn't know.

The next few days were very busy for all of us. This was to be the central clearinghouse for casualties from all over the district. Once the field hospitals had stabilized their condition, the wounded would be brought to us. We would perform the more involved surgeries that the field hospitals couldn't or didn't have time for. From here, the seriously wounded would be returned to their homeland for full recovery, or for the disabled, to be processed out of the service.

The first casualties to arrive were from the battles at Feodosiya and Kerch. These were two small port cities in the South and West of the peninsula. Kerch had just fallen to the Germans on the day that we arrived at Simferopol. All our army's attention was now to be directed towards investing the large Russian naval base at Sevastopol. No one realized at the time, but we hadn't heard the last of either Feodosiya or Kerch.

The nurses, nurse's aides, and the orderlies were housed in an apartment building adjacent to the hospital while the doctors stayed in the hospital itself since they were always on call. We couldn't believe our good luck. Though the apartments were very plain and almost totally without furnishings, they seemed like heaven compared to the tents at Odessa.

Each apartment had a small stove at the center of its one-and-only room that could burn either wood or coal. We immediately made good use of these since the rain had stopped and the temperature had plunged to below-freezing only two days after our arrival.

Four people were assigned to each apartment. Naturally, Maria, Elaine, Sasha, and I arranged to room together. We found that it was best that we work different shifts so that there would always be someone in the apartment to keep the stove burning. Once again, we were fortunate. The army provided wood or coal for all their personnel, though we had to carry it up to our third-floor room. There was one toilet for each wing of each floor in the building, but the plumbing didn't work. I doubt that it ever had. We did most of our toilet at the hospital while on our shift if we had time, that is. We became busy with casualties very quickly. Our hospital served both German and Romanian wounded, and there were too many of both. Even though this was a German show, there were several brigades of Romanian troops in the Crimea. Just as the influx of wounded from Feodosiya and Kerch began to taper off, we started to get a steady stream of injured from the fighting around Sevastopol.

From the wounded we treated, we discovered where the eighty thousand Russians that withdrew from Odessa had gone. They were all in Sevastopol along with about one hundred thousand other defenders. That meant that our men were facing almost two hundred thousand enemies who were entrenched in what was probably the strongest fortress in Europe.

For the rest of November and the first half of December our armies, under the command of German General Von Manstien, surrounded the fortress of Sevastopol. While this was going on, I resumed my habit of visiting the wounded whenever I had time. Since most of them were German, out of necessity, I began to learn their language.

It was through talking with these men that I came to realize how unprepared our armies were to carry on a prolonged struggle. Virtually no provision had been made to supply our troops with any clothing or equipment designed for use in the coming winter. The temperature had been falling steadily since our arrival in the Crimea and by mid-December the average temperature was well below zero, yet our men had no winter overcoats or boots designed for cold weather.

Actually, the Germans had it worse in their nice-looking uniforms than our Romanian troops did in their more functional clothes. Our uniforms had never been as dressy as the German's, but at least our men didn't wear tight-fitting hob-nail boots that transmitted every bit of the cold directly to the feet. Also, our troops' conical lamb's wool winter cap, called the Caciula, may have been laughed at by the Germans, but it was much warmer than anything that they had. Our men were not too proud to use any of the wonderfully warm Russian

Valenki felt boots that might be "liberated" from the enemy, whereas the Germans were much more reluctant to admit that anything Russian might be superior, at least in the beginning. I should know, I treated thousands of cases of frostbite that first winter.

There was much bad news in December. First, we got the news that the rest of Army Group South, which had advanced across the Nogai Steppe to capture the major industrial city of Rostov, had been forced to abandon their prize and were now fighting for their lives on the open plains. Even worse, was the news from the central front. Army Group Center had been forced to go over to the defensive after reaching the very gates of Moscow. Hordes of Asian troops from Russia's far eastern provinces had counter-attacked all along the line in front of the Russian capital, where they were even now forcing our armies away from our ultimate goal.

It is hard to describe the gloom that the news of the Moscow retreat brought to our spirits. Up until the first week of December we had expected Moscow to fall momentarily. Then the war would have been over. How could the Russians continue with their political, spiritual, and industrial heart cut out? That thought above all had motivated our troops to try their utmost. Now the hope of a quick victory was gone, and we were facing a bitter Russian winter on the open field of battle. I knew enough history to know that this same situation had spelled doom for Napoleon.

Oh, we were still confident of victory, but now we knew it was going to be a very long, cold winter. It was probably all this bad news that generated the emotions that led to a confrontation between Elaine and myself.

I had just reentered our apartment after working my shift at the hospital next door and had carried a scuttle of coal up to the room with me. Elaine was getting dressed to go on her shift (she should have already been on duty) when I entered.

"Throw some more coal on the fire, Anna. It's so cold in here that I can't stand it," said Elaine. Her tone of voice seemed to exclaim that the world was treating her unfairly.

I hooked the door of the small stove open with the poker and looked in. There were two lumps of coal already there, burning merrily, so I said, "There's plenty of fire there. You know that we have to conserve heating materials. Our army has already appropriated most of the civilian supplies around here."

"Oh, for Christ's sake! Throw some coal on the fire!" exclaimed Elaine. "I'm freezing."

I had just assisted with an operation to remove the frostbitten toes of a soldier, so I was not in the mood to be diplomatic as I replied, "You're freezing? You should try living in a hole in the ground twenty-four hours a day with no source of heat except to lean against the man next to you!

"And you shut up, Maria," I added quickly, to forestall some sort of suggestively snide remark that I could see brewing behind Maria's shining eyes as she devoured my confrontation with Elaine.

"Damn you, Anna!" shouted Elaine. "You're such a fool. I think you like it here! Don't you realize that people are trying to kill us? The damned Russians tried to bomb the hospital again last night."

"Yes," I said, feigning thoughtfulness. "I seem to remember something about that. Let's see...where was I? Oh, yes. I was *in* the damned hospital at the time, as I remember!"

"See what I mean. You weren't even on duty, and you were in that miserable place. You like it here!"

"I like helping people," I answered. "But if you think I like this war, you're more crazy than you say I am."

"Well, at least you have compensation for being here," said Elaine.

"What compensations?" I asked this very calmly, even though I thought I knew what was coming. I noticed Maria's expression go from amusement to worry.

Elaine continued with an air of superiority. "Your boyfriends, of course. Even though you couldn't find your wonderful Peter here, at least you have your German Captain to fall back on...or under."

I was speechless for a moment. It was true that my biggest disappointment so far in this whole war had been finding out that Peter had continued on towards Rostov with the other part of the Third Army instead of coming here to the Crimea. I suppose that if I had been able to look deeply enough into my soul, I would also have realized that I was feeling a little guilty at enjoying Captain Roiders' attentions while being betrothed to Peter.

I replied as coldly as I could. "As you well know, we have all been too busy for any kind of social life. Captain Roider stops once in a while to say hello. That is all."

"He doesn't stop by to say hello to the rest of us," said Elaine. "He doesn't bring us little presents like chocolate bars either."

"I always share anything he brings me with all of you."

"That's not the point, is it? said Elaine.

At this point I noticed that Maria had maneuvered herself between the two of us. I asked her, "What are you doing? Do you think I am going to try to kill the little...her?"

Before Maria could answer, Elaine said, "I'm tired of having people trying to kill me. I quit! I'm telling them today that I want to go home."

"But what about your nursing certificate?" asked Maria.

"I don't care about the nursing certificate." Elaine was answering Maria's question, but she was looking at me. "I'll get my certificate eventually. But Anna will stay here, even if she earns a dozen certificates. Just so long as she can *save people*."

I didn't say anything, but I was thinking, *Your damned right, you coward.*

Thinking back on this time as I write down my story, I realize that Elaine was not guilty of being a coward. She was only guilty of being sane in an insane world. It was myself and the rest of the world that were wrong. At the time, however, I was not so objective.

The re-laying of track in European gage to Simferopol was completed shortly after our fight. Elaine was on the first trainload of wounded to leave, and at the time I was glad to see her go. I have never heard what happened to her, or even if she made it home alive.

It was not long after Elaine's departure that I found that I didn't know as much as I thought about my other friends. Once again, our little coal stove seemed to be the catalyst for a "lesson" in my education of how the world works.

It was atypically slow at the hospital for a change, and my supervisor sent me home to our apartment in the middle of our shift to get some extra rest. After Elaine's departure, Sasha was the only one using the apartment at night as Maria and I were both on the night shift at the hospital. Since it was about midnight when I climbed the stairs to our flat, I was very careful to open the door quietly to avoid waking Sasha.

Lighting the paraffin lamp, I hurried to change into my nightgown. The pathetic little coal stove in the center of the room barely kept the temperature above freezing, it seemed. There were only two beds in the room. Each shift used the same beds when the other was on duty. In the military, they call it hot bunking. Sasha was by herself now and could use either bunk she wanted; though she was in the one I considered "mine." I hesitated a second, and then began to get into the bed Maria usually used. Sasha's voice coming from the gloomy darkness made me jump.

"Am I in your bed, Anna? I'll move if you want."

"What? Oh, no. You stay there, where you're warm. We can switch around in the morning when you go to work," I said.

As I began to pull the covers down on "Maria's" bed, Sasha said, "I have a better idea. I'm freezing even under the covers. Why don't you join me in here? There's plenty of room and we can share our body heat."

"Oh, that's okay. I'll warm up in a little while," I said as I contemplated the idea of crawling into those frigid sheets.

"Come on Anna! What are you afraid of? That people will talk? I tell you; I'm freezing. Come over here, *please.*"

"All right, you talked me into it," I said. As I hurried over to Sasha's bed, she lifted the covers and I quickly jumped in.

As she lowered the covers over us she said, "See? Just like a pajama party." Then she giggled a little, and so did I.

I thought she would roll over facing away from me, but she didn't. She did pull the covers over our heads, saying, "Let's conserve our heat as much as we can."

"Okay," I said. "Now let's get some sleep."

I was a little uncomfortable with the situation, but I had to admit it was nice to crawl into an already-warmed bed. To breath better, I stuck my head out of the covers while Sasha stayed curled below them. I was becoming drowsy when I felt Sasha squirming around under the covers. She seemed to be wiggling closer to me. Soon, she seemed to have her head buried between my breasts.

I was going to roll over to face the other way, but she laid one of her arms over my waist. I thought she was already asleep, so I didn't move so as not to awaken her.

I was getting very uncomfortable as she seemed to be rocking her head against my breasts. I was just getting ready to say something to her when her hand slipped from my waist and went between my thighs.

"Sasha! Sasha, wake up." I whispered.

To my surprise, she answered me immediately and with no sleepiness in her voice. "I'm awake. What's the matter?"

"You're…touching me," I said.

"I know. You are very soft."

"What? What are you saying?"

"I need you," she said.

I began to roll out of the bed, but her grip on my thigh tightened painfully and her other hand grabbed my arm. "What's the matter, Anna? Don't you like me?"

"Of course I like you, Sasha. You're like a sister to me. But I'm not…*like that.*"

"Well, I am *like that*. And I need someone to be with."

When I tried to roll from the bed again she held me tightly. "Anna, please! Listen to me. If you do, I'll let go and you can run from me if you want."

"All right, I'll listen, but I'm not interested in a…girl, girl relationship," I said.

By now, Sasha's head was above the covers and we were face to face in the dim lamp light. "You don't have to have sex with me," she said. "I don't even know if that is actually possible in a technical sense. But I really, really need to be *with* someone right now. With all the death and suffering I see every day I need some comforting."

"I see the same things daily," I said. "And I don't jump into bed with other women for comfort."

"That's because you're 'straight' and you would; have to jump into bed with a man for that kind of comfort, and you wouldn't do that would you? No, because you're *honorable* and think of yourself as belonging to your doctor Peter. Well I don't have anyone, and I wouldn't have a *man* if I could."

"Why not?" I asked in a whisper.

"Let's just say I had all the men I needed growing up with a sicko father and two over-sexed brothers. I started having the pleasure of a man's company at a very early age."

"You mean they...? Oh, my God, that's terrible. No wonder you don't like men."

"Who said I don't like men? I like people. Why do you think I became a nurse? I don't think being...used, can cause a person to become a lesbian. That's a character trait like being happy or hating Bananas or something.

"Do you know why I like you? You try to help people no matter how much it costs you. So just think of me as a patient who needs therapy. You would do anything for one of our boys, wouldn't you?"

"I wouldn't have sex with one of them!" I said.

"Only because it would be morally wrong, not because you wouldn't do anything you could for them. And besides, like I said this isn't 'having sex', it's just helping me when I need it.

"Please stay with me. You don't have to do anything."

"I must have 'sucker' written all over my face. Okay, I'll stay. But I'm still not into girls, just my friends."

So, that is how I come to be sleeping with a member of my own gender. She happily tucked her head back under the covers and was soon suckling one of my nipples. Frankly, it turned me on in spite of myself. But when she began to touch me between the legs, I firmly removed her hand.

Soon her hand was between her own legs and I could tell she was having an orgasm as she nearly bit down on my breast. When she finished jumping and squirming around, she wrapped her arms around me and fell asleep. I pulled her head to my neck and rested my chin on her soft brown hair, falling asleep almost immediately.

I awoke the next morning in the same position to find Maria standing over us with the most enigmatic smile I have ever seen on her face.

I gave her my most severe scowl and motioned with a tilt of my head that she should be on about her business. My movement must have awakened Sasha because she raised her head from under my chin and looked at Maria. I thought she would be flustered or embarrassed, but instead she said, "Hi, Maria. Am I late for shift again?"

Then she simply got up and dressed quickly, as Maria got ready for bed. No one said anything more, but Maria kept smiling the whole time. When she was dressed, Sasha pulled on her coat and started out the door. But instead of leaving straight away, she turned back and came over to me. Still saying nothing, she kissed me on the cheek and then hurried from the room.

As I stoked the small stove and combed my hair Maria continued to watch me with that stupid grin on her face. Finally, I turned on her and shouted, "What!?"

Shaking her head, Maria said, "Nothing, nothing at all."

"Just...well, she got to you, didn't she, with that poor, poor, pitiful me routine?"

"What do you mean?" I stammered.

"Do you believe that family abuse story?" Maria asked.

"You mean she told you?"

"Of course she did. She uses it for sympathy, but I think it's real."

"Why did she tell you her story?"

Maria finally began to chuckle, "She thought she needed it to get me to sleep with her. But she needn't have. She is really pretty sexy once you get her into bed."

"What!? You slept with her? How could you?"

"Ha, look who is talking. You just got out of her bed, but I bet you didn't enjoy it the way I did, did you?"

"You mean you're…?"

"Hell no! But I can enjoy an opportunity when it presents itself, though I must admit that I prefer boys."

"Well, so do I," I said.

"Bull, you are so uptight I bet you haven't slept with even one patient."

"Like you have," I said. Then looking into Maria's smiling face, I said, "Oh, my God. You have slept with them!"

"Not all of them," she said defensively, "only the reasonably healthy ones."

"I'm living in a human cesspool," I moaned.

To which Maria said, "I must say, you are taking this all much better than Elaine did."

"What do you mean?"

"When our little Sasha hit on Elaine, she really freaked," answered Maria.

"I'm going to bed now…by myself," I said. Unfortunately, Maria's chuckling kept me awake for quite a while.

On another occasion, Maria and I had words of a sort, though the outcome was less surprising to me. It was the middle of the night, and I was asleep in the apartment when Maria came in. Making noise as usual, she woke me as she began undressing.

"Be quiet," I said. Then as my brain began to wake up, I asked. "Did you just get off duty?"

"Hell no," she answered. "I just got off Private Baum…or the other way around. I really can't remember which."

"You're drunk!" I accused. Then I realized what she had said. "You don't mean that you, uh…slept with another soldier, do you?"

"Slept hell, we weren't sleeping. Boy, are you a prude."

As Maria began dropping her clothes all over the floor in preparation for getting into bed, I sat up fully awake now. "But you can't just sleep with any man that comes along," I scolded.

"Look, I already told you we don't sleep. And I don't go with just any man. He has to be cute…or an officer. Besides, it's none of your business. If you want to keep your…self, for one man, that's up to you. Personally, in view of the fact that any of us could be killed at any time, I plan on having some fun while I can. And if my fun lifts the morale of one or two of our soldiers, so much the better."

"One or two?" I sneered.

"OK, a whole battalion if you want! It's still none of your business.

"Put out the candle, will you? I'm really tired," she said.

"I'll bet!" I snipped.

"Oh, shut up."

Maria was on duty, and I was in the flat alone one evening in early December when Sasha came rushing into the room. She was trying to say something, but she was out of breath from running up the three flights of stairs.

"Take it easy and slow down," I said.

In a few seconds, having regained her breath, she began again, "The Japanese have attacked the British and Americans! They are at war now! We have a new ally!"

I was surprised, of course. Mostly because I had thought of nothing but our own little piece of the war for so long that, for me, the rest of the world had virtually ceased to exist. "You say that they attacked the British *and* Americans?"

"That is what the radio said," she answered.

"Then we have a new enemy in the Americans as well as a new ally," I said. "Did the radio say if the Japanese attacked the Russians also?"

"They didn't say anything about the Russians," said Sasha.

"Well, if they didn't attack the Russians, then they are no help to us."

"But they'll have to attack the Russians if they are Germany's ally, won't they?"

"I don't know," I said. "But I think we are likely to see Americans coming over the horizon before we see any Japanese." Unfortunately, this was one of my better predictions.

As the month of December moved into its second half, our army began to press its attack on Sevastopol with greater intensity. This meant that the flow of wounded into our hospital began to increase again. The word amongst the troops was that General Von Manstein wanted Sevastopol taken by Christmas. I wondered if he meant it to be a Christmas present for Hitler. Christmas day brought big news all right, but not what everyone had hoped for. Even though it had been obvious for several days that Sevastopol wouldn't be in our hands by Christmas, everyone was determined to celebrate the holiday as much as possible. A Christmas tree had been set up in every ward and decorated with whatever could be found. There was even a nice holiday meal with many dishes for the patients and staff alike.

Frankly, I was having a little trouble swallowing my roast chicken as I thought of our men on the front lines when the news broke. At first, it was just a rumor, but it was soon confirmed by radio. The Russians had landed an entire army at Kirch, on the Eastern end of the Crimean Peninsula. In thirty degrees below zero weather, they had crossed the narrow Straits of Taman and waded ashore against a single division of German infantry under the command of a general named Von Sponeck. After quickly securing bridgeheads on either side of the town, they were now threatening to surround the Germans there.

This attack against the rear of our army was obviously intended to distract us from our attack on Sevastopol. The next five days showed, however, that the Russian strategy had failed. The German division defending Kirch wiped out one of the landings and contained the other in its beachhead without having to draw any troops from the Sevastopol attack.

Unfortunately, the Russians weren't done yet. On the thirtieth of December they landed another army at Feodosiya on the southern coast of the Crimean Peninsula. We had virtually no troops defending Feodosiya at the time, and if the landing went unopposed, our troops that had done such a wonderful job defending Kirch would be cut off from the rest of our army. This latest landing even threatened to cut off the entire eleventh army from its' supply bases on the mainland.

This time there could be no other choice. On the last day of the year of nineteen forty-one, with our troops already fighting their way through the last defense lines of Sevastopol, the attack was called off so that units could be rushed to Feodosiya. A few days later, I found out how close we had come to taking that formidable fortress from one of the men injured in that last attack.

I had been wandering the wards after my shift, exchanging a few words with those wounded who couldn't sleep, when I came across a young German soldier who seemed even more distressed than most. I introduced myself in my broken German and asked him if there was anything I could help him with. I could see the tracks of tears on his cheeks and thought that he might be in pain.

Trying to hide the tears, he said, "No, there's nothing you can do, unless you happen to have Fort Stalin in your back pocket."

My German wasn't very good yet, so I thought that I had misunderstood him. "I'm sorry, I don't understand. What is Fort Stalin?"

"Fort Stalin is that miserable piece of hell that I and most of the sixteenth regiment got our asses shot off trying to capture."

He sounded bitter, so I tried to soothe him. "Casualties have been heavy everywhere, and you can't blame yourself if you didn't achieve your goal. I'm sure you tried..."

"That's just it!" he interrupted. "We had it in our hands! We had gotten across the Belbek Valley under fire from the Russian artillery and mortars. We got through the mines and the barbed wire. We fought through the machine-gun fire and climbed the glacis wall. We were in the fort and clearing the Russians out of each trench and pillbox. And then what? Then they told us to withdraw! Withdraw for god's sake! There were only sixty men left in my entire regiment. I got shot in the back...withdrawing!"

I could see now that his tears were not from pain or fear, but from rage and frustration. I took a cool damp cloth and wiped away the beads of perspiration that had appeared on his forehead, saying as I did so, "Try not to get upset, it will only aggravate your wounds. I know you're frustrated, but you must be confident that your comrades' sacrifices were not in vain.

"The Russians have landed two armies in our rear and if we don't send forces to stop them, they could cut all of us off and trap us here in the Crimea. We can't let that happen, can we?"

My attempt to get him thinking of the big picture may have helped a little. Grudgingly he conceded, "No, I guess not. But they never tell us what is going on. They just say, 'Go here, do that, do this.' They never tell us why, or even how."

"Well," I said. "It sounds like you have just described what being in the army is all about."

He didn't laugh, but at least he did smile a little. I held his hand, and we talked about his home, a little village called In Den Pier near Frankfort, until he drifted off to sleep.

The enlisted men weren't the only ones feeling the pressure, as I was to find out only two days later. Captain Roider had been uncharacteristically absent for over a week when he hailed me as I left the hospital one evening.

"Anna," he called from his Kubelwagen as he and his driver pulled up to the curb in front of me. "Hop in. I want to talk to you." When I hesitated, he added, "I know you are tired. I promise not to keep you too long."

I *was* tired after my ten-hour shift, but as I have said, having the attentions of a handsome army Captain was very flattering. He jumped out of the car and held the door to the back seat open for me. I smiled and got into the little vehicle. To my surprise, he didn't resume his place in the front seat, but instead, went around the car and got into the back seat with me.

The back seat had very little leg room so that even a small person like me had to sit a little sideways. When the Captain got in, the seat was suddenly very cramped and of necessity our knees rubbed together. When that happened, I felt an odd tingling sensation run up my leg. I tried to not let anything show on my face, but I don't know if I succeeded. For a few seconds I thought that Captain Roider had engineered this situation just to achieve this kind of intimacy, but he seemed not to notice our contact and began talking immediately.

"I am very sorry that I was not around to celebrate the new year with you, but I have been very busy. Let me make it up to you by taking you to dinner. Then I'll be able to fill you in on what has been happening."

I wasn't as interested in "what has been happening" as much as where he would find someplace to go for dinner. Russian cities were not noted for their fine dining, and I thought that anything that there might have been, would not be open now anyway. I had to find out. "Dinner?" I asked. "Where?" With his usual charming smile he said, "Why, at the officer's club, of course. They just opened one over by headquarters. I don't know what the food is like yet, but it can't be any worse than your unit's mess hall, and you have to eat anyway."

I shook my head yes, and we were off. On the short drive to the club, he explained that after the crisis touched off by the Russian landings, he had been briefly assigned to army headquarters to help with the routing of units to their new defensive positions.

When the car stopped, the Captain jumped out and hurried around to my side to open my door for me. I felt that I could get used to this kind of treatment. Speaking of feelings, that same warm tingle went up my spine when he casually put his arm around my back to guide me into the officer's club.

The feeling was so distracting that I almost missed seeing the first attractive building I had come across in Simferopol. It gave the appearance of a sprawling log cabin, but much more splendid. The huge hard-wood logs that made up the walls had been hand hewn to an almost perfect symmetry. The numerous windows had their glazed panes set off with an intricate wooden latticework, while the steep, wood tiled, roof overhung the walls by a good meter. At the entrance was a beautifully carved wooden door.

I marveled to Hans, "I haven't seen anything like this anywhere in Russia."

"It was the local commissars' Dacha," he explained. "He was responsible for the political 'purity' for this region. As you can see, all communists are equal. It's just that some are more equal than others."

"I didn't think the communists could build anything this beautiful," I said as we entered the oak paneled dining room.

"Oh, I'm sure they didn't build this. It must be left over from the days of the 'evil Czars.' It probably belonged to a noble family...before they were shot. But let's not dwell on their misfortune. Instead, let us enjoy a nice meal for a change."

By normal standards I suppose that the meal was nothing special, but to me it seemed like an elegant feast. I enjoyed my meal while Captain Roider talked of his work in organizing the defense of the Crimea. After a while, the Captain lowered his voice and leaned across the table to address me in a rather conspiratorial manor.

"Did you know that they have arrested General Von Sponeck?"

My eyes widened in surprise as I said, "But wasn't he the General commanding the division that defended Kerch so well?"

"Yes, but when the Russians landed behind him at Feodosiya he retreated across the isthmus to rejoin the rest of the army!"

"Well of course he did," I said. "His division would have been surrounded and destroyed if he had not.

"True, but he had orders to hold his position at all costs. He tried to say that he didn't receive those orders, but Von Manstien isn't buying it."

"What will they do to him?" I asked.

"I don't know, but he is of noble birth. Ordinarily, I would say that he would get off with a reprimand, but I hear that Hitler himself is livid with anger."

For a change, I chose to keep my mouth shut. Personally, I had no use for "Der Fuhrer", but I knew that Hans held him in the highest regard. I was about to find out just how high.

Looking around again and lowering his voice even more, he continued. "This Von Sponeck affair is nothing compared to what has happened on the Central Front. The Fuhrer has sacked Guderian!"

This time I really *was* surprised as I said, "You mean General Heinz Guderian, the father of the German armored corps?" I knew that I sounded like a propaganda newsreel, but after hearing it a thousand times, it seemed the only way to refer to him. "Yes," said Hans. "The Fuhrer says that Guderian has become defeatist. That he has lost his nerve. I can't understand it though. I served under his command in France when I was with the Tenth Armored Division. During our drive from Sedan to Dunkirk he virtually dragged the rest of the high command along behind him. They were actually afraid of his tremendous success. Even when the British counterattack at Arras threatened to cut off the spearhead formations, he maintained the advance while General Rommel stopped them with the anti-aircraft guns and saved our bacon."

"But I thought that your victory over France was almost inevitable due to your superiority in tanks and planes," I said.

"Ha, that's a laugh," he barked. "You bought all that propaganda, didn't you? Our Luftwaffe was outnumbered two to one and the French alone had three tanks for every two of ours. On top of that, their tanks were better than ours in many ways. Their Somuas had better armor and guns than most of ours and the Char-B... well, we had nothing to compare to them. Thank God they only had a few.

"I know how your Romanian army complains that we only give them obsolete equipment, but the captured French tanks we have given them are almost as good as anything we have, even now. No, we beat the French through superior training and leadership. That's why I can't figure this Guderian thing."

"Then the Fuhrer must have it wrong," I said.

That was the first time I had seen Captain Roider get really angry. For a moment he regarded me with an ugly look that actually scared me. Then he said, "The Fuhrer is never wrong. I was too old to join the Hitler Youth organization when it was started, but I have helped to train many of those young men. And even the youngest of them knows that the Fuhrer is always right. Just look at what he has done for our country. He brought us out of economic slavery and put Germany back on top where it belongs. He led us through Anschluss and rearmament. He has led us back to our former greatness, and now he is settling both the Jewish and Bolshevik problems. He is a genius...and he is *never* wrong!"

My blood ran cold as I realized that I was looking into the eyes of a fanatic. A few seconds later, I could see the fires of his fanaticism fade and the light of human reason return to his face. He smiled and said, "Let's not spoil dinner by talking politics." He pointed to my plate and said, "You've hardly touched your dessert."

I returned to my meal, but inside I shuddered to think what would happen if I ever revealed my Jewish heritage to this man. On the ride back to the hospital the occasional contact between us just didn't have the same spark for me.

In the end, the Russian invaders were sealed up on the Kerch peninsula. Their attempt to surround our army had failed. In one way, however, they had succeeded in their objective. The attack on Sevastopol had been called off and could not be attempted again while our army was split between two fronts.

For us in the Crimea, the war had become a stalemate that would last through the early months of nineteen forty-two. To the North, the war was going even worse for our armies. Massive attacks by seemingly unlimited numbers of Russian troops continued to force the central front to fall back farther and farther. The enemy was trying to surround our armies there. For the most part, they failed. However, there were two exceptions.

At Demyansk, the Soviets surrounded one hundred thousand German troops, while at Kholm, they surrounded another thirty-five hundred. All throughout the terrible winter months of February, March, and April, a massive effort by the Luftwaffe's supply squadrons kept these isolated units supplied from the air.

When these units were liberated from their encirclements during the spring offensives, everyone breathed a sigh of relief. We had no idea at that time that these successful operations would spell doom for virtually the entire Romanian Army along with hundreds of thousands of German troops at a time not too far in the future. All we knew was that we were tired, overworked, and yes, bored. There were only three of us in the apartment now that Elaine had gone. Since we were as short of staff as we were of everything else, our not getting a replacement for her came as no surprise.

Through the long winter months, one of the things that bothered us most, was the close proximity of the "Russian Riviera". As I said earlier, Simferopol sat in the foothills on the northern side of a small mountain chain. The mountains were called the Yalya Mountains. Less than one hundred kilometers to the south, over those mountains, lay the Black Sea coastline. Even though the temperature here was usually twenty to thirty degrees below freezing, along the coast, dotted with its' picturesque fishing villages, and warmed by the southerly sea breezes, the temperature was always well above freezing.

The coastal area was called the "Russian Riviera" because all the important people in the Soviet Union would take their vacations there in the summer. Needless to say, to exchange this depressingly cold city for an almost tropical coastline, any one of us would have traded our soul. *And it was so close!*

But, of course, no one was allowed to go there. The officially stated reason was that we couldn't spare the staff for "vacation time". While this was true in the short view, I was sure that a few days off, on a rotating basis would have improved morale and efficiency more than enough to make up for the lost man (or woman) hours.

It was Captain Roider who confided the real reason for our restriction to me. The high command was afraid that the Russians had more landings planned for the coast and didn't want to let anyone go there, lest they be captured. To Hans this reasoning was absurd. He said that if the Russians had anything left up their sleeve, they would have used it long ago.

He was so convinced that it was safe that he conspired to take us to the coast for a day. Actually, he offered to take *me* to the coast, but I refused to go without my friends. After some persuasion, he agreed. Sasha was too chicken to go on our little adventure, so that it was just Maria and me who went with the Captain and his driver.

A strong wind swirled the twenty-below-zero air around us as we piled into the captain's little auto early in the morning. To Captain Roider, I remarked, "I see you got your cast removed."

"Yes," he answered. "I couldn't have very much fun on the beach with that thing on, so I insisted that the doctor remove it."

The auto's engine roared, and soon we began climbing into the mountains surrounding Simferopol. The vehicle's weak heater fought a losing battle with the cold as we gained altitude toward the high passes. Soon, however, we descended into a small valley between ranges where the temperature climbed a little. Then we were climbing over a second range of gradually ascending mountain slopes. Once over the second set of passes, the mountain slopes dropped off sharply. We wound our way down twisting, narrow roads, amidst numerous streams of snowmelt as they leaped and splashed their way to the sea below. It was a fine, clear day, and we could see far out over the dark waters of the Black Sea. Below the snow line, we entered forests consisting of Oak, Beech, Pine, and many other varieties of trees. A little lower on the slopes, we entered orchards of fruit trees These were followed by vineyards covering vast areas of hillside.

Even though it was mid-winter and the vegetation wasn't at its peak, it was wonderful to see any living plants at all, after the monotonous white of snow drifts in Simferopol. Once we got down to the coastal plain, the temperatures seemed absolutely warm.

Along the way to the beach, we saw several more Dachas dating from the Czarists' times, as well as the ruins of some medieval castles and even the ancient remains of a Greek trading post. What we were all really interested in was the beach, of course. We drove right onto the sand within a kilometer of Yalta and piled out of the car.

The air temperature was probably only about twenty degrees centigrade, but after the frozen high plains it seemed like heaven. We found a spot on the sand that was in the sun and protected from the breeze by a rocky outcropping where we laid out our blankets. Somehow the army blankets seemed out of place on the beautiful sunny beach, but we didn't care.

I'm not normally a sun worshipper, but I quickly peeled off my coat and then my dress. Underneath, I had worn my swimsuit. It was a very conservative one-piece suit with an attached skirt that came almost halfway to my knees so I didn't feel over-exposed, even in mixed company, as I stretched out on the blanket.

The water was too cold for swimming, so we contented ourselves with wading in the shallow surf and sunbathing. I felt bad for poor Lutz. I knew he felt out of place relaxing with his Captain and two "civilians."

Late in the afternoon, we ate the lunch we had brought with us. The only beverage we could get from the mess hall that would keep for the trip was water, so we drank that with our food. As we were finishing our meal, Captain Roider said that it was a shame that we had to drink water when we were in one of the best wine producing regions in Russia.

He told Lutz to take the car into Yalta and see if he couldn't get a couple bottles of wine for us. When he insisted that Lutz take Maria with him to see the sights of Yalta, I began to get a little nervous, but I said nothing. Maria seemed to look at me strangely as she and Lutz disappeared around the rocks. Now I was *really* nervous.

When I heard the sounds of the little car fading in the distance, I got up and went into the surf to wade. The captain watched me from his blanket for a few moments and then called to me.

"Anna, it's too cold to be out in the water. Come out and get warm."

I pretended not to hear him and waded around for a few more minutes. Finally, I *did* get very cold and returned to my blanket. As I said, "Wow, that water really is cold," I wrapped myself up in the blanket like a mummy.

Hans just smiled at me and shook his head. I wondered why so many people did that when they were around me as he got up from his blanket. Dressed only in his khaki shorts and loose unbuttoned shirt, he moved around behind me. I tried to follow his movements with my eyes without moving my head, but I lost sight of him. That is why I jumped so much when his hands closed on my upper arms from behind.

Saying, "Relax, I only want to warm you up," he began rubbing his hands up and down vigorously on my arms.

As the friction of his hands (to say nothing of his closeness) warmed me, I said, "Umm...that feels good."

That is when he said, "So will this," and slipped his arms around me from behind. At first, he just held me around the waist, and I said nothing. Then his hand slipped upward over my ribs to cup my breast through the blanket. With my heart pounding, I smiled a little and said, "Now, now captain, what about your proper military bearing?" As I said this, I tried to twist away from his enfolding arms. His hands tightened on my breasts until it was uncomfortable, and he pulled me back against him.

All I could say was, "Captain! Don't!"

As he roughly turned me to face him, he said, "Call me Hans, Anna."

I could see that his face was flushed, and his eyes seemed to burn into me. I was becoming very frightened. He pushed me backwards, and even though I tried to remain on my feet he forced me onto my back in the soft sand. Looming over me, he forced a kiss on me. His tongue tried to probe my mouth, but I clamped my teeth shut and rolled my face away from him. With the side of my face pressed into the sand, I said, "No, Hans! Think what you are doing!"

He didn't answer, but instead pulled the blanket from around me. The blanket flipped me onto my stomach, and I immediately tried to crawl away. His strong hands grabbed my hip bones and literally slammed me back over onto my back. Dropping to a crouching position over me, he placed one knee between my legs and tried to force me to spread them apart.

This whole time I was yelling, "Hans, no! Stop it! Stop it!"

He had gotten both his legs between mine and was pulling the shoulder strap of my suit down when I got one of my hands free and slapped him as hard as I could, in the face. This stunned him for a second, which I took advantage of. I leaned up off the sand and screamed into his face. "I am engaged to the man I love and the only way you will have me is by force! If you do that, I'll hate you forever!"

I could see emotions battling on his face as what I had said registered. I don't know what the decision would have been, because just then we could hear the noisy approach of his car.

He stood up and turned his back to me, mumbling the single word, "Sorry."

By the time Maria and Lutz came around the intervening rocks, the captain was staring out to sea, and I had pulled the blanket back around myself. I'm sure something showed on our faces as Lutz looked grim and Maria actually looked shocked.

Since the captain was still standing with his back to us, Maria mouthed the question, "Did he...?" I shook my head, but my denial must have been too vigorous because Maria didn't look convinced. The wine was consumed in an uncomfortable silence and we soon started on the return trip. The drive back was also a rather silent affair. Although

Maria and I tried to start conversations about the beautiful scenery on several occasions, the talk always sputtered out quickly.

The only time Captain Roider responded in anything except monosyllables was when I commented that he might expect to be reassigned to an armored unit now that he had the use of both arms again. I hadn't intended this comment as a snide remark, honest to God. I didn't even realize the double meaning it carried until after I had said it.

Fortunately, he didn't seem to take it the wrong way. He just complained that the chances of his being assigned to an armored unit were remote because there were no armored units in the entire army of the Crimea.

We got to Simferopol very late and went straight to our apartment building. As we prepared to get a couple hours of sleep before our shift began, Maria whispered to me so as not to wake Sasha, "Did he try to force himself on you?"

"Uh, no... not really, "I stammered. "He got some ideas in his head, but I talked him out of them...I think. But I am glad that you hurried Lutz to return to the beach."

"I hurried Lutz?" Maria said. "Ha, that's a laugh. I thought he was going to kill us the way he flew into town, grabbed the first two bottles of wine he saw, pointed to the wharf and said, 'There's the fishing fleet,' and took off for the beach again. We weren't gone fifteen minutes."

"You weren't?" I said in shock. "I thought you were gone for at least an hour. How about that. I'll have to have a talk with Lutz someday...to see what all the hurry was about."

It would be quite a while before I had a chance to ask Lutz about his actions that day. Throughout the rest of January and the months of February and March we were fully occupied with the business of running a wartime hospital. We treated two cases of frostbite or pneumonia for every casualty by enemy action. The nurses' aides assisted with the routine procedures, washed patients, changed sheets, and cleaned uncounted numbers of bedpans. On occasions when there was a shortage of nurses available, or an overabundance of patients, we even assisted in surgery.

Throughout that long, cold winter we were never at a loss for work to do. Captain Roider's official duties brought him to the hospital frequently. Because of that, it was impossible to avoid him completely, but I did so as much as possible.

At first, he seemed as reluctant to confront me as I was to see him. However, after almost two months, he began to approach me once again. I would only speak to him as my duties required and refused to engage in any personal conversation. After a time, however, his repeated apologies and requests to explain himself began to wear down my resistance. Call me a fool if you will, but I was still flattered that a handsome man of his important position felt that he needed to explain himself to me.

Finally, the day came when he managed to corner me alone. I was climbing the stairs to my apartment when I looked up to find him sitting on the steps above me. My heart leaped into my throat when I realized that there was no one else nearby. I wanted to turn and run, but at the same time, I wasn't going to let him know that I was afraid of him. Instead of running, I decided to say something clever.

"What are you doing here?"

Okay, it wasn't that clever, but what *was* I going to say?

"Waiting for you," he answered.

"Let me by!" I demanded.

To my surprise, he just stood up and moved to the side of the stairwell.

I hurried past him, turning back towards him once I was several steps above.

"That's it?" I asked.

"I just wanted to prove that you can trust me. I can't apologize enough for my behavior, but I can't stand having you mad at me either. I don't know what came over me on that beach...Well, I guess I do. It was you. You were so beautiful there in that romantic setting. I guess that I thought that you felt as lonely as I did. I honestly thought that you felt something for me like I do for you.

I'm beautiful? He's lonely? What does he feel for me? As I have said, I'm a fool, and this fool's heart was beginning to thaw out. I wasn't about to forgive that easily though.

"You nearly raped me!"

"But I didn't, did I? Once you made your feeling clear I stopped, didn't I?"

"Yes, you did," I said softly. At the same time that I said this, I was muffling that little voice in the back of my mind that was saying that he really didn't have any choice.

He looked like a little boy asking to open his Christmas presents early as he said, "Am I forgiven then?" "We'll see," I said. "For now though, I'll let you carry this scuttle of coal up to my room." He smiled his usual charming smile as he carried the heavy scuttle to my door where I promptly closed it in his face, saying, "Thank you." Placing the coal next to the small stove, I wondered if I was relieved or disappointed that he had scrupulously maintained his distance on the way up to the flat.

I saw nothing of the good captain for the next two weeks. I was just beginning to wonder if he had been playing some sort of game with me when he came hurrying up to me in the hospital pharmacy. I was preparing the intravenous medications for use on the next shift when he found me.

"Sorry I haven't been around lately," he began. I've been assigned to assist at headquarters again."

"I suppose that means that we will be getting busy around here again," I speculated.

"Umm...I can't say," he evaded. "Top secret and all that, you know."

Trying to use my driest tone of voice, I said, "Right. So if you can't say anything, why are you here?"

"You're in luck. I'm being sent on an inspection tour of some units on the Sevastopol front, and you get to go with me."

"You call an inspection trip to the front luck? And what makes you think I would go anywhere with you?"

"No, no. It's all right," he protested. "I've arranged for Maria to come with us. And I promise that I won't try to get you alone with me, no matter how much I might like that idea. I just think you'll find our destination interesting."

With raised eyebrows, I asked skeptically, "Just you, me, and Maria?"

"And Lutz, of course," he replied.

"So, when is this 'holiday outing' to take place?"

"Tomorrow. I'll send Lutz to pick you up an hour before dawn."

"Lovely," I said. But I was already speaking to the captain's retreating back as he hurried away.

"What have you gotten me into?" grumbled Maria. Shivering in the predawn darkness, our flat lit only with a single paraffin lamp, we struggled to get dressed before we froze to death, since the stove had burned low during the night.

"Me? This wasn't my idea!" I said.

"Why didn't you just tell him no? After what he tried, how can you trust him?

"He's all right," I said. "I really think that he just got carried away, there on the beach. Besides, you and I aren't going to be more than an arm's length apart for this whole trip. And after all, he did get us out of the hospital for the day."

When the captain's car pulled up to the apartment building, I was glad to see that Lutz was alone in the little vehicle.

Once we were both in the back seat, he said, "I am to drive you to headquarters where we will pick up the captain."

"Fine," I said. "Say, Lutz?"

"Yes, frauline?"

Motioning towards Maria, whose ugly frown did her no justice, I said, "When the two of you left me with Captain Roider on the beach outside Yalta, she said you seemed to be in a very great hurry to get back to us. Why?" Lutz turned to face me, as much as he could from his seat, and said. "The captain is a fine officer, but I have a daughter your age at home, and I wouldn't leave her alone with him."

"Oh, dear," I said. Maria's frown had turned into a smirk as I asked Lutz, "Do you think we will be safe with him today?"

"Today? Yes, I would say so. He is on duty today. He would get into trouble if he didn't stick to business."

Captain Roider joined us outside the headquarters building, and we were off as the sky began to lighten towards dawn. By that light, I could tell that we were headed west, but that was all. After a two-hour ride along the twisting and turning roads of the mountain foot-hills, I had no idea where we were.

When I mentioned this to the captain, he said, "Good, you're not supposed to know where you are when you meet Karl and Dora."

"Who are Karl and Dora?" I asked.

"They are the reason for this inspection trip," he answered. "You'll meet Dora this afternoon, but for now, we are almost to Karl."

I thought about questioning the captain's semantics but didn't get a chance for just then the car rounded a sharp curve and was stopped at a checkpoint by a serious-looking German sentry. Captain Roider's papers seemed to satisfy the sentry, and we drove a short distance into a pine forest. As he exited the vehicle, the captain said, "We have to walk from here. Don't worry, it isn't far."

The weather was getting warmer now, with the snow slowly turning to slush, and Maria and I were glad for the boots that I had insisted that we scrounge from the discarded clothing left behind by the wounded that were invalided back home. We walked several hundred meters through the woods. All along the way I noticed German soldiers spread out amongst the trees. I could even glimpse an occasional machine-gun position hidden here and there. Whoever Karl was, he must be important to have so much protection, I thought.

When the trees began to thin out a bit, Captain Roider turned to me and asked, "What do you see up ahead?"

There, among the pine trees, I could just make out a large rectangular structure that seemed to be about twenty meters long and four meters high with a flat roof. From the top of the structure there protruded what appeared to be a short, fat chimney. Only this chimney was tilted at a considerable angle.

"It looks like some kind of factory," I said.

With a mischievous smile on his face, the captain said, "Oh? Well, let's go and have a closer look, shall we?"

Drawing nearer, I could see that the entire structure was made of metal. Even more surprising was the fact that the whole thing was supported on the kind of treads you would find on a tank, running the entire length of it.

"Good Lord," I said. "This can't be a tank. It's far too big to move under its own power, isn't it?"

"Actually," said the captain, "it can move on its own, but only at five kilometers an hour. You're right, though, it's not a tank. It's a mortar. The largest mortar in the world. It fires a shell that is twenty-four centimeters across and weighs more than the car we came here in. Not only that, but it can shoot up to fifteen kilometers."

"That's very impressive," said Maria. Then, when Captain Roider turned to admire his prize once again, she turned to me and whispered, "Boys never outgrow their fascination with dinosaurs, do they?" I was stifling a laugh when the captain asked us if we would care to climb to the top of this monster. I could see a metal ladder hanging down over the tracks at each corner. They led to further rungs going all the way to the top of it. We both declined his kind offer to try to break our necks and contented ourselves with wandering around the vehicle while the captain conferred with the commander of this unit.

Half an hour later we were walking back to our car when I thought of a question. "Hans...I mean captain, surely they didn't drive that thing here from Germany at five kilometers an hour. How did it get here?" "You're right,' he said. "It travels hung between two special rail cars when it has to go any distance. There is a spur line back there in the woods that was laid to bring it in here."

"Ah, I see. Then making rail travel more comfortable for us nurses wasn't the only reason that your army was in such a hurry to convert the Russian rail system to European standard."

"That's true," he said with a smile. "But your comfort is the much more important reason. Now, let's go see a truly big gun."

"But you just said that Karl is the biggest mortar in the world," said Maria.

"Biggest *mortar*, yes," he said.

Then he refused to say anything more as our little car wound its dizzying way through the hills and valleys surrounding Sevastopol. We traveled the winding roads for a couple more hours until we arrived atop a hill overlooking a small valley. Hans told Lutz to stop the car so that we could all get out. Encompassing the valley with a sweep of his arm, Captain Roider asked, "What do you see down there?"

To Maria and me it looked very much like every other valley that we had been in and out of all morning. The rocky, snow-covered landscape, broken only by the occasional forested area seemed very ordinary.

To Captain Roider I said, "I don't see much of anything. A few trenches and some anti-aircraft guns like usual." Then I looked more closely at the edge of a wooded section on the valley floor. I said, "I think I see a short length of railroad track coming out of those woods down there. No, it's a pair of tracks, but they don't go anywhere."

"That's very good, Anna," he said. "Too good actually. I'll have to tell them to cover those tracks better. If you can see them from here, Ivan can spot them from his aircraft."

"Ivan," was the term used for the Russians, of course, but I couldn't think why they would be interested in a pair of dead-end rail lines.

We got back into the car and started our descent into the valley. We hadn't gone more than a hundred meters, when we came to the first of several checkpoints that we would pass through before arriving at the valley floor. Captain Roider's papers got us through all the checkpoints quickly, and soon we were entering another wooded area.

Men and guns seemed to be everywhere. Half the German army seemed to be hidden in those trees. After yet another check point, we pulled into what could only be described as a small city made of tents, there under the concealing trees.

Two artillery officers met us and led the way through the tent city. From the backward glances that they threw our way, I got the feeling that they thought that we shouldn't be here. I know that *I* certainly felt out of place. I'm sure that Maria and I were the only women for kilometers around. As we rounded a large kitchen tent, we came into view of a gun larger than anything I could have ever imagined. It was a railway gun, of course, and I had seen railway guns before. But this behemoth must have been twice the size of anything I had ever seen.

Captain Roider must have seen the surprise on my face. He said, "Really something, isn't it?"

Apparently, Maria wasn't as impressed as I. She said, "It's a big cannon, so? Can we go home now? I'm really cold."

I don't think Hans even heard Maria's complaining. He started upon a description of the gun that made him sound like a proud father describing a prodigal son.

"This isn't just a big cannon. It's the biggest in the world. It's bigger than anything... even the guns on the world's biggest battleships. It fires a shell that is almost a meter across. And it can shoot it up to fifty kilometers. The armor-piercing shell from this thing weighs seven tons."

Since he was obviously going to tell us everything about this gun, I decided to play dumb. "What on earth would you shoot a seven-ton armor-piercing shell at? You could never hit a tank with this thing." He missed my sarcasm completely as he answered. "No, no. you don't shoot at tanks with it. It's for destroying those damned forts that Ivan has all around Sevastopol. A shell from this thing can penetrate more than thirty meters of concrete.

He went on to tell us that it took two parallel sets of rail lines to hold it when it was fired and that there were over four thousand men assigned to the unit that operated it.

After he had raved on about it for several moments, I said, "It sounds as if you are ready to transfer from the armored corps to the artillery."

"Oh, no," he said quickly. "These guns are fascinating, but they don't move fast enough for me.

"Well, Maria and I are going to go over to the kitchen tent and hunt up something to eat."

"And get warm," added Maria.

"When you are through admiring this wonderful product of German engineering, you'll know where to find us," I said.

Walking to the tent, I whispered to Maria, "Men and their toys!"

A sneeze was her only answer.

Maria and I had coffee and biscuits in the mess tent while the captain conducted his tour.

"You know what all this means, don't you?" I asked Maria.

"It means that I'm going to have a cold for weeks," was her thoroughly self-centered answer.

"No! It means that they are almost ready to start the attack on Sevastopol again. They know that they can't keep all this preparation secret very long. Besides, the spring thaw should start soon and Von Manstein will want to start the attack before the ground turns to mud.

"Like you know about this stuff," grouched Maria.

"Haven't you learned anything about this war?" I asked. "Don't you ever listen to your patients? You can learn a lot from them if you pay attention."

"That may be," she said. "But frankly, I'd rather not learn any more about this lousy war than I have to."

I had to agree with that, but I felt that I had learned much from our soldiers. I said, "They'll start the attack on Sevastopol within a week, I'm sure."

I was completely wrong of course.

CHAPTER IV

Sevastopol falls at last

Yes, a major battle did start a few days later, it just wasn't anywhere near Sevastopol. It seems that General Von Manstien had decided to remove the Russian threat to our army's rear before launching a renewed assault against the fortress. In early May he unleashed a ferocious attack against the Russian forces dug in on the Isthmus of Parpach.

The hospital had been put on alert to expect increased casualties. As usual, we had to await the arrival of the first of those casualties to hear any of the details of the battle in progress.

Let me say right now that most of the medical personnel, myself included, dislike the term "casualties." It is just a sanitized way of referring to those unfortunate soldiers who suffer unbelievable pain and loss to accomplish the aims of their leaders. It looks good on reports along with troop strengths, supplies delivered, and objectives captured. It avoids mentioning the unpleasant effects that enemy bullets and shrapnel have on the human body. It was dealing with those terrible effects that was our daily routine. Amongst the first wounded to arrive from this latest attack was a young German private with severe burns over his back and legs. The severity of his injuries required that we sedate him with some of our limited supply of morphine crystals, an item of which we never had enough.

Even sedated as he was, the pain kept him awake as I went through the slow and painful process of removing his hastily applied field dressing.

He talked almost continuously as I used forceps and saline solution on his dirty bandages.

He told me how proud he was that his regiment from Bavaria had been chosen for a special mission. His unit had boarded inflatable boats after dark on the evening before the attack and paddled out into the Black Sea. In the dark, they had rowed their boats along the coast toward the enemy lines. When our artillery lit up the pre-dawn darkness with a tremendous barrage all along the front, they had started their outboard motors and charged straight toward the end of the Russian lines.

It seems that the Russians had dug an anti-tank ditch, eleven meters wide, across the entire width of the isthmus. At its Southern end, it ran right into the Black Sea. The assault boats simply sailed right into the ditch and surprised the defenders there, overwhelming them. It had not been all one-sided, however. Along with several machine-gun posts, there had been some flame-throwers built into the sides of the trench. It had been one of these that had started my patient on his long and painful journey to our hospital.

When he asked me about my accent, I explained that I was Romanian. He seemed especially pleased to hear this. He said that the troops that eventually broke through to his surrounded unit were Romanian. This news didn't make me particularly happy. It just meant that I would soon be seeing some of my fellow countrymen under similar circumstances.

Fortunately, this tempo of operations didn't last long. Despite a short period of rain that turned the countryside into sticky clay, the Russians were completely defeated in a little over a week of intensive operations.

When the last of the Russians had surrendered at Kerch, we all knew that it wouldn't be long before the assault on Sevastopol would begin again in earnest. Captain Roider's absence lent strength to our suspicions of an impending action since he was routinely pulled away from his liaison duties with us to help with staff work when army headquarters were particularly busy.

On the evening of the first of June, as I was getting off my shift at the hospital, Julius approached me. "Anna," he called. "Wait a moment. I need to ask you something."

"Hello Julius," I said. "I haven't seen much of you lately. Where have you been hiding?"

"Under a mountain of work, that's where," he replied.

"So, what do you want with me?"

"I want you to share in my good fortune."

At my puzzled look, he explained. "I have finally gotten a choice assignment. Tomorrow, I will be driving one of our motor ambulances to a field hospital near Balaclava to deliver a load of field dressings. Then I'll be heading over to Yalta to pick up more medical supplies. Compared to cleaning and paperwork, I consider this a vacation trip."

"That's nice," I said. "But what does this have to do with me?"

"They said that I can pick an assistant to go with me, and I pick you."

"Me? Why me? I can't drive a lorry and I wouldn't be particularly helpful loading supplies."

"Oh, I don't need help with the loading or driving. I just need someone to talk to so I can stay awake while driving. And besides, I heard about the... um, difficulties you had on your last attempt to see Yalta. I thought you might like to go with someone you can trust."

"You heard... Oh, brother, you can't keep anything secret around here. Well...okay. I'm not scheduled to work tomorrow. But you knew that, didn't you?"

He just smiled and said, "See you at oh-five-hundred tomorrow." Then he quickly disappeared down the crowded corridor.

As I walked back to my apartment, I reflected on how you could feel that you could trust one man and not another. If Captain Roider had proposed this, I wouldn't even have considered going with him. True, Julius was an older man, but not *that* old. No, you could just tell that he was someone you could rely on.

That night, I regretfully cut my evening visiting with the patients short so that I could get some sleep. Then, punctually at five AM, I was climbing sleepily into the cab of a German-made, Opel lorry. The rear of the vehicle was arranged as an ambulance, though today it was filled with crates of bandages. Many of the bandages we used were not the proper gauze type, but merely sterilized rags collected from the home front. Sometimes they weren't even white.

At this early hour I was much too sleepy to reflect on how unprepared our country was for a war that, truth be known, we had been all too happy to jump into. I'm afraid that I wasn't much company for poor Julius for those first few hours as we bumped and bounced over the typically atrocious Russian roads. By now the spring rains had let up some and the roads were at least passable again.

Yes, spring had finally come to this arid, high plateau and the wildflowers were a riot of color all along the roadside. Getting away from the hospital's depressing sounds and smells and seeing new life sprouting everywhere lifted my spirits, despite the continuous drumming of distant artillery fire. Even when we drove past the "British Cemetery" just outside of Balaclava, the resting place of so many British Empire troops from a previous war, my spirits remained high. A major battle had been fought here the previous winter. Many of the stones, and even some of the graves, had been churned up but I was more interested in the gaily colored flowers than the thousands of disturbed headstones. We arrived at the field hospital, where Julius skillfully backed the ambulance up to a large tent. While he went to collect several men to carry the crates, I climbed into the back of the lorry and prepared to hand them out.

When he got back, he said, "I told you that you don't have to do any work. We can handle this." I wrinkled my nose and squinted my eyes at him and said, "I suppose you think that since I am just a *woman*, I can't do anything. I'll toss the crates out. You men just try to keep up."

The crates weren't heavy, and I tossed them out as fast as I could. But no matter how quickly I worked, there was always a pair of hands ready to catch the next box. When the last container was gone, I had worked up quite a sweat, despite the cool air. I climbed out of the lorry to congratulate Julius and his crew on keeping up. Before I said anything, however, I noticed that Julius' "several" men had turned into several dozen.

When I raised an inquiring eyebrow at Julius, he said, "When they heard that there was a pretty nurse in camp, I suddenly had more help than I could use." I imagine that I turned a brighter shade of red than the cross on the side of our ambulance. They were all smiling and trying to make polite conversation as Julius hustled me into the cab like a mother hen.

In seconds, we were on the road again as I turned to Julius and asked, "A *pretty* nurse? Julius, you exaggerate too much."

"I don't exaggerate at all," he said. "You just don't give yourself enough credit. If I had a daughter, I would want her to be as pretty and smart as you."

"Why Julius, I don't know what to say. You're not planning on turning into a Captain Roider on me, are you?"

"Oh God no, Anna! I didn't mean anything like that."

I tried to maintain a stern countenance, but finally I had to laugh at Julius' consternation.

We descended from the heights of Balaclava towards the coastal plain where we had a marvelous view of the Black Sea and the open, almost cloudless sky above. Once we reached the coastal road, we turned east towards Yalta. I was enjoying the warmer temperature and chatting with Julius when I saw one of the strangest sights I have ever seen.

As we traveled a stretch of road that ran immediately along the sandy beach, a totally naked man arose from the surf and scrambled across the sand to stand in the road directly in front of us. He waved his arms for us to stop, and we could see that he had no intention of moving out of our way.

As soon as Julius had brought us to a stop, the man was at his window shouting excitedly in German. Julius made him understand that we were Romanian, and he would have to speak more slowly. Between the two of us, we pieced together his story.

He was a lieutenant of General Von Manstien's staff and had just swum ashore from an Italian torpedoed boat. The General was on that frail craft observing Sevastopol from the seaward side when they had been attacked by Russian fighter planes. The boat was disabled, with several dead and wounded aboard. The Lieutenant needed to get to Yalta as fast as possible to take another boat out and tow the General's boat back to port.

I hastily climbed into the back of the ambulance as the naked Lieutenant jumped into the passenger seat that I had just vacated. I really don't think he even noticed me. I sat on one of the litters and hung on for dear life as Julius raced the few remaining kilometers to Yalta. We drove straight onto the pier where the German jumped out and commandeered another torpedo boat. As the boat raced out of the harbor, I could see one of the Italian sailors bring the Lieutenant a pair of pants.

While Julius and I awaited the arrival of the crippled boat, with its injured passengers, we asked the harbor personnel where the nearest military hospital was. It turned out that it was the same one that we had been heading for before our interruption by the naked Lieutenant. It was another twelve kilometers down the road. If there were any seriously injured on the boat, it would be up to us to stabilize their condition long enough for the ride there.

I went through the ambulance to see what equipment we had with us. Unfortunately, it had been mostly cleaned out for our supply mission. At least the litters were still there, folded against the interior sides. I found one simple first-aid kit and thank the lord, one field surgery pack.

After that, all we could do was wait. It seemed like an eternity before we saw the two boats approaching from the open sea. The first boat towed the disabled one right up to the pier where a swarm of men made it fast.

Julius and I were amongst the first to jump aboard the battered little ship. Aircraft cannon shells had torn holes everywhere along the wooden deck, leaving jagged splinters of wood protruding for the unwary to impale themselves on. We found three wounded men laid out side by side on the deck. We quickly determined that two of the wounded were only slightly injured and would be all right with proper care. The third man wasn't so lucky. He was bleeding heavily from a wound to the upper thigh. When I removed the shirt that was tied around the wound the bleeding increased even more, coming in spurts.

I yelled to Julius, "It's the femoral artery! We'll have to perform a ligature right now."

"We need a doctor for that...don't we?" asked Julius.

"I've assisted with dozens of them. Give me a pair of forceps, the small clamp, and that curved needle with some suture on it."

Theoretically, it was a simple procedure. You only had to use the crescent-shaped needle to sew the artery closed with the clamp. The problem came in getting the artery to a position where you could work on it. I was using the forceps, attempting to recover the severed end of the artery from the groin. The bloody stump was extremely slippery, and I was just thanking my lucky stars for the bright sunlight when a shadow fell across my work.

"Get the hell out of my light!" I yelled without looking up. The shadow moved away immediately. Then, as he leaned near to me to hand me the suture, Julius whispered in my ear, "That is no way to talk to a general, Anna."

I was frustrated from my largely unsuccessful attempts to retrieve the artery, so I snapped at Julius. "I don't care if he's Abraham himself. He'd better stay out of my light."

Finally, I captured the bleeder and clamped the end. It took only seconds to suture the end of the artery.

"This one needs a hospital and transfusion as soon as possible," I said as I wiped my bloody hands on my uniform skirt, the only clean place I could find.

The three wounded men were quickly loaded into the ambulance. I sat on the empty fourth litter to tend to them as Julius sped the ambulance towards the field hospital.

"Will he be all right?" asked an unfamiliar voice from the front seat.

I was surprised to hear a strange voice since I hadn't realized that anyone else had boarded the ambulance with us. I looked up to find a worried-looking face gazing back at me. It was the rather grandfatherly face of an older gentleman. The full, round face, with a prominent nose and well-groomed mustache, had a rather aristocratic appearance. And this aristocrat was wearing the uniform of a German general. With a start, I realized that I was face to face with the army commander, General Von Manstien.

Hiding my surprise at his presence as best I could, I said, "I don't know. He has lost an awful lot of blood."

In a sad voice, the general said, "I hope he makes it. I don't know what I would do without him."

At my puzzled look, he continued, "He has been my batman...and friend, since this war began. He is really a fine man. We've been through so many close calls that I was beginning to think that we were both immortal."

I thought that he wanted to say something more, but he didn't.

To break the gloomy silence that followed, I said, "Was that you that I yelled at back on the deck? I'm sorry, I shouldn't have been so short with you."

"No, no, don't be sorry. One of my staff interpreted your Romanian and you were quite right. I was only getting in the way."

"His name is Fritz, you know."

I hadn't known that, but I nodded my head and went back to tending the wounded man. There was really nothing more that I could do for him at this point except to keep him warm. His pulse was weak and thready, and I would have bet that he had no blood pressure to measure.

It was then that the general said something that made my heart stop. In a very soft voice, he said, "You know that a gentile would have sworn in the name of Jesus, not Abraham."

I pretended not to hear the general's comment as I worked on my patient. I just couldn't think of anything to say. Finally, when the silence grew unbearable, I raised my eyes to look into the general's face. The kind look in his eyes and his gentle smile reassured me that I had nothing to fear from this particular Aryan.

We were just coming into sight of the field hospital when I lost all sign of a pulse. With a slight sigh, his respiration stopped also. The loss of blood had just been too much for poor Fritz.

I looked up to find the general looking sadly upon his friend's face. I don't know why this man's passing should bother me so much. I had seen hundreds die in the last few months. Perhaps it wasn't his death at all, but the effect it was having on his friend. In a war, most die amongst comrades-in-arms or even complete strangers, but seldom real friends.

Whatever the reason, I had a tear in my eye when I said, "He is gone. I am so very sorry."

The general's face was composed but resigned as he answered. "Don't be sad little frauline. He died a soldier's death, and I know that you did everything possible."

"What is your name, little one?"

"Anna Tompchin," I answered.

"Well, Anna Tompchin, if our soldiers fight with as much heart as you do, we'll do all right in this war."

I knew that he was trying to cheer me up and wondered at that. After all, it was I who should be trying to help him. Maybe generals don't need help.

While Julius and I supervised the transfer of the other wounded to the hospital I saw the general talking to the units' adjutant. I supposed that he was making arrangements for his friend's body. A few moments later, two orderlies arrived and removed the body with more than the usual care shown for the deceased.

I saw the general get into his big Horst staff car, which had followed us from Yalta. As the powerful vehicle pulled away, the general looked at me and touched the brim of his hat in salute. I nodded in return, and he was soon out of sight in the cloud of dust raised by his car.

We picked up our supplies and drove back to Simferopol. It was a quiet drive. I for one, was emotionally drained. At one point, Julius did say that he was sorry that I had lost my first patient. He said that, as far as he could tell, I had done everything right. I found little consolation in his words, but thanked him anyway.

After a short pause, Julius continued in a quiet voice. "Anna...was the general right? Are you a...?"

"Jew?" I said, finishing his question for him. "Would it matter to you if I was?"

He hesitated only shortly before he replied. "Yes, but not the way you think. I would only be bothered by the possibility of your being found out."

"Well, don't worry. Let's just say I have some relatives that are Jews."

"Okay," he said. "But if you don't mind, I'll just keep my mouth shut and worry a little anyway."

Despite everything, I had to smile as I realized that Julius was an even better friend than I had thought.

The following day, at the hospital, Captain Roider approached me. He seemed unusually subdued as he asked to talk to me. Steering me to a reasonably quiet spot amongst the usual confusion, he said, "I am very impressed, Anna. You seem to be traveling in some very powerful circles these days."

"Hans," I said. "I am very busy. What are you talking about?" Adopting a very official tone of voice, he said, "General Von Manstien sends his compliments, and requests your attendance at the funeral of his batman tomorrow."

"I am very flattered, but I can't take any more time away from the hospital," I said.

"You don't understand, Anna. A general's request is an order. It has already been cleared with the hospital. His car will pick you up at oh-four-hundred tomorrow morning and have you to the cemetery at Yalta in time for the dawn funeral."

"The funeral is at dawn? My God, doesn't anyone ever sleep in this army?"

With a sly grin, Captain Roider said, "Tomorrow you will see why it is a dawn funeral."

So, it came to be that I was standing in the sad but lovely cemetery of Yalta as the light of dawn of the third day of June, nineteen forty-two began to break. Once the chaplain had delivered his sermon, the general said some very lovely farewell words for his friend. The honor guard then fired a salute to their fallen comrade.

I thought my ears were playing tricks on me when the echoes of the salute refused to fade out. The roaring actually seemed to be getting louder. I looked up and behind me to find the sky virtually filled with German warplanes winging their way to the west.

The general was standing to my left. I turned to him and said one word, "Sevastopol?"

He nodded and said, "This time there will be no stopping until it is in our hands."

"Then there will be much for me to do soon. With your permission, I will return to the hospital."

"My car is ready to take you back," he said. "God go with you little one."

Ordinarily I didn't care for references to my petite build. But from this sad and gentle person, somehow I didn't mind. I simply said, "God be with us all."

Sevastopol did fall. But only after thirty more days of hellish fighting in the bunkers, trenches, and gun pits of that terrible fortress.

In the days that followed, as I went from one broken body to the next, I thought of those huge guns of which Captain Roider had been so proud. I realized that if our troops were suffering so, how much worse it must be for the enemy on the receiving end of those thousand-kilogram shells. The Grim Reaper was certainly having his day. I began to wonder if any amount of reclaimed territory was worth this price.

When the Crimean Peninsula was declared secure, we knew that we would soon be moving on. At first, we thought that our army would move directly east to cross the narrow Kerch straits. From there we could move into the Caucasus and on to the Soviet oil fields.

Then came the startling news that General Von Manstien was being transferred to the Leningrad front in the far North. Along with him, many of the best units of our army were also being transferred. The remaining combat units of the Army of the Crimea, including us Romanians, would backtrack across the Perikops Isthmus and then turn east to join the rest of Army Group South in its attack towards the Don River.

The hospital was a beehive of activity as we prepared for the move. We had been in one place so long that I had almost forgotten that we had to go wherever the army went. Even though the hospital would continue to serve the Crimean Military District after our departure, we had to move out as many patients as possible before the reduction in staff. They were to be either returned to the front or sent home for extended recuperation or separation. Rumors abounded about how soon we would leave, but no one knew anything for certain. I was helping patients onto a homeward-bound train when I heard a familiar voice calling to me. It was Captain Roider.

"Anna, there you are! I missed you at the hospital and I was afraid I wouldn't get to see you before I left. I'll be on the next train out and I wanted to say goodbye."

"You're leaving us?" I asked. "Have you been transferred to General Manstiens' staff permanently now?"

"No, they are already on their way to Leningrad by air. I have a much better assignment."

He was all smiles and as happy as a child at Christmas time, so I said, "Don't tell me. Let me guess. You have been transferred to an armored unit."

"The 22nd Armored Division," he said proudly. "They arrived in time to take part in the attack on Kerch and have made quite a good name for themselves, after a slightly shaky start, that is."

"So you are going back to your tanks, where people shoot at you and you can be blown to bits at any second," I said. "And this makes you happy? I just don't understand men."

"I'll be back in action. Leading men in combat and taking my chances along with the rest of the soldiers. I don't expect you to understand. After all you're only a..."

"Woman?" I interrupted. "I'm glad I'm not a soldier. I really don't think I could kill someone, even if my life depended on it!"

"I was going to say that you are only a civilian and don't understand the camaraderie of men in combat.

"Of course, the likelihood of being promoted to Major is also an incentive to get back into it.

"Will you miss me?"

"Yes," I said. "But then I would also miss a toothache when it was gone." But inside, I felt a sense of loss even though this man frightened me sometimes.

He leaned forward and said, "How about a farewell kiss, leibchen."

That dispelled any feelings of remorse I had at his leaving. The anger I felt must have shown in my eyes because he pulled back quickly as I said, "I'm not your liebchen, *captain!* Have a nice trip."

I pointedly ignored his stare as I returned to loading the wounded onto the train.

A few days later, Maria, Sasha, and I were on a train of our own, headed back across the Pericops Isthmus towards the Nogi steppe once again.

After we had been moving for a while, I noticed Sasha looking at me out of the corner of her eyes. But whenever I looked her way, her attention would suddenly be directed out the window.

Finally, I said, "What's the matter, Sasha? Is my nose on crooked, or something?"

She didn't answer me. Instead, she looked at Maria, who returned her glance with an angry look of her own. Now I was really worried.

"All right, what's going on," I demanded.

Looking resigned, Maria gave a sigh and said, "We just heard some news from home before boarding the train. I'm sure it means nothing."

"What means nothing?" I could feel a tightness developing in my chest.

"We heard that the Americans bombed...Ploesti, last week," said Maria.

"What? That's my home! How bad was it? Was anyone hurt?"

"All we heard," said Maria, "was an official broadcast that said the Americans launched a failed attempt to bomb the oil fields at Ploesti. From the sound of it, they didn't accomplish much and there was no mention of casualties."

"But how can they be bombing us?" I protested. "They've only been in the war a few months.

"And why bomb us? The Japanese are the ones that attacked them. Why not bomb them? Or the Germans? Why us? Why *my* family?"

"Anna! Don't get hysterical," said Sasha. "I'm sure your family is fine."

"Sasha is right," said Maria. "The Americans probably flew a few planes over from some base halfway around the world, just so the British won't feel so alone." For a change, she was mostly right. But I wasn't about to be consoled so easily. I said, "But I'm the one who chose to go to war. I'm the one who volunteered to get bombed and shelled and take my chances, not my family. With the damn slow mail around here, they could all have been killed and I wouldn't know about it for months." By now I was actually crying, something I thought I had gotten over, working in the hospital. Sasha and Maria did their best to cheer me up, but I was still quite upset when the next blow to my spirits fell.

After several hours on the train Maria said, "Look, we're stopping in Caplynka. Isn't that the little town where the peasants thought that we were crusaders when we passed through last Fall?"

I tried to break out of my depression as I said, "Yes, they thought the iron crosses on the vehicles were church crosses and we were there to rid them of the 'Godless communists.'"

We hurried from the train hoping to enjoy a break in the pleasant little town.

Once we got off the train our break was anything but pleasant. The road leading to the station was lined with telegraph poles. From each pole hung a dead body. They were all hanging by the neck and had been dead for some time. The faces were blackened, and the tongues protruded from their mouths, showing that they had all died of strangulation rather than a broken neck. The eyes had been plucked out by birds. It was a ghastly sight, even for us, and we had been dealing with violent death for months.

We all stood dumbfounded, staring at the bodies. I don't think any of us could believe what we were seeing.

Julius hurried up to us and said, "Let's go inside the station. You don't need to see this."

None of us could seem to make our feet move, however. Finally, I said to Julius, "What the hell is this? What happened here?"

"I heard that an SS unit was ambushed by partisans near here," said Julius. "These people were hanged as spies and saboteurs."

Angrily, I turned on poor Julius. "Spies and saboteurs? These are old men, women, and even children! How could they be partisans? These people were murdered! Who did this!"

Julius moved close to me and said very quietly, "The SS did this. I heard that they included as many Jews in their vendetta as they could find. Now be quiet and let's go inside."

"Be quiet?" I asked loudly. "The whole world has gone crazy, and you want me to be quiet? I'll not..."

"Shut up, Anna!" yelled Maria. She had tears in her eyes as she nodded her head towards several SS men lounging on the railroad platform. They were watching us closely.

First my home was bombed, and now this. I wanted to go over to those soldiers and scream in their faces, but I also wanted to go on living, so I let Julius lead us into the station and away from that

Once in the station, Julius got us all seated at a table and brought us some vile-smelling ersatz coffee.

As Julius took his seat at the table with us, Sasha said, "I heard what you said about them looking for Jews to hang. How could they know who they were?"

"All the Jews were required to register with the authorities when this area was first occupied," answered Julius. Then he looked directly at me and added, "Just like back home in Romania."

Sasha didn't seem to notice that the last remark was aimed at me when she asked, "But not all the Jews are spies... are they?"

There was silence at the table until I turned to Sasha and said, "No, Sasha. Not all of them."

When I continued, I was speaking mostly to myself as I said, "I know that no one but the Iron Guard zealots were happy about jumping into this war, but at least I thought we had good reasons for doing what we did. I thought that we deserved to get our territory back. But nothing is worth this... nothing."

CHAPTER V
Moving east again

From Chaplynka we traveled by rail and road across the Nogai Steppe. This is the southern part of Russia that borders on the Sea of Azov to its south. Our destination was the major city of Rostov where the great Don River empties that sea on its northeastern corner.

At this time, mid-July, the city was still under Russian control after having changed hands several times since the previous summer. We expected the fighting there to be over by the time we arrived since we had over 600 km. of empty steppe to cross before we got there. We weren't making very good time either. It seemed that ammunition and fuel always had priority over the service units, even the medical ones.

Once again, our armies were successful everywhere. The word was that we were moving even faster and farther than during the opening phases of the war, a year ago. I heard from some of the German officers that the Russians were no longer standing and fighting the way they had before. Now they withdrew when they were pressed.

Personally, I thought that sounded preferable to fighting for every inch of ground. But the army was complaining that they were no longer capturing great numbers of enemies with each encirclement. What puzzled me most was why were we fighting so hard here in the south and we were hearing nothing about Moscow anymore. Last year we were told that taking Moscow was "absolutely necessary" to win the war. Now it was "On to the Caucasus! On to Stalingrad!"

Where was Stalingrad anyway? And why was it so important now? Well, I'm just a foolish nurse. What do I know? I only go where they tell me. As the days of travel stretched on, it occurred to me that most of the soldiers in our army had come all these hundreds of kilometers on their own two feet. Even though the tanks got all the notice it was the infantrymen, walking under their own power, that made up the bulk of the army. They had crossed every dusty meter of this seemingly endless plain with only the occasional dry riverbed, called Balkas, to break the monotony.

Actually, when we reached Taganrog, where we briefly set up our field hospital, we found that many men were suffering from depression. This condition was brought on, not by battle or fear of death, but simply by the huge open spaces. Both our troops and the Germans were used to mountains, forests, and towns. Here there was nothing but the distant, flat horizon. It could make a person feel very insignificant, even lonely in the middle of an army.

The reason that we were halted at Taganrog was that Rostov hadn't *quite* been taken yet. Where had I heard *this* before.

Finally, on July 28, we moved into Rostov to set up a more permanent facility. We could hear the occasional firing still going on at various locations around the city as we drove through the deserted streets. The signs of battle were everywhere. Many streets were missing their cobblestones because they had been pulled up by the defenders to build barricades. Every side street seemed to have lorries and wagons overturned in an effort to stop our tanks. Many street-level windows had been sandbagged for strong points. All the walls were covered with the pockmarks of bullets, with holes blown in many of them.

In some places, the bodies of Soviet soldiers were still lying where they had fallen. The victors hadn't bothered to remove them yet.

"We are too close to the front," said Sasha, as we jostled along in the back of our motor lorry.

"It must be safe enough," said Maria. "They wouldn't risk noncombatants unnecessarily... would they?"

Our lorry was just squeezing past an artillery piece that was being unlimbered from its horse team when we heard the whistling.

"What's that?" asked Sasha.

No one answered. We were too busy grabbing handholds to keep from falling from the lorry as it sped up suddenly and turned abruptly into a side street.

"Everyone out!" yelled the driver as he slammed the lorry to a stop. He was already running for the cover of the street-side buildings before we recovered from our shock and began to move.

We were still in the back of the lorry when the explosions came. Fortunately, they were around the corner, in the street we had just vacated. Even so, we could feel the heat and pressure of the blasts. We heard the debris and shrapnel crashing into brick and mortar as we finished evacuating the vehicle. All of us ran to the nearest wall and cowered there waiting for the next volley of shells to fall, but it was all over.

When no more shells came for some moments, I crept back to the corner of the building and peered around it. The artillery piece we had just passed was now lying on its side. There was no sign of the crew, but two of the horses from the team were in sight, amidst the rubble. They were a pitiable sight. One was lying on the pavement with both its rear legs broken while it struggled to rise using only its forelegs. The other one was standing stock still with its intestines exposed and hanging onto the ground around its hoofs. Both of the poor beasts were emitting the most horrible screams. They sounded like human babies crying out in pain.

I couldn't shut out the terrible sounds, even with my hands pressed as hard as possible against my ears. I was just about to run towards them when one of the gun's crewmen staggered up from the rubble. As he stumbled past the wounded beasts, appearing dazed and confused, a shot rang out. To my horror, the top of his head exploded in a fountain of blood and brains.

"Sniper!" yelled Julius from just behind me. He grabbed the back of my blouse and literally threw me to the ground behind the corner of the building. When I picked myself up my eyes must have been as big as saucers. Julius looked at me and said, "They must have had this site pre-zeroed. They were just waiting for a target to show up. There must be a spotter in one of those buildings across the street, and he has a sniper with him.

We couldn't get away down our side street because it was completely blocked by crumbled buildings on either side. The only way out was back into the main street where the sniper waited. "We just have to sit tight until some of our infantry comes this way and flushes out the sniper," said Julius. "If he could see down this street, we would already be dead."

As we sat there, huddled against the side of the ruined buildings, we could hear the piteous crying of the horses from around the corner. Their every scream pierced my heart until I was crying uncontrollably. Finally, I said to Julius, "I can't stand this. We have to stop their suffering."

"No one can go out there without getting shot," said Julius.

"We are medical people, aren't we? I'm wearing the Red Cross. I should be able to go out there under a flag of truce."

"They are Russians...and you are part of an invading army destroying their country. And remember, they never even signed the Geneva Convention. What would you do in that sniper's place?" asked Julius.

"I wouldn't shoot," I said without hesitation.

"That may be, but you don't know what that man out there will do."

"Okay, you win," I said. "But those animals are suffering."

"It can't be helped," said Julius. "Stay put while I see if I can find our driver and get us out of here somehow."

I nodded assent, but as soon as Julius was out of sight, I began tearing a strip of material from the bottom of my white slip.

From beside me, Maria asked, "What are you doing?"

"I'm helping those poor animals," I said as I tied the material to a strip of wooden window frame that I found lying at my feet.

"I'm getting Julius," said Maria.

"Too late," I said, as I thrust my white flag around the corner of the building. When no shots rang out, I slipped around the corner and into the street.

Holding my flag in one hand and my nurse's cap with its red cross on it, in the other hand, I walked slowly to the center of the street. My every muscle was as tight as a bowstring as I awaited the sudden blow of a bullet entering my body. When several seconds passed and I was still alive, I replaced my cap on my head and knelt down beside the sniper's victim. I pulled the pistol from the dead soldier's belt and held it high. Still, I lived. I began to pick my way through the rubble of brick and cobblestones towards the wounded animals, always being careful not to look in the direction of the sniper, lest he think that I was trying to locate him.

I approached the standing horse from its head. Once I was within a few feet of the animal it quit its crying and looked at me through dazed eyes. I raised the pistol and pointed it at the animal's forehead from a few inches away. When I tried to focus on the gun's sights, I found that I couldn't see clearly through the tears in my eyes. I blinked away the tears, clenched my teeth, and pulled the trigger. The recoil took me by such surprise that the gun nearly flew from my hand. By the time I had brought the weapon back down to point once again at the animal, it had dropped to the pavement and lain still.

Still crying profusely, I stumbled over to the other poor animal lying nearby. Its cries also stopped as I drew near. I like to think that I saw gratitude in its eyes just before I pulled the trigger. This time I used two hands to control the recoil and saw the animal roll onto its side and sigh one last time before it died.

I threw the gun from me and began to retrace my steps back to the relative safety of our side street. That is when I saw another one of the gun's crewmen lying hidden in the rubble. He lay on his back, eyes open and bleeding from the mouth. He was almost certainly dead, but I felt I had an obligation, as a nurse, to find out for certain.

When I started towards him, however, I heard a shot ring out. Simultaneously, a bullet hit a section of shattered wall just in front of me. My face was peppered with sand and gravel, and I froze where I was. So that was how it was... I was permitted to put animals out of their misery, but not help an enemy soldier. My heart was trying to leap from my chest as I reluctantly turned to rejoin my friends. As soon as I turned the corner, I sat down with my back against the apartment wall and drew my legs up before me. I hugged my knees in an effort to stop shaking. I looked up to find Maria, Sasha, and Julius looking down at me. Maria and Sasha just looked on in shocked silence, but I could tell that Julius was angry. I couldn't meet his eyes, so I buried my head between my knees and cried.

I heard him mutter, "Damned little fool."

Then Maria added her little bit by saying to Julius, "I used to think that she was a fool, but now I know that she is just *crazy*."

I think that was the only time I ever heard Julius swear. We stayed where we were for another hour until a German infantry company swept through the area searching for our animal-loving sniper. I don't know if they found him or if he vanished back into the battered city.

Our unit was withdrawn from the combat area for two days while the city was "cleansed" of such isolated resistance. We didn't reach our goal, a battered hospital building in the center of the city, until three days after the sniper incident. By then, all my friends were talking to me again.

We didn't spend much time in Rostov. Our armies were moving beyond the city very quickly by the beginning of August. The German High Command had decided to split Army Group South into two separate Army Groups called simply A and B. This was done to allow us to pursue the "defeated" Russians in two different directions.

Maria and I were in a wrecked surgery room trying to salvage usable equipment when Sasha rushed in.

"Don't work too hard getting this place cleaned up," she said. "I just heard that we are moving east again very soon."

"East...not south?" asked Maria.

"That's what I heard. We'll be following Army Group B towards Stalingrad. And I must say that I am just as glad that we are. It's already too hot right here. Can you imagine what it will be like with Army Group A heading down south into the Caucasus? If they go far enough, they'll be meeting the Arabs in Iran."

"I don't think Iranians are considered Arabs," I said.

"It doesn't matter," said Sasha. "What is important is that the Third Romanian Army will be with our group."

I had to smile at that. It was common knowledge by now that I was becoming almost desperate to find Peter. I had received a letter from him telling me that he was now assigned to the 1st Romanian Cavalry Division. And they were with the 3rd Army. If we were all assigned to the same Army Group, I still had a chance to catch up with him sometime this summer.

I should point out that the area between Rostov and Stalingrad is mostly flat land, drained by many small rivers, all of which run into the great Don River, since that river surrounds this part of Southern Russia on three sides. This area is known as the Great Don Bend because that river swings hundreds of kilometers east, from its southward path from central Russia before it swings southwest again to empty into the Sea of Azov at Rostov.

Into this wedge-shaped section of Russia, half the size of all Romania, the German 6th Army was advancing from the northwest. At the same time, our Army Group B, the 3rd Army included, was to advance east and north. All these forces were converging on a small city called Kalach. This unfortunate town sat where the Don reaches its furthest eastern point. From there, it was only forty more kilometers of open steppe to the city of Stalingrad on the Volga River.

Of course, we were completely ignorant of all this as our medical unit repeatedly moved east, from stop to stop, behind the advancing army units through the month of August. For us, it was just a continuing blur of drive, stop, set up camp, treat patients, pack up camp, and drive on again. With the lack of any significant towns throughout this area, we were operating from our tent hospital once again. It was during this period that I had another one of those odd experiences that could only happen in wartime.

I was attending four lightly wounded patients in the back of a motor ambulance. The ambulance was making its slow way towards our field hospital located outside a small town called Morozovsk. I say we were making slow progress because we were traveling at only a few kilometers an hour through a dense nighttime fog. All my patients were stable, so I poked my head into the cab to see how the driver was doing.

How is it going?" I asked.

"With these miserable blackout headlights, I can't see a damned thing." answered the young driver.

"Uh...sorry. I didn't mean to swear, nurse."

"Don't worry, I've heard *much* worse at the hospital," I said.

"It's just that with this da...darned fog, I can't see three meters."

"You're doing fine," I assured him. "I had a meteorological department patient last week. He said the frequent fogs in this part of the country are caused by great masses of cold damp air coming down from the North Sea, meeting hot dry air coming up from the Arabian Peninsula. According to him, there is only flat ground all the way from Leningrad to the Caucasus with no mountains in the way to stop the air flow.

Can you imagine the distances that air must travel to bring us this nice fog? It must be thousands of kilometers."

"I just know that it seems to be foggy all the time around here," he said.

My prattling seemed to be calming him somewhat, so I continued. "Just be glad you're not a pilot. There is a big German airfield at Morozovsk. They have to fly in this stuff all the time."

As if to accentuate my point, just then, we heard the drone of aircraft engines passing low overhead. We both craned our necks to look up, but it was just as foggy above as in front.

About thirty minutes later I was in the back of the ambulance once again when I was thrown from my feet by the sudden breaking of the vehicle.

"I hurried to the cab and said, "What's happened? What's wrong?"

The driver pointed through the windshield and said, "There's some crazy man on the road in front of us."

I looked out to see the dark silhouette of a man outlined against the fog. He was waving his arms over his head, signaling for us to stop. For an instant, a picture of the naked lieutenant on the beach road at Yalta flashed before my eyes.

This time it wasn't a lieutenant, and he wasn't naked.

A fully clothed Captain of the German Luftwaffe walked up to the driver's door.

"I need your help," he said to the driver, who didn't speak any German.

Answering across the driver from my side of the cab I said, "You'll have to speak to me. He doesn't speak any German."

The Captain seemed surprised to hear a female voice coming from the darkened cab, but he recovered quickly. "I need you to guide me to the airfield at Morozovsk."

"Sure," I said. "Hop in."

"No, no, you don't understand. I am the lead pilot for a flight of two dive bombers. We haven't been able to find the airfield in this fog, so we landed on a hilltop just north of this road.

I need you to guide our planes to the field."

I was bewildered when I answered. "But how can you fly behind our ambulance. We couldn't move fast enough for that, even if it wasn't foggy."

He chuckled and said, "I intend to taxi down the road behind you, while you lead the way."

"But it's 20 kilometers to the airfield," I protested.

"I didn't say I thought it would be easy," he answered.

It wasn't. As a matter of fact, it was more difficult than I had imagined. Even after the two airplanes had been slowly taxied down the hill and onto the roadway behind the ambulance, we still had *big* problems.

By big, I mean that the planes themselves were huge. They were a pair of the famous Stuka bombers. They were also the biggest single-engine aircraft I had ever seen. With their bulky landing legs hanging down from the inverted gull wings, and their tail wheels dragging the ground, the nose must have been a good 4 meters above the ground. That meant that the pilot, seated over the wings at the middle of the craft, couldn't see over the nose of the plane when it was on the ground.

"We have to zigzag along our path," explained the Captain. "First we look over the left side, moving at a 45-degree angle to our intended path and then we swing around and look over the right side."

"But this road isn't wide enough for that," I said.

"That is exactly why I need your lorry. Someone will have to sit on the roof, at the rear, holding an electric torch for me to follow. I'll be able to see that through the arc of the propeller."

When I translated the plan into Romanian for the driver, he gallantly volunteered to ride on the top of the ambulance and hold the torch. I then reminded him that I didn't know how to drive a lorry. And this was no time to learn.

"But if the plane behind us misses a signal, the propeller will chop this ambulance into kindling, and you would be the first to go," he pointed out.

I thanked him for reminding me of that and began climbing onto the roof. A rope stretched across the top gave me a tenuous handhold while my legs dangled over the rear of the vehicle.

I suppose that our little convoy would have seemed quite funny to anyone along the roadside. To me, it was anything but funny. With that 3-meter propeller never more than five meters behind me in the fog it was up to me to keep the torch held up to where the pilot could see it. If we slowed or stopped, I was to wave it from side to side to alert the pilot. It worked surprisingly well...for a while.

After a while, it seemed that I had been floating through that fog forever. My arms felt as if they would drop off if I held that damned torch one more minute. As time went on, I was getting drowsy, even with that thousand-horsepower engine droning along just a few meters from my face.

Then the ambulance stopped suddenly. I nearly toppled off the roof, but I grabbed the rope quickly and began waving the torch frantically. But the spinning blade continued to approach. Was the pilot asleep? I couldn't tell but I had to do something quickly. I could jump and maybe only get a broken neck, but what would happen to the wounded men in the ambulance below me?

When the propeller was within 2 meters of me, I threw the torch at the pilot's canopy. It didn't get past the propeller, but it caused such a bang and shower of sparks that it alerted the pilot. He hit the brakes instantly, but even so, I could have reached out and touched the spinner on the nose of the plane by the time it stopped. The driver even had to pull the ambulance forward to allow me to climb down. Then the Captain came storming up.

"What was the idea of that? You could have ruined my propeller!"

"And you could have ruined my whole day!" I yelled back.

I really hadn't intended it as a joke, but the Captain laughed anyway.

It turned out that the driver had stopped because we were approaching an overpass where another road went over ours. The opening was too narrow to let the aircraft through.

The determined Luftwaffe Captain tried to taxi his planes around the overpass but got bogged down in a roadside ditch. By now we were within a kilometer of the airfield, so we gave the Captain a lift while his crews watched the planes. He was already rounding up a rescue party for his aircraft as we left.

"He didn't even say thank you," said the driver.

As we plowed back into the fog I said, "That's okay. "I'm just glad to be rid of him. I've had men follow me before, but this one really made me nervous."

Hey, in a war, you have to get a laugh whenever you can.

By the middle of August, the Germans had captured Kalach and were regrouping to continue the advance on Stalingrad. Also, during this period, the 4th Romanian Army returned to the front, having completed their rest and refitting after the Odessa campaign.

For a while I was worried that our unit might be returned to the control of 4th Army, and so move me farther from Peter. Soon however, we heard that the 4th Army was to join the Germans in their assault to the south of Stalingrad while the 3rd Army, our unit included, was to move north to secure the German 6th Army's left flank. That flank lay along the Don River where it flows southeast towards Kalach.

Even though our unit was moving north, and not towards Kalach, I did manage to get as far as the bridgehead there. Our unit was ordered to send two lorries and some experienced personnel to that location to pick up some supplies. This seemed an odd order since supplies are supposed to come from the rear, not the front.

I didn't care about that though since any eastward movement should bring me nearer to the 1st Cavalry Division, and Peter. Naturally, I volunteered for the mission. I even volunteered Maria. Boy was she ever happy about *that*. "If I choke to death on this dust, it will be all *your* fault," groused Maria as we bounced along yet another atrocious road. Actually, we weren't even actually on the road, but somewhere alongside of it. There was so much military traffic moving east that much of it just drove along the hard, flat ground to either side.

"The dust *is* a bit thick," I admitted through my scarf.

Actually, it was as thick as the frequent fogs that plagued this God forsaken land. All this traffic was headed for the bridgehead at Kalach to support the German drive on Stalingrad. Our little group broke away from the mass of vehicles to head north just before we entered Kalach.

Even so, I could look back from the slightly rising road we traveled to see the mass of vehicles pouring through the little town and onto one of several bridges across the Don. The town's one bridge appeared to have been captured intact, while several pontoon bridges had been built not far from the original.

"Where the hell are we going now?" asked Maria.

"I don't know," I said. "They just said that there are some supplies around here that we are supposed to get."

"All I want to get is a bath," said Maria as she shook dust from the bandanna that she had been breathing through.

"Look," I said. "That looks like a train up ahead of us. Over by that station building. See?"

A few moments later we were pulling up beside a desolate looking steam train. I say desolate because the engine and cars were all riddled with bullet holes. The engine sat forlornly, with no sign of steam or smoke from its riddled boiler.

As we jumped down from the lorry Maria said, "What's this? Is this where we are supposed to be?"

I had no answer for her, but a German Lieutenant standing nearby did.

He said. "You are the Romanian medical people?"

When we nodded our heads in assent, he continued. "Welcome to our 'manna from heaven.'"

To our puzzled looks, he explained. "Our Russian hosts were kind enough to run this train right up to this station just after our panzers had captured it. When they realized their mistake, they tried to back away, but we persuaded them to stay." Saying this he pointed to the many bullet holes in the cars.

My curiosity made me bold enough to speak up. "So, what is on this train that makes it so important that we should drive 50 kilometers out of our way?"

"What isn't on it?" he answered.

His self-satisfied tone was beginning to wear on me, but he continued.

"It is full of wonderful presents from our friends across the sea. The Americans, I mean. Everything on this train came across the Atlantic, through the Arctic Ocean, and all the way down here from Murmansk... just for us.

It is full of guns, ammunition, and lorries. And such lorries! Let me show you."

He led us down the side of the immobilized train to a line of flat cars loaded with the largest lorries I had yet seen. They looked streamlined and shiny new. (Well at least as streamlined and shiny as any green military lorry could look.)

"My God," I said. "These things are twice the size of any of the Russian-built lorries I've seen. And you say that the Americans are giving these to the Bolsheviks?"

"That's right. But if the Russians keep handing them over to us, I won't complain."

"What has this to do with us?" asked Maria.

"The lorries...nothing," he said. "But come with me." Then he turned and led us down beside the train once again. It was a very long train. Eventually he stopped beside an enclosed boxcar. Sliding the door open, he said with a flourish, "Medical supplies."

The intern, who was nominally in charge of our group, quickly climbed into the car and began rummaging around. Soon he was back at the door with a happy look on his face.

"Bandages, surgery supplies, antibiotics, everything we need," he said.

When he hopped down from the car he came up to Maria and me and said, "Look at this." In his hand he held a small object that looked as if it were made of glass with one pointed end.

"I've heard of these, but I never hoped to see one in this God forsaken land."

"What is it?" I asked.

"It's a morphine ampoule. It's an individual, pre-measured dose of morphine with its own needle. With these, anyone can treat a wounded man quickly to keep him from going into shock.

You just have to be careful how many you use. One will deaden the pain for most wounds, while two will render even a large man unconscious. Three would kill most people."

"Well, since shock is what kills most wounded, these will come in very handy," I said.

I turned to the Lieutenant and said, "And you are just giving this stuff away?"

"We have been ordered to share it out equally with all medical units. even the non-German ones."

Did I detect a bit of contempt in his tone? No matter, what was important was this cornucopia of supplies. So it was, that on this last day of August, our lorries began their return trip to our unit. Coincidentally, it was the same day that the German 16th Division reached the Volga River at Stalingrad. That event meant nothing to us at the time. But it would have dire consequences for all of us before long.

It took three days to locate our unit since it had been moving north behind the 3rd Romanian Army while we were gone.

It took the Germans *much* longer than that to take Stalingrad.

Our army took up positions facing north along the Don to protect the left flank of the German units involved in the Stalingrad fighting. We caught up to our unit as they were setting up the tent hospital by the small village of Pronin, a couple kilometers North of the Chir River.

Headquarters decided that they didn't trust the medical orderlies in the field to use the morphine ampoules, so they were divided between the medical personnel of the hospital. I had some in my medical bag for use in triage. Otherwise, our side trip was soon forgotten in the hustle of setting up the field hospital.

The land around Pronin was as dismal a stretch of steppe as you were likely to find, and we hoped that we wouldn't be there long. In that, we were to be greatly disappointed. We sat there throughout all of September and October while another Russian winter prepared to roll over us. And this time we would be in tents on the open plains. The only saving grace was that our sector remained relatively quiet, with only occasional probing attacks by either side along the entire 100-plus kilometer front.

The same couldn't be said of the Stalingrad fighting. For those two months we heard every day of the terrible fighting that went on in that doomed city. One day the radio would say that the city had fallen. The next day we heard of yet more new units being committed to the attack.

It was at the end of September that we nurses' aides had to make a decision. Our year of training with the army was up, and we could go home if we wanted to. As we sat in our tent discussing our options, Sasha said, "I think we should take our nursing certificates and go home. There is just as much need of nurses as ever in civilian life and this living in tents is for the birds."

"You're right about the tents," agreed Maria. "But the army still needs us as badly now as when we first came here."

"You know how cold it's going to get around here soon. Do you want to face another winter in Russia? And this time living in a tent?" asked Sasha.

"I know," said Maria. "You're being awfully quiet Anna. What do you think?"

"I don't want to say anything," I said.

"Why not?" Asked Maria.

"Because I have already made up my mind, and I don't want to influence either of your decisions," I said.

"You're staying, aren't you?" said Sasha. "Elaine was right. You won't leave until this is all over."

The mention of Elaine's name still angered me, so I said, "That's right! What right do we have to return to our warm, safe homes while our men are out here suffering and dying! Are we in this thing to do our duty, or only to get a good-paying job?"

They were both quiet for a moment and I realized that I had done exactly what I had not wanted to do. I had tried to shame them into staying. *Do I want them to stay because the men need them, or because I need them?* I wondered.

In the end, we all stayed, and I am sure that my soul will have to pay the penalty for what happened.

I managed to find out that Peter's 1st Cavalry Division was at the far eastern end of our front. It was close to Stalingrad, but thank God, not involved directly in that fighting.

One night I was on one of my usual nocturnal visits to the wards, chatting with the men, when I heard quite a commotion on the road in front of the hospital. When I went to investigate, I found a column of lorries, each towing a cannon, stopped on the road.

"Hey!" I yelled. "Can't you keep the noise down. We have injured men in here that need their sleep."

"Sorry," said a sergeant. "One of the guns has broken a wheel and we are trying to fix it."

"Fine. But keep the noise down, okay? Say, you wouldn't be headed to the 1st Cavalry Division, would you?"

I was disappointed in the answer. "No," said the sergeant. "We are headed directly north, to the front lines. We have to get these new guns up there as quickly as possible.

They sure are beautiful, aren't they?"

"The guns? I suppose so," I said. But I was thinking, "Damn men and their war toys." He continued with obvious pride, "They are the best in the army. They're French 75mm's on German platforms."

"They look like any other gun to me. Why do you say they are the best in the army?"

"I say it because they are the biggest anti-tank guns in the Romanian Army."

"Those? I said in surprise. "The Germans have hundreds of those."

"I know, but these are the first four that they have given us," he said. "The rest of ours are 37mm's."

"Ha! The Germans call those 'door knockers.' They are useless against the new Russian tanks. Even I know that."

"That may be, but it's all we have," he replied glumly.

"Well, if that is the case, I'm glad we have the Don River between us and the Russians.

"Um...that's not exactly true. About the Don River, I mean. We never pushed the Russians quite all the way back over the river. Our lines are a few kilometers this side of it.

I couldn't believe what I was hearing. Everyone knew you were better off to defend behind a river. "You mean our lines are out in the open steppe? What is supposed to stop the Russians if they come?

"These guns...if we ever get them there," he said.

"You mean all four of them? Ho, I feel much safer now!" I'm afraid that my sarcasm was beginning to show.

"We should have set up the hospital south of the Chir River, not up here with the Russians so close."

"Don't worry," he said. This whole front is quiet. The Russians won't attack."

He was no better at predicting than I was.

All through October and the first half of November the temperature dropped. By now, all those who had been complaining of the summertime heat were freezing their tails off, along with the rest of us, I might add. I, for one, couldn't remember the last time I had been warm.

Living and working in the tents, heated only with charcoal stoves as the frigid north wind howled across the steppe, we barely managed to avoid becoming frostbite casualties ourselves.

On the night of November 18, we were trying to get warm enough under our blankets to fall asleep, when Maria said to me, "Tell me again Anna, why we decided to stay on when our year was up back in Sept."

"Well...I guess it was sort of my idea, wasn't it?" I said.

"And a stupid idea it was!" she blurted.

"Lay off her, Maria," said Sasha "We each decided for ourselves."

"Oh, like I was going to go home and leave Anna here by herself in the middle of a war," said Maria.

"I can't tell you how much safer I feel with you to save me from those nasty Ivans," I giggled.

That night, as the wind crept under our tent flaps, I had a hard time falling asleep. At 0400, I was awakened by the rumble of distant artillery fire to the north. I said a silent prayer for whoever was on the receiving end of that barrage. As I slipped back to sleep, I had no idea that I was hearing the beginning of the end of the world as we had known it.

CHAPTER VI

Disaster on the Don

By 0800 the next morning, I'd had breakfast and was already assisting in my first surgery of the day. Still, the rumble of distant artillery fire filled the air. When Julius entered the surgery bringing more towels, I called to him through my sterile mask.

"Hey Julius, any word on what's happening at the front?"

"Not yet," he answered. "But somebody is really catching it. And those can't be our guns firing."

"Why not?"

"Because we don't have that many guns or ammunition. General Dimitrescu has been begging for more men and guns for months, but there are no more to be had. But don't worry, our good friends, the Germans, have everything under control."

"Oh? How do you mean?" I asked.

"They have put a whole battle group behind us, to back us up, *fifty kilometers* behind us.

"Fifty kilometers!? What good is that?"

"I don't know, but you'll be glad to know that the 22nd Panzer Division is with them."

"Captain Roiders' unit? How interesting," I said.

"I hear that he's a Major now," said Julius.

"I'm not surprised. He's a man in a hurry."

"In more ways than one," said Julius, giving me an insufferably smug smile.

I was about to tell him to mind his own business when I was cut short by the doctor's sharp rebuke. "Watch what you are doing, nurse!" I had just stuck him with a scalpel while not watching my hand-off.

Julius left the surgery quickly, barely stifling a laugh.

When I stepped out of the surgery tent for a breath of fresh air an hour later, my attention was drawn to the road that ran through our camp. It had the usual flow of soldiers and military vehicles, but something was wrong. I was trying to determine what was different when Julius came up to me.

"The artillery fire has stopped," he said.

"So, it has. That's good, isn't it?"

"It depends," he answered. "If it means that the attack is over, it's good. But it could mean that the attack has outrun the range of its supporting guns. That would be bad."

I was still watching the flow of traffic on the road as we talked. Suddenly it hit me. For months the traffic had been moving north almost exclusively. Now it was reversed, with everything headed south.

To Julius, I said, "I think you should go over to the road and ask some of those people what is going on."

Julius' complacent look was replaced with one of worry as he realized what I had noticed. He hurried to the roadside and was deep in conversation with some soldiers there when the doctor's insistent voice called me back into the tent for our next operation.

By the time I next emerged from the tent, Julius was nowhere in sight and the traffic on the road was still moving south. But now it seemed to be moving faster. Just then, Julius rushed up to me and began speaking in a hurried whisper.

"You were right. There are rumors of a Russian breakthrough at the front. They say that there are hundreds of Russian tanks headed this way. Our orders are to pack everything up and move south as fast as possible."

"But we have a full surgery schedule this morning!" I protested.

"It's canceled," said Julius. "Tell everyone in there to pack up *now*. We'll try to save what we can."

Within minutes we were throwing all our supplies onto the lorries and wagons, while the orderlies loaded the stretcher cases into the ambulances, carts, or anything with wheels.

As my lorry began to move south, I called to Julius where he was loading more wounded. "Julius, the tents! What about the tents?"

"No time for them," he called back. "Who knows, this whole flap may be a mistake. We may be back here by dark."

We never saw our tents again. By now it was even difficult to get into the flow of south-bound traffic. But once on the road, we were swept along at a rapid pace. Maria and I were in a lorry together while, due to the confusion of our rapid departure, Sasha was in the lorry behind ours.

"Look at the soldiers on the road," I said to Maria.

"What about them?"

"Most of them have no weapons," I said.

"So, what of it?" asked Maria.

"So it *means* that this isn't just a withdrawal. It's a rout. I think we're in big trouble."

We had traveled less than 2 kilometers when the traffic came to a standstill. I could see that the flow of refugees (it could no longer be called an army) was backing up at the bridge that spanned the Chir River. Even though the temperature must have been at least ten degrees below freezing, the river hadn't frozen over completely, so that the only way south was over that single span.

As our group inched towards the bridge, we could see that some of the retreating soldiers were completely out of control, pushing and shoving their way across the span. The panic redoubled when, just as our lorries moved onto the bridge approaches, the unmistakable clank of metal on metal announced the approach of armored vehicles coming from the north.

People began to scramble in all directions, with some even being knocked over the sides of the bridge into the freezing water. Our lorry lurched to a stop as the driver jumped from the cab and ran for the nearby ditch. Maria and I began to move to the rear of the lorry in order to jump to the ground when I saw the source of the noise. They were tanks all right, but they were ours.

Just as we were beginning to breathe a sigh of relief, we saw a new danger. Our tanks were driving full speed for the bridge and not stopping for anything. We saw them crush a hand cart and scatter men in all directions as they rushed forward. Even without shooting, they were doing as much damage as any enemy might.

To Maria I said, "Stay in the lorry. We're not in their path so they should miss us with no problem."

"Okay," said Maria. Then looking over my shoulder at the lorry behind us she said, "What the hell is she doing?"

I turned to see that Sasha had jumped from her lorry and was running into the roadway.

"That ambulance is in the path of those tanks and the driver has run off," I said. "She must be trying to move it."

Sure enough, with no time to climb into the driver's seat, Sasha ran to the head of the two-horse draft team and began leading them to the side of the road. She almost succeeded in getting the ambulance full of wounded out of the way. Unfortunately, the rear corner of the ambulance was still in the road as the tanks roared past.

Our pathetic little lend-lease tanks may have been of no use against the Russians, but they were more than a match for a wooden wagon. The lead tank clipped the rear wheel, shattering it into a thousand pieces and jolting the ambulance sideways. It was still intact, but the traces to the horses snapped just as those frightened beasts surged forward.

I had the brief, horrible sight of Sasha falling under their sudden rush. The powerful hooves of the two large draft horses spun poor little Sasha around and around as they ran over her.

I don't know where the tanks or the horses went. I was too focused on reaching Sasha to see anything other than her limp body lying face down in the mud beside the road.

As orderlies and interns began removing the wounded from the ambulance, Maria and I ran to Sasha. She was literally pressed, face down, into the half-frozen mud. From the unnatural angle that her leg was bent it was obvious that her left femur had a compound fracture. Even so, we had to roll her onto her back to allow her to breathe. When we turned her over, I had to use my fingers to clear her mouth and nose of the sticky mud.

She showed no reaction to the movements we put her through despite the extreme pain that it must have caused her. I could detect no signs of life, so I bent over her and blew into her mouth. With a gasp, Sasha drew a breath, and her eyes began to flutter open. Her gasp was followed by a stifled scream as the pain hit her.

"You're okay now," I said. "Everything is going to be all right." While trying to reassure her, I tried to brush some muddy hair from her face. She stiffened and groaned when a flap of her scalp came loose in my hand. It was all I could do to keep my fear for her from my face.

Sasha seemed to be trying to speak but didn't seem to be able to get enough air to talk. Her panic-stricken eyes began to focus on my face, and I could see bloody foam forming in her nose.

Turning my head away from Sasha, I whispered to Maria. "She has a punctured lung. Get a doctor and a surgery pack over here *stat*. She can't be moved. We'll have to operate right here."

Once Maria had run for help, I leaned over and kissed Sasha on the forehead, saying, "Maria is getting the doctor. We'll have you on your feet in no time."

While I was talking to her, I was opening her coat and blouse. From my medical bag, I pulled a pair of dressing shears and cut open the army issue undershirt she wore. I had to cut away her bra also. Now I could see that one of the draft horses had stepped directly on her chest. Her left breast was almost completely covered with an ugly bruise in the shape of a horse's hoof. There had to be several broken ribs under that bruise, and at least one of them had punctured a lung.

When Maria returned with help, Sasha was gently lifted onto a stretcher. The stretcher was then placed across several packing crates to form an operating table. We attached a tarp to the side of the disabled ambulance and draped it over the entire area to form an ad hoc operating room.

While Maria and I assisted with Sasha's operation I was dimly aware of the continuing flow of traffic past our little operating theater. By the time we were finished I was confident that Sasha would recover, although for her, the war was over.

While Maria and I helped tear down our temporary shelter to get ready to move on, I noticed a young lieutenant with a pistol in his hand. He was standing beside the road, pulling any infantrymen he saw from the line of refugees. Whenever he had collected a group of men, he would turn them over to an NCO and send them back north, up the road.

When I had a moment, I went up to him and asked, "What are you doing?"

"I'm rebuilding our front lines," he said.

"All by yourself?"

"We have to start somewhere. Besides, I'm not by myself. I have you and your unit to thank."

"I'm afraid I don't understand. What does a bunch of doctors and nurses have to do with rebuilding our front line?"

"Well, whenever these men wanted to keep running, I just had to show them how your group was calmly working there beside the road. When they saw that you were not worried about the Russians, how could they keep running?"

"But we *are* worried about the Russians," I protested.

"So am I. But we don't need to tell the men that. All they need is some leadership to make them as good as any soldiers in this war."

Soon we were on our way south again. With Sasha lying in the back of our lorry between Maria and myself, we rolled over the bridge at last. I waved farewell to the young Lieutenant as we passed out of sight of his little unit of refugees. At least now I had some hope that the Russians wouldn't be able to roll right over that bridge to continue chasing us.

The days are short at this latitude in November, but this day seemed to last for an eternity. It was well after dark when we caught up to the rest of our unit. They were camped alongside the road in the middle of nowhere again.

Because we had left most of our tents behind, many of the wounded had to spend the night in the ambulances. What sleep the staff got was taken in the back of the lorries. We even had to send out scouts in the morning to find a field kitchen so we could feed our patients.

All this notwithstanding, we had actually been very lucky. The Russians never did get across the Chir thanks to the efforts of the brave lieutenant, and many others like him. I have to admit, however, that those brave men weren't the only reason we weren't overtaken by the enemy.

We didn't learn for almost a week, but our good fortune was largely due to the fact that the Russians turned their attack to the southeast once they had shattered our lines. We hadn't even been their main goal. What they really wanted was to capture Kalach and thereby encircle the German 6th Army at Stalingrad. Along with powerful forces coming from the south, which shattered the 4th Romanian Army, they succeeded in capturing Kalach in about three days. The 6th Army was now surrounded in that long-suffering city.

On the day that we saw Sasha off on the first leg of her journey home, I was beside myself with worry and guilt. *How much had I been responsible for Sasha's decision to stay with the army?* And my worry wasn't for Sasha only. Just days before the Russian attack, I had received word that Peter's 1st Cavalry Division was at Kletskaya, only a few kilometers from our hospital. I had actually been scheming how I would get a ride there when the attack started. Now I had no idea what had happened to Peter and his division.

We continued to minister to the wounded as well as we could from our makeshift camp for several days. I noticed that we had mostly walking wounded to tend to. It was some time before I realized the reason for this. Most of the seriously wounded who hadn't already been at the hospital had been left behind due to the speed of the withdrawal. Their care was now up to the advancing Russian army. Even though this made our workload lighter during these difficult times, I shuddered to think of how our men might be treated by the enemy. All we could do for them now was pray.

Somewhere around the end of November, Julius came to the small tent that Maria and I shared as living quarters. He had some interesting information for us.

"I have some news for you," he began.

"Good or bad?" asked Maria.

"Both... I think," he answered. "First, Field Marshal Von Manstein has taken command of our army group."

"Field Marshal?" I asked.

"Yes. He has been promoted since we served with him in the Crimea. Also, we are moving back to the Morozovsk area to set up a proper field hospital. It will be a combined German and Romanian operation since our armies have been so thoroughly mixed together since that last attack."

"Yeah," I said. "They are mixing Germans into all our units, even down to the squad level. I don't think they trust us anymore."

"That may be. But at least we will have better weapons and more ammunition this way. And this Morozovsk... they call it Moro for short, is farther from the front lines."

"Okay, that's the good news," said Maria. "What's the bad?"

"Well... it's not all bad," said Julius softly.

He was stalling, and that made me nervous.

Finally, he continued. "I found out what happened to the 1st Cavalry Division."

My heart was in my throat so that I could hardly speak when I asked, "Peter's unit? Where are they?"

"They were pushed east by the Russian breakthrough. They should be safe... I think. They are with the German 6th Army."

"Trapped in Stalingrad? You call that safe?" I almost yelled at poor Julius.

Suddenly I was having trouble breathing. I began pacing around the small tent. The Russians had completely surrounded Stalingrad. We had been pushed back more than 40 kilometers from that city. The men inside that circle were virtual prisoners of the Russians.

"Don't worry," said Maria. "The 6th Army has more than a quarter of a million men in it. The Germans won't let them be cut off for long. You'll see." "That's right," added Julius. "I hear that Reichsmarschall Goering himself has pledged the Luftwaffe to supply the army by air for as long as necessary. And now that Von Manstien is running things, you know that he'll think of something."

"Yes," I said. "He's a good man and a great general. I guess I'll have to leave Peter's future in his hands."

Then, quietly, to myself I added, "and God's."

The next day we began moving south towards Moro. There was pathetically little to pack after our last hurried retreat.

Moro was not just one base, but a complex of bases located around the town of Morozovsk. There were two airfields as well as numerous army installations in the area. It had been a major supply base during the army's advance. Now it would supply that same army during its siege, this time from the air.

By the time we had set up our hospital, with tents mostly borrowed from the Germans, the great airlift was already underway. The skies were darkened with the comings and goings of hundreds of aircraft. Not only were the sleek fighter planes and ugly Stukas in evidence, but now we saw ever-increasing numbers of the boxy-looking Junkers transport planes.

Even as the airlift gathered momentum, the weather worsened. By the first week of December, the temperature had dropped to 20 degrees below zero while the wind blew the snow across the open steppe in blinding sheets. Amazingly, when the snow and wind weren't causing havoc, dense sub-zero fog would spring up, reducing visibility to nothing.

With all the air activity it would have been easy to forget that the army was busy also. That is, it would have been easy if it weren't for the wounded that continued to arrive at our hospital in need of all types of care. The onset of winter had brought pneumonia to the troops in almost epidemic proportions. Many wounded came out of Stalingrad on the return flights of the transports, but we also received many from much closer at hand.

On one occasion we received a young patient whose arm was badly mangled. He was unconscious when he came in and was rushed directly into surgery. Despite the determined efforts of the doctors, the arm couldn't be saved and was amputated just below the shoulder.

That evening I made sure that I was in the recovery tent when he awoke. Many young men have a very violent reaction to the loss of a limb, especially when they had no warning. I wanted to be there in the event that he needed someone to vent his feelings to. I needn't have worried, however. He surprised me at how well he took the news, after the initial shock. Coming out of the anesthetic, he seemed eager to talk about his accident.

"You say it was an accident?" I said. "Does that bother you more than if it had happened in combat?"

"No, not really. It happens all the time in tank-killing school," he said.

"You are an anti-tank gunner, then?"

"Ha, nothing so easy as that. We don't have as many guns as the enemy has tanks, so in this school, you learn to kill tanks by hand."

"How can you fight tanks by hand?" I asked.

"With magnetic mines, hand grenades, or even petrol bombs," he said. "But first you must get very close to your enemy. I was trying to climb onto a moving tank when I slipped and got my arm caught in the tracks."

I realized that he was running on nervous energy, so I let him talk as much as he wanted. He explained the blind spots of a tank, how to get close to them, and how to stop them in some of the most unlikely ways. He went on for more than an hour before he fell back into a restful sleep. By this time, I had become quite an expert in fighting tanks, though I never thought I would ever need my new knowledge.

You learn a lot from the wounded. They know what it is really like at the front. From the wounded coming back from Stalingrad I learned that the airlift wasn't working. The men in the pocket, that which was now being called the cauldron, weren't getting nearly everything they needed. They were becoming short on food, medicine, weapons, and ammunition. I was beginning to wonder if our air force was trying its best, until I had a chance to talk to a Luftwaffe sergeant who was being treated for frostbite of the fingers.

As I was wrapping his blackened fingertips I said to him, "We see an awful lot of frostbite cases with you mechanics. I thought that you had fairly decent quarters at the airfield." "Our quarters are all right. We have our tents and some of the lucky ones even have some peasant huts to live in."

For a second, my first view of a Russian peasant's hut flashed into my mind. Back when we were on our way to Odessa, we had thought those huts absolutely disgusting. Now, you were lucky to get one.

The sergeant continued. "It's just too bad that Tante Ju can't fit inside the huts with us."

"Aunt Judy? Who is Aunt Judy?"

"That's what we call the Junkers tri-motor transport aircraft. They have been around so long that they are like an aunt, old, dependable, and slow. They even have the wrinkled skin of an old aunt." He laughed over his reference to the corrugated metal skin of the outdated aircraft.

He grew serious again as he said, "Unfortunately they need a lot of maintenance. That's our job, but there are no hangers out here on the steppes. We have to do all our work out in the wind and weather. And that's why we are always coming to you with frostbite. You can't fix a motor with your gloves on."

"That must be terrible," I said.

"It is. But the worst thing is how many planes we are losing. Between the fog, storms, and enemy fighters, soon we won't have any planes left. I don't know how we are going to keep this airlift going much longer."

Trying rather unsuccessfully to keep my voice steady, I asked, "Have you heard anything from inside the pocket? My fiancée is there with the 1st Cavalry Division."

"He's inside the pocket? That's too bad. I hear that it's very bad there. The Russians are attacking from all sides."

He must have seen the distressed look on my face because he quickly added in a whisper, "But don't you worry. I've heard that General Hoth is to lead a relief attack to break through to the pocket. They have even recalled some divisions in from the Caucasus. I'm sure they'll be able to get the 6th Army out. Don't tell anyone, though. It's top secret."

I didn't tell anyone, either. That is, no one except my closest friends like Maria and Julius. I wasn't really surprised to find out that my "top secret" was no secret at all. Even so, I felt much better with the hope that Peter might soon escape from the Russian trap.

I even felt good enough to challenge our hospital's commander, Colonel Petrovici, on the dress code again. While we had been at Pronin, we had won a small victory by getting his permission for the medical personnel to wear combat boots in the mud and the cold. But he had remained adamant that we nurses continuing to wear our uniforms with their skirts and light blouses. When we had been at a real hospital building in the Crimea the cold had been bearable. But here in the field, with the cold wind lifting both the tent flaps and our skirts, it was damn uncomfortable.

"What are you doing?" asked Maria as she hurried through the flap to our small tent and began quickly retying it closed against the wind.

"Getting ready for my shift," I answered as I lay on my back on the hard army cot that served as my bed. I was tugging both legs of a bulky pair of army fatigue pants on as I answered.

"You can't go on shift like that," said Maria. "Colonel Petrovici will have kittens."

I stood up and placed my rear close to the charcoal stove that tried to heat our miserable little mud-floored quarters. I pulled my "new" army tunic over my head and said, "He probably won't even notice."

"Why not?"

"Because it won't show...much," I said. I then pulled my nurse's skirt and jumper over the army uniform leaving only the sleeves and lower legs of it showing.

"He'll notice," said Maria dryly.

"Look, he said we had to wear our uniforms, but he didn't say what we had to wear under them."

"No, he didn't," agreed Maria. "But you could get in trouble."

"Maybe, but what can he do? Send me to Russia?"

That got a laugh out of Maria.

That evening the colonel had been in the surgery for a half hour before he noticed my modified uniform. When his eyes narrowed and his eyebrows nearly became one above his sterile mask, I thought I was in trouble. He didn't say anything, however, and the next day nearly all the nurses were sporting the latest "winter uniform".

On the tenth of December General Hoth's relief attack aimed at Stalingrad got under way. As his divisions advanced steadily against strong resistance my spirits rose with each kilometer gained. I went about my duties with renewed enthusiasm even though the battle was already increasing the number of wounded arriving every day.

My happiness was short-lived, however. On the seventeenth the Russians launched another offensive. This time the blow fell on the Italian army. They had been holding the line west of where our Romanian army had been stationed. The Italians were no better equipped to face front-line Russian formations than we had been.

The enemy quickly punched a 60-kilometer-wide hole in the Italian front. The Russians pouring through that gap threatened to sweep over the entire area we occupied in the Don bend. That included not only the rear of the Stalingrad relief attack, but our air-lift fields also. With the Russians advancing on us from the north, General Hoth was forced to first cut back on his push for Stalingrad, and then abandon it altogether.

Now it was a fight for survival of not only our army group, but also the Army of the Caucasus. On the 24th of December we received the frightening news that the airfield at Tazi had been overrun by the Russians. Tazi was actually several kilometers west of us. That put the enemy between us and our homeland. Terrible as this news was, worse was to follow.

That night we began transporting patients to the airfield at Moro to be flown out at first light. For the next few days at least, the airlift to Stalingrad would have to be put on hold while we flew as many wounded and non-combatants out of the threatened zone and back to the Rostov area as the transports could handle.

All personnel were pressed into service to move the patients. That is why Maria and I were at the airfield instead of the hospital as dawn broke on Christmas Day, 1942. I say it was dawn, but the only way you could tell was by a very slight lessening of the gloom. All our frantic efforts to be ready at first light were being defeated by the weather. Not only was it below freezing with a steady snow falling, but there was a thick fog making take-off almost impossible.

"Should we return to the hospital?" Asked Maria.

"I don't think so," I answered. "Someone has to look after the patients till the planes can take off."

To Julius I said, "You go back with the ambulance for the next lot. Maria and I will tend the men already on the aircraft."

Julius and the ambulance disappeared into the fog while Maria and I climbed into the door located on the side of the aircraft, just behind the wing. Because it was a tail-wheel type of plane, the floor sloped steeply upwards towards the nose where the pilots sat. That meant that we had to be sure that each of the stretcher cases was securely strapped in to avoid sliding around during take-off. The plane was not heated, so we had to be sure that each patient was well wrapped in blankets also.

While we were occupied with the patients, Maria turned to me and said, "What was that?"

"What was what?" I said. "With the engines running I can hardly hear *you.*"

"I heard explosions. I'm sure of it. Do you think there is an air raid?"

"With this fog, I don't see how."

Just then the pilot came running back through the plane. "Ground control just radioed that there are Russian tanks attacking the field," he said. "All aircraft are ordered to take off immediately! If you two aren't flying to Rostov, you have to get off right now. I'm closing the door."

For a second I was tempted to stay on the plane and fly to safety along with the wounded. The same thought occurred to Maria; I could see it in her eyes. But we were needed here, so we jumped to the ground before the door could be closed.

The plane began taxiing immediately. In the fog, I couldn't see how they could know which way to go. Indeed, no sooner had our plane disappeared into the fog, than another one came taxiing across the same spot in another direction. The field looked like a chicken coop after the fox breaks in. With the roar of accelerating aircraft engines coming from all directions, Maria and I moved away from the field to keep clear of the hurrying machines. We had just moved next to a small shed when I heard Maria scream.

Pointing across the field, she said, "I saw a tank! Do you think it was a Russian?"

By the time I looked, the fog had closed back over the spot Maria was indicating so I said, "I don't see anything, but we had better find some cover quickly in case it was."

"Let's get into this building," said Maria.

"Don't you listen to your patients?" I asked her. "A wooden structure is just a target for a tank. It wouldn't give us any protection at all. There should be some slit trenches around here for use in air-raids. We need to find one."

Just then a light anti-aircraft machine-cannon opened fire on some unseen target. The luminous tracer shells disappeared into the fog, but the muzzle flash of the gun had given away its position.

"That way," I yelled as I began running towards the gun. "They will have a trench dug near their gun for emergencies."

Maria followed me and we soon found ourselves climbing down into a narrow slit in the ground. It was long enough to fit about six men, but it was only four feet deep. We had to crouch down to get our heads below ground level.

"They should have dug this deeper," I said.

"What do you know about it?" asked Maria angrily.

"I know that the deeper the better when someone is shooting at you."

Maria's answer was drowned out by the anti-aircraft gun firing again. This time there was return fire. A shell exploded halfway between the gun and our trench. I heard the shell fragments rip through the air above our heads.

"We're non-combatants," shouted Maria. "They aren't supposed to be shooting at us!"

"In this fog, anything that moves is going to be shot at, so keep down," I said.

The engine noise of the scrambling planes was just beginning to fade some when we heard a loud explosion and saw a patch of flame erupt somewhere out on the field. Two aircraft must have collided in the fog. While our attention was drawn towards the flames, another loud bang rang out behind us. The anti-aircraft gun had been blown up.

Before I could say to Maria that we should look for wounded, I saw movement on the far side of the gun's position. A tank was emerging from the fog.

"Is that a Russian?" asked Maria in a whisper.

It rolled directly over the gun and kept coming in our direction, so I said. "It must be." It was less than 50 meters from us and still crawling straight towards us on its metal treads

"We have to run!" shouted Maria.

"No," I said. "We have to stay right here in this trench. They can't see us here and even if it passes right over us, we won't be hurt if we keep low."

The iron beast kept to its course directly at us. When it was only ten meters away Maria screamed something unintelligible and jumped from the trench. I grabbed for her but lost my grip on her arm and tumbled to the bottom of the trench. In that instant I had to decide whether to chase after her or stay hidden.

I chose to hide. I heard the tank's machine gun firing just above my head, but that sound was quickly drowned out by the noise of the clanking treads and the roar of the engine as the iron monster passed directly over me.

I had landed on my back in the bottom of that hole-in-the-ground and found myself staring up in horror at a steal link of the tank's tread less than a meter above my head. The upper edges of the trench crumbled dirt into my face, but the walls held the tons of iron off me until the monster had passed over. A blast of hot diesel fumes from its exhaust signaled its passage, as it moved away from me.

I lay still for a moment, fully expecting to see Russian soldiers looking down on me at any second. When nothing happened, I sat up and peered around. There was no one in sight. Even the enemy tank had disappeared into the mist.

I knew which direction Maria had run, so I quickly set off after her in a low crouch. I found her only a few meters from the trench, lying face down in the snow with both her arms outstretched above her head. There were two bloody holes in her back. I knelt beside her and rolled her over into my lap. The front of her coat was a mass of blood, and I thought that she was already dead. But as I cradled her head with my arm and tried to straighten her long beautiful blond hair, her eyes opened and looked into my face.

It wasn't me she saw, however, as she said, "Mother? Mother it hurts. Help me mother."

I lifted her face to my shoulder and whispered into her ear. "It's all right. Mother will take care of you."

When I lowered her back to my lap, her eyes were closed for the last time. I checked for a pulse and found none. Hugging her to me, I thought, *so now I know… it isn't only the men who ask for their mother in their last moments. Why had I let her run? I should have held onto her somehow. I should have run after her…knocked her to the ground… done something. I'm the last of our little group left. Why am I still alive while a lovely girl like Maria lies dead in my arms? Did I kill her when I talked her into staying in Russia?*

I don't know how long I held her lifeless body, but the fog was lifting when a German soldier came up to me. When he asked if Maria were dead, I said, "yes." Then he asked me if I was all right. I couldn't answer that.

It turned out that the raid on the airfield had been a mistake. A few Russian tanks had become lost from the main assault and had stumbled across the field. That mistake had cost Maria her life. It cost me the last of my optimism about the war. I realized now that Peter would never return from Stalingrad. Even though we held onto the field at Moro for another week, we were finally forced to withdraw to the next line of defense, behind the Donets River. The supply flights to Stalingrad now had to cover more than 100 kilometers instead of the previous 40 to 50 from Moro.

It was obvious that the 6th Army would be captured by the Russians sooner or later. And when it marched into captivity, so would my fiancée, if he lived at all. With the loss of my last close friend from home, and Peter's fate sealed, I may have started losing touch with reality. I don't know how else to explain the plan that now began to form in my mind.

CHAPTER VII

A desperate plan

Our new location was now a few kilometers east of Sahty, a fair-sized town that was still mostly intact due to the fact that our advance through this sector had been almost unopposed the previous summer. The organizing of our field hospital was rather chaotic, partly because this was our third move in two months, and partly because our equipment and personnel were arriving piece-meal. Some of the non-military personnel such as myself had been flown out of Moro, while other members of the staff, and virtually all of the equipment, were transferred by either train, lorry, or in most cases, horse-drawn wagon. Each unit's arrival was dictated by how much the enemy's rapid advance had interfered with their journey.

I took advantage of the confusion to put my plan into action as soon as I arrived at our new site. On New Years Day I arranged to ride to the airfield accompanying a shipment of medical supplies bound for Stalingrad. Once at the field, I assisted with transferring the supplies from the lorry to the aircraft. When the loading was nearly complete, I made sure I was one of the last on the plane.

As the medical staff filed off, I fell in at the end of the line and simply dropped down behind a crate in the tail of the Junkers. From my hiding place I watched the pilot secure the door and climb back into the pilot's cabin at the nose. While the engines ran through their pre-take-off run-up, I slipped out of my nurse's dress, leaving only the simple fatigue uniform I'd had on underneath. I pulled a Red Cross arm band from my pocket and put it on.

As I stuffed my skirt and blouse into a corner of the tail, I prayed that my additional weight wouldn't be too much for the old plane to lift from the snow-covered runway. I knew that each aircraft was loaded beyond the normal limit due to the urgent need for supplies by our surrounded army. At my heaviest, I had never massed much more than 100 lb. Now, with the limited food and heavy work schedule, I was probably no heavier than 90 lb... Even so, I worried that my presence could cause a disaster for the plane and its crew. It is a measure of my desperation that I was willing to risk innocent lives for my scheme.

Everything went well despite my misgivings, and soon the old trimotor was lumbering slowly higher and higher into the frigid air. The plane had no windows in the tail where I was hidden, but even so, I had an excellent view of the ground dropping away. I only had to look through any one of several jagged holes in the corrugated metal skin. The holes were usually in pairs, one where the shrapnel from the anti-aircraft fire had entered the body of the plane, and one where it left. By this time there wasn't one aircraft flying that wasn't sporting its share of holes from flak and machine gun bullets. Even this far along, I knew that my plan had a good chance of failure. Between the weather, the fighters, and the anti-aircraft fire, more than half of all flights were forced to return without delivering their loads. I was lucky this time. Despite a brief attack by fighters on some other planes in our formation and some very scary flak over the enemy lines, my plane made it all the way to its destination. Pitomik was the larger of the two airfields held by our forces within the siege perimeter. After landing my plane taxied rapidly to the edge of the field and stopped abruptly amid the squealing of overtaxed brakes. I knew that all loading and unloading had to be accomplished as rapidly as possible on these fields because the arrival of any of our planes was an invitation for enemy artillery to begin firing in the hope of catching new targets helplessly on the ground. Indeed, I was counting on the hurried, and hopefully disorganized, unloading of the planes to allow me to mingle with the unloading crew.

The aircraft was still rolling to a stop as the co-pilot came running down the narrow center isle and quickly popped the loading door open. Immediately, half a dozen men, dressed in the shabbiest uniforms I have ever seen, began to climb into the plane. My heart sank as I realized my plan to mingle with the workers was not going to work. They were Hiwis, Russian prisoners of war who were willing to work for their captors in exchange for certain privileges, such as extra food. With their heads and feet wrapped in rags and their tattered uniforms, I could never have been taken for one of the work crew.

As I tried to think of what to do, a large prisoner walked directly to the crate I was hiding behind and lifted it from in front of me. He froze in his tracks, staring open-mouthed when he saw me. He crossed himself and mumbled something in Russian as his sunken, red-rimmed eyes looked on my face in disbelief.

I had to do something quickly before other members of the unloading crew noticed his odd behavior. I dredged through my meager knowledge of the Russian language, acquired from my father's mother. She had been from Russia and had always told us stories in her native language.

Standing as tall as I could, I came about to the Hiwis' chest. In what I hoped was a commanding voice I told him to be quiet and go about his business. If I remember my grandmother right, I probably told him to, "Be quiet, little one."

He merely stared at me as I lifted one of the smaller crates and hopped down from the plane. There were sporadic explosions from artillery rounds landing on the field as I started off in what I hoped was the direction of Stalingrad. I hadn't gone 10 meters when I heard a challenge shouted in German. "You there, stop! What are you doing here?"

A junior-grade lieutenant caught me from behind and grabbed my arm, spinning me around to face him. I almost dropped the crate I was carrying. When I saw that I was faced with a junior officer rather than a grizzled old veteran, I decided to try to brazen my way through.

"Watch it you fool," I said. "You nearly made me drop this, uh...sulfa powder. We need it desperately at the hospital! It may be the last we get for a long time."

"You...you're a... woman," he stammered.

Despite my bulky uniform and the Caciula cap pulled low over my hair, there had never been any realistic chance of my passing as a man, once my beardless face and high voice had been discovered. I said, "I'm not a woman. I'm a nurse, and I am to report to the 1st Romanian Cavalry Division medical office."

"But certainly, they are not allowing women to come into the perimeter," he protested.

"I'm here, aren't I?"

At this point he fell back on his army training, saying, "Let me see your papers."

I had no papers, of course. But I thought I could see my salvation approaching. True to form, the arrival of new aircraft had triggered an increase in the tempo of harassing fire coming from the Russian artillery. I could see a salvo of explosions moving progressively closer to our position. I began stalling for time while hoping that my unwitting accomplices didn't run out of shells. "Here, hold this," I said as I thrust the case of sulfa powder into the young officer's hands. I then proceeded to search slowly through all the pockets of my borrowed uniform. All the while I searched, grumbling to myself, the explosions came closer and closer. Finally, the Lieutenant became aware of the danger approaching from behind. At last, he yelled, "Take cover." Then he threw himself into a nearby trench. I scooped up the sulfa case and ran for the edge of the field. By the time the barrage of shells had passed, the Lieutenant was nowhere in sight. He probably thought that stupid non-combatant had gotten herself blown into little pieces. At any rate, I'm sure that he didn't spend much time looking for me.

By the time I reached the perimeter of the field, the aircraft I had flown in on was already accelerating down the runway for its return flight to the outside world. For better or worse, I was in. All I had to do was join the flow of soldiers on the road headed east. I call it a road even though it was barely visible under the blowing and drifting snow.

Here inside the perimeter, there was no petrol to spare, so nearly all traffic was either on foot or by sled. Most of the sleds were drawn by Panjes, the hardy little Russian ponies. They were small, but incredibly tough and able to stand the winter weather better than our horses could. By now, most of the army's horses were already dead from overwork and lack of fodder anyway. Fodder was much too bulky to be flown in, so the horses died.

Even in death, the poor animals performed one final service for their former masters. All along the snow covered track I could see the frozen carcasses of horses that had been butchered for food. Horse meat was now the principal source of protein for an army of over 250,000 men.

Horses weren't the only carcasses littering this road to hell. Hundreds of dead soldiers, their bodies frozen in the most grotesque attitudes of violent death, lay everywhere. Many times, only an arm or a leg protruded from a snow drift, while in some places, the bodies had been stacked like some sort of macabre cordwood.

At one point, the pony pulling the sled ahead of me let out a pathetic wheeze and dropped dead in its tracks. Instantly, a dozen ragged, starving men, fell on the carcass and began cutting it up.

I turned to a soldier sitting on the side of the trail and asked, "Why are they in such a hurry? Surely there must be enough for all of them."

"With the temperature this far below zero, the body will freeze too hard to cut within a few moments," he answered.

"Why aren't you joining them? Aren't you hungry too?" I asked.

"Oh, I'm hungry all right," he said. "I just don't care anymore. I walked all the way out here because they said my specialty was too important to lose and I would be flown out. When I got to the field, they had changed their mind and told me to go back to the city.

"Go back to what, I ask you? Why should I go to all the trouble to go there to die when I can do that just as well here? Besides, I hear that freezing to death isn't a bad way to go. You just go to sleep and don't wake up. That's better than a bullet in the head or being blown to pieces."

"But you can't just give up," I said. "If you do, then the enemy has already won."

"I have news for you," he said. "They *have*. Now go away. I want to die in peace."

I didn't want to leave him, but what could I do? Already, my few moments of inactivity in the 20 degrees below zero temperature had me shivering inside my parka. I moved on and left the defeated man to his fate.

It was less than 10 kilometers from the airfield to the city, but with the snow and the slow pace of the bone-weary travelers, that seemed to be walking in their sleep, it took several hours to reach the city proper.

Actually, once I got there, I realized that there really wasn't any city left. From the low hills west of the city I could look out over a scene of almost unbelievable devastation. It looked more like the surface of the moon than a part of this earth. There were whole square kilometers where nothing recognizable as a building remained standing. Only gray rubble, mostly covered with a sooty snow, was visible. Even the outline of the streets had been erased.

Continuing to move with the flow of inbound traffic, I finally came to what appeared to be a command post. It was situated in a corner formed by two partially standing cement walls. There was no roof, of course, but the walls broke the wind somewhat.

I was hesitant to talk to anyone there lest they try to stop me in my quest. But I had to have some idea where to go. Stalingrad may have been flattened, but it still spread for a dozen kilometers along the Volga River. When I finally got up the nerve to ask someone, they didn't seem concerned about my gender at all. I don't think anyone cared much about anything anymore.

I was informed that what was left of the 1st Cavalry Division was in the northern factory district of the city and that the medical section would almost certainly be situated along the banks of the Volga. I was assigned to a squad of German soldiers headed into the city as reinforcements for the street fighters there. Soon we were trudging along a barely discernible path through the rubble that I think had been a street at one time.

We had covered several kilometers when the patrol leader signaled for everyone to spread out and keep low. From that point on we moved from cover to cover, always keeping below the level of the piles of rubble.

At one rest break, I asked the soldier next to me, "Why we were sneaking around so? I thought all the enemy were outside the city, surrounding us."

"Oh, no," he said. "We never got all the Ivans out of the city. They still hold some key points and sections of the riverbank cliffs. The real problem is that they keep using the sewer system to come around behind us. And if I were you, I would take off that armband. That red cross makes a great aiming point for the snipers."

"Don't the Russians respect the Red Cross?"

"Not here, they don't. To them, one dead corpsman means a lot of other soldiers will die of their wounds."

I took the armband off and stuffed it into my pocket.

Just then, the squad leader motioned for us to move up to the corner of a street that was, almost miraculously, mostly clear of rubble.

"We have to cross here," he said. "I don't like the looks of it, so we cross one at a time...and quickly."

When he tapped one of the men on the shoulder, the man took off across the street like the devil himself was on his heels. Nothing happened, so two more men ran across. This time a machine gun opened fire, but both men made it across all right. In ones and twos, everyone crossed the street until only the squad leader and myself were left.

He turned to me and said, "You should go back. I don't know why you are here, but it can't be worth your life."

"Is your life worth any less than mine, just because I'm a woman?" I asked. "Besides, why I'm here *is* my life."

Before he could say anything else I said, "See you on the other side," and began running. Even over the hammering of the unseen machine gun, I could hear the pounding of the squad leader's boots behind me.

I dove the last 2 meters, landing headfirst in a pile of brick-and-mortar rubble. I suppose it should have hurt to land like that, but I was too elated to have survived to care about a few bruises. I turned to laugh at the squad leader and his fears, but he wasn't there.

He was lying on his back in the middle of the street, not moving. I scrambled to a crouching position, preparing to sprint back to him when a hand grabbed my shirt collar from behind and yanked me off my feet. I landed in a ruined ground-floor room with the other soldiers.

The corporal whom I had been talking to earlier was the one who had grabbed me.

Putting his face right into mine, he yelled, "He's dead! And even if he wasn't, no one could get to him and live! Two dead bodies out there won't make things better.

"Now we have to get moving up this block. And I mean *now.*"

"We can't," I said sullenly. "You just said that no one can survive in that street."

"When you can't go up the street, you go through the houses," he said. "Get back. We are going to blow out a wall."

We all took cover behind the remains of someone's furniture while a short fuse detonated an explosive charge placed against the wall. When the dust cleared, there was an open passage into the next building. Whenever there were no convenient doors or windows we progressed in this manner until we were clear of that entire block of buildings. By now it was dark, and we halted within a somewhat less damaged building for the night.

The soldiers produced a surprising array of food from their packs and pockets and began to eat their cold rations. I hadn't thought to bring any food, so I decided to settle for quenching my thirst with mouthfuls of snow.

"Don't do that," said the corporal. "You'll lower your body temperature too much before you ever get enough to drink. Didn't you bring any rations?"

When I shook my head, he said, "Here, eat some of this bread. I have some cooked meat too."

Then he produced a canteen of water from under his coat. "It keeps it from freezing," he explained.

I accepted the bread and water. But I couldn't face the meat, knowing from where it had most likely come. While we were eating, he pulled a pistol from his belt and held it out to me.

"You may need this," he said.

"No, thanks, I swore to save lives, not take them," I said.

"If the Russians get their hands on you, you may change your mind."

I just shook my head and said, "No, thanks," again.

The night passed uneventfully if you didn't count the frequent outbursts of firing and the continual drone of artillery fire. At first light, we were on our way once again. We crawled through ditches and over mountains of rubble. Bodies were everywhere. Usually, they were covered with piles of bricks or mortar. Sometimes only snow covered the remains of those who no longer suffered as the living did. I noticed that many of the bodies were civilians who had been caught in the holocaust of Stalingrad.

Once, when some mortar shells fell fairly close, I jumped behind a pile of rubble and found myself straddling a frozen body. It was the corpse of a young child lying where she had fallen. She was naked, with no visible marks on her. I had seen this effect before. Most likely the same explosion that had stripped her clothes from her had killed her with the concussion yet left her untouched otherwise. As I stared at the body, the corporal said, "Stalin refused to allow the civilians to evacuate the city before we got here. He wanted all of them to help in the battle, even the women and children."

At last, toward mid-morning, we came to the edge of a bluff. The ground dropped off steeply to a broad, frozen river below.

"That's the Volga," said the corporal. "Now that it is frozen all the way across, the Russians are coming at us from that side also."

Just then, a group of Romanian soldiers carrying stretchers with wounded men on them came along the edge of the bluff, heading north.

"Are you going to the 1st Cavalry aid station?" I asked.

They said they were, so I bid a hasty farewell to "my squad" and followed the group of my countrymen. They were carrying the stretchers with one man per handle, probably because they were all so weak from the difficult job of hauling the wounded over such irregular ground coupled with their poor diet. I had long since strapped the case of sulfa powder onto my back to keep my hands free for scrambling over the rubble, so when I noticed that one of the stretcher bearers was having difficulty holding up his corner of the stretcher, I offered to carry it for a while.

"You're too small and scrawny to do a man's work," he scoffed. "Get away from me. You don't belong here."

"Maybe I don't belong here, but I'm in better shape than you. When was the last time you had a good meal?" He didn't answer, so I continued. "I had a hot meal just the day before yesterday. And I'm a lot stronger than I look."

He still didn't say anything, but one of the bearers at the front of the stretcher turned his head and said, "She's right, Heimmy. You're just slowing us down with that wounded wing of yours."

That was when I looked at the man's other hand and saw that it was wrapped in blood-soaked bandages. "You're wounded," I said. "Why are you carrying a stretcher when you should be in a hospital yourself?"

"I'm on my way to the aid station now. You don't think that they are going to send any more able-bodied men back from the front than they have to, do you?"

"Fine, then just worry about getting yourself to the aid station," I said. Then I stepped in front of him and took the stretcher handle as I bumped him away.

"Careful, Miss," said the bearer at the front of the stretcher. "Heimmy hasn't been that near a woman in a long time." Then he added, almost to himself, "Come to think of it, none of us has."

"Then I guess that you will all have to get used to it again," I said.

The whole group continued their passage with grins on their faces. Perhaps I can get assigned to Stalingrad as morale officer, I thought.

Soon the trail began to descend into a gorge that ran towards the river. The trail became steeper and the footing more slippery as we descended. Finally, it was a struggle just to keep our feet. We had to stop and strap the patients onto their stretchers to keep them from being tumbled onto the ground. The only thing we had to strap the wounded in with was our belts.

I felt pretty silly for the rest of the descent, holding the stretcher with one hand and my pants with the other. I had the feeling that the others in my group were just waiting for me to take a tumble and let go of something. At last, we reached a level area about halfway to the bottom.

"Here we are," said the lead bearer.

"Here, where?" I asked.

"The aid station," he said. Then he pointed to a large rectangular opening in the gorge wall. It was a cement pipe, about three meters on a side, with a trickle of water coming from the lip. The water was tinted red and running into a shallow stream, where it quickly froze before it could reach the river below.

"That's a sewer!" I said.

"No," he said. "It used to be a sewer. Now it is heaven."

All I could do was look at him as if he had lost his mind, so he explained. "That used to be a storm drain for the city. Now it is our hospital, storage depot, barracks, and whatever else we need. But most of all, it's warm...compared to out here anyway."

As we climbed into the open end of the sewer, he continued, "Everything above ground is open to bombing and shelling. In here, we are safe from almost anything.

The Russians showed us about the luxuries of sewer living. While we bombed and blasted everything in sight, they kept coming around behind us. After a while, we figured it out and took to the sewers ourselves. Even the Russian commander, General Chuikov, lived in the sewers around here until we drove him out. Now, they are attacking, and we are hiding in the sewers."

I thought the interior was going to be pitch black until the men at the head of our group pushed through a tarpaulin that had been draped across the tunnel as a blackout curtain. All precautions had to be taken to avoid revealing the tunnel's location to the watching enemy.

Once past the tarpaulin, the tunnel was lit with candles and kerosene battle lanterns. The dim light produced a gloomy and depressing scene, but at least it was much warmer and relatively safe. We filed past armed men near the entrance. Beyond them were stacks of crates and boxes. Further in, smaller tunnels branched off at intervals. They were all occupied by stores or troops trying to get some rest or to warm up and get a meal before going back out into that city of death and destruction.

We must have been fifty meters into the tunnel when we turned into a branch that had a hand-lettered sign at the entrance saying, "Aid Station." I forgot my sore, blistered hand and my arm that felt like it was about to fall off. Instead, all I could feel was my heart pounding in my chest as I realized that I was finally about to see my beloved Peter.

The branch we were now in was lined along both walls with army cots, leaving barely enough room for us to carry our wounded. All the cots were occupied with wounded men, while orderlies moved up and down the rows tending them. At last, we reached an area with enough room to put down our burdens. Orderlies quickly checked the tags on the wounded men and directed them to what space was available for them.

"Peter...I mean Dr. Peter Pickmann. Do you know where he is?" I asked the orderly who took the crate of sulfa from me.

Nodding his head towards a side-tunnel, he said, "He's in surgery now. You can't bother him until he's done.

So he *was* here! After traveling thousands of kilometers, only a privacy curtain separated us. I wanted to rush through that insubstantial barrier and throw my arms around his neck. Instead, I indicated the wounded stretcher bearer, Heimmy, standing behind me.

"This man needs attention," I said.

"The dressing station is down there," said the orderly. "We'll get to him as soon as we can."

The orderly sounded very tired, or maybe he had just given up. Either way, I wasn't going to let a wounded man stand around any longer than necessary. I led Heimmy to the indicated dressing station and had him sit down.

"Unwrap your bandage," I said. When he did, I began to inspect his hand. "Where did you get this shrapnel?"

"A grenade," he answered. "Ivan and I were trading grenades back and forth between our basements... I lost."

"I have to extract the pieces and get some antiseptic on this."

When an orderly passed, I asked him, "Where do you keep the anesthetics?"

"Anesthetics are only to be used for major surgery," he said.

"What about some hydrogen peroxide for cleaning the wound?"

"Sorry, were out of that. But there is boiled water over there," he said, indicating a small petrel stove with a large pan of water on it.

"This is going to hurt," I said to Heimmy.

"He nodded, and I began to extract the meal fragments with a worn-out pair of forceps. The pain must have been considerable, but he didn't complain, and I soon had his hand clear of fragments and cleaned as well as I could with the boiled water. I opened one of the sulfa packets that I had carried all the way from the airfield. As I dusted the antiseptic powder over his hand and then began to wrap it in fresh bandages, I glanced up at the surgery curtain once again.

"He must be some kind of man," said Heimmy.

"Who?" I asked.

"The doctor who's on the other side of that curtain. You haven't taken your eyes off it since we got here."

"I'm sorry. Have I been hurting you?"

"No, it's not that. You've done a great job. But I can't believe that you were sent here to work in a hospital that will soon be overrun by the Russians. You came here because of that Peter fellow, didn't you?"

"He's my fiancé. I had to come. Any woman would have, in my place."

"If that were so, why isn't this place crawling with wives and girlfriends?"

I had to smile. "They just didn't have access to a Junkers, the way I did."

"Like I said, he's a lucky man."

Just then, the curtain was pushed aside, and my Peter emerged from the tiny operating theater. As though by a will of their own, my feet began to carry me towards my beloved, even as my eyes registered the changes that had come to his face. His eyes had a haunted look. His face, never very full, was now almost skull-like. Even his raven black hair was showing streaks of gray, while several days' worth of stubble covered his cheeks.

When I got to him, I couldn't speak. I just stared up into his face, a full head above me.

He was talking to another doctor, facing partially away from me when he became aware of my presence. I must have changed quite a bit myself, for when he turned to me, he didn't seem to recognize me.

"Can I help you..." he began. Then he got a very puzzled look on his face. That was quickly followed by a look of shock. Then, thank God, a look of happiness that lit up his whole face.

"Anna? Anna, it can't be you...can it?"

I could barely squeak out a whispered, "It's me."

For a moment we simply stared at each other, while around us, the rest of the world ceased to exist.

Finally, I managed to find my voice again. "Please don't be mad. I just had to come to you. I love you too much to let a few Russians come between us."

"I'm not mad..." he began, but I cut him off as I jumped up to wrap my arms around his neck and kiss him as hard as I could.

He wasn't mad at me! He was glad I was here! He still loved me!"

My leap took Peter by surprise, and we almost tumbled to the floor. I didn't care. I wouldn't have cared if we rolled on the floor in front of everyone. I had found Peter!

"You're off duty for the next six hours," the other doctor said to Peter. "The surgery won't be used for at least that long, so why don't you and your...friend use it to get reacquainted in privacy."

He smiled and walked away as the orderlies, now finished with cleaning the surgery, pushed past us in the narrow corridor.

Our eyes never left each other as Peter lifted the privacy curtain with one arm and, with the other around my waist, guided me into the small room. His touch sent tingles up my spine. The operating room was just another section of the storm drain with an antiquated surgery table in the center and a few lanterns scattered about. Above the table were several worn electric torches for use during operations. There was no place to sit except on the table, so Peter lifted me to the disinfected tabletop while he stood before me.

"How in hell did you get here?" he asked.

When I briefly described my flight in and the trek through the city, he kept shaking his head. Finally, I ended my tale with, "And that is when you came through the curtain and proved that my efforts hadn't been wasted. I'm so glad to find you in one piece. Now we can work together helping the wounded."

"You are *insane*," he said. "You can't stay here. Do you know what is happening? We're trapped here. There is no way we will ever get out. We'll all be prisoners, or dead, soon."

"So I'll help as long as possible. Then, when the end comes, they will still need medical people to care for the prisoners."

"You little fool, don't you know what the Russians will do to a woman?"

"They are people just like anyone else. I'm sure they will respect the fact that I am a nurse and let me do my duty."

"Oh God! You have no idea what this war has done to everyone. The men, on both sides, act like animals. I'm amazed that our own men treated you as well as they did."

"But they *did* treat me well. I think you are overreacting, and I don't want us to spend our time arguing." With that, I took his hand in mine and lifted it to my face. "I just want you to touch me the way I want to touch you."

He raised his other hand and placed them both behind my neck, pulling my face close to his. Softly, he whispered to me, "Your being here is both a nightmare and a dream come true. Let's live the dream for now."

Gently, he pulled me to him and brushed my lips with his. Suddenly, my arms were around his neck, pulling him to me. I pressed my mouth firmly over his and opened my lips. I wanted him to know that I hadn't come to this stinking hell, risking my life all the way, for anything less than to have him make love to me. I had timed my arrival for my fertile period, as well as I could determine. In my mind, I knew that if I couldn't get Peter to leave with me, I could at least take a part of him with me.

As I had said before, Peter and I had made love only once. I had been a virgin then, and I think he was also. So, when my tongue pressed into his mouth with all the urgency that I felt, Peter may have been surprised, though he didn't show it. His tongue slid against mine, forcing its way into my mouth as we tasted the built-up passion of our long separation.

While our mouths explored each other, my hands slid down his chest and over his stomach. I was satisfied to find a growing hardness between his legs that I encouraged with my stroking. I had actually been afraid that, after all the hardship Peter had endured, he might be physically unable to respond. Now, I was no longer worried.

I began to untie his surgery gown. The ties in the back made it that much more enjoyable as I pressed my body against his to reach them. I was sure to rub my breasts against his chest. They may not be large, but by now my nipples were hard with anticipation. I was bursting with desire as I helped him undress.

Then he was unbuttoning my uniform shirt and pulling the army-green tee-shirt over my head. I wore no bra, and soon he was cupping my breasts with his hand while he kissed and suckled on my nipples. It was all I could do, not to cry out. But that would have brought an instant investigation from the other side of the curtain, and I couldn't have that. Not yet at least.

I unlatched my web-belt and quickly slid the rough wool pants down my legs. My only concession to civilian comfort, my soft cotton panties, soon followed the trousers as I stood naked before my love. I am happy to say that his eyes couldn't seem to get enough of me as his hands slid down over my hips and caressed my buttocks.

I untied the drawstring of his surgery pants and lowered them along with his underpants. I smiled hugely when his manhood saluted me. We were standing beside the surgery table enjoying the sight of each other when his gentle surgeon's fingers began to caress the flesh between my legs. I held him, stroking him gently as he separated my lips and slid his fingers into my moist canal.

I couldn't wait any more. I pulled him to me violently. Perhaps too violently, as his manhood jabbed me far too high, due to our large difference of height. We laughed a little. Then he lifted me by my hips and placed me on my back on the table.

We were very serious again when he climbed onto the table with me. He placed himself over me with his knees between my outspread legs.

With my arms wrapped around his neck, he lowered himself onto me. He looked as if he were afraid, I would break under his weight. When the tip of his penis touched lightly against my mound, I took one of my hands from around his neck and guided him into me. His stiff penis felt incredible as he pressed slowly deeper and deeper into me.

On his first thrust, he penetrated me as deeply as possible and then began to pull slowly back. Again, I almost screamed with delight. Soon he was too involved with his own needs to worry about my apparent frailty as he began to pump up and down into my vagina. I used my vaginal muscles to try to milk every stroke for maximum feeling.

When he came into me, I swear I could feel his stream enter my womb. Spent, he dropped heavily onto me, his sweat making my breasts slippery and sticky at the same time. When he realized that he was putting his full weight on my small body he tried to pull away.

I locked my arms behind his back and wrapped my legs around him, trapping him in place. "I want to remain one with you as long as possible," I said.

He relaxed back down onto me, though I could tell that he was holding some of his weight in his knees and elbows. "That was better than I could have ever dreamed," he said.

I guided his head down onto my shoulder and said, "I want to touch you while I have you." And that was true, as far as it went. But I had another reason for not wanting him to pull out of me too soon. I knew that my chances of conception were greatly improved by keeping him in me for as long as possible.

I nibbled his ear as I felt him slowly shrinking inside me. Finally, he slipped from my wet canal. I rubbed my face against the crook of his neck, tasting his sweat, smelling him, trying to memorize the feel of him. Slowly, he lowered all his weight onto me as his breathing became regular. He was asleep. I realized how exhausted he must be, and briefly felt a pang of guilt at using him this way. But I was only doing what I thought was necessary. Of course, I *had* just flown over enemy lines, crawled through hell, and seduced my lover in a sewer, so I might not have been considered sane by some.

I slid my legs together enough to feel his limp manhood hanging against my crotch. Then I began to move my thighs against him. It took most of an hour, but at last he began to respond. His penis swelled with passion even as his brain remained mostly asleep. I wiggled an arm between us and somehow managed to insert him into me once again. With my legs wrapped around his buttocks I began to rock up and down. I couldn't produce much motion, but Peter soon awoke enough to respond and began to pump into me again. This time it took much longer and felt that much the sweeter for it. I actually achieved my first orgasm before I felt him shoot into me the second time. Once again, I held him in place, though his sleep-drugged mind put up less resistance to remaining in me than he had previously.

I was ecstatic. I had taken his seed twice and managed to remain on my back for a long time after each coupling. If I was ever to get pregnant, this should do it, I thought. However, now my mind ran on a different tangent.

It made no sense, but now I wanted to stay here with Peter and share his fate. Perhaps I was already becoming irrational, but I was determined to persuade him to let me stay once he awoke. For now, however, I would just enjoy him touching me all over, even if it was a little hard to breath.

I slid partially out from under him and stretched as far as I could to pull a surgery sheet from a nearby table. Using my hands and feet, I awkwardly managed to spread the sheet over Peter's back to keep him from freezing. After all, even though it was warmer here underground, we *were* still in a sewer. I decided to remain only half under him since it made breathing easier, but I continued to cradle his head on my shoulder as I enjoyed the feel of his body on mine.

I could have happily stayed in that position forever, but of course there was a war on. All too soon I heard voices coming from just beyond the curtain. Next, Heimmys' head was poking around the curtain.

"Sorry to interrupt, but they want their surgery room back. I told them to give you a few minutes...to get it ready."

"You've been out there all this time?" I asked.

"Sure. You didn't want any interruptions, did you?"

"No we didn't. Thanks, Heimmy."

"No trouble," said Heimmy as his eyes dropped from my face to my chest where one of my breasts was not covered by the sheet. I made no move to cover myself, and his eyes lingered a second until he disappeared behind the curtain once again.

I should have felt embarrassed, but I didn't care who saw us. Besides, didn't I owe Heimmy a little something, or was I just making his situation worse. Maybe I was just being selfish. After all, I was with Peter and I was happy. Nuzzling the side of his neck, I said, "Wake up, sleepy head. They want their operating room back."

He didn't answer so I stuck my tongue in his ear. That woke him!

His head came up suddenly while his eyes tried to focus. When he saw me he smiled and kissed me gently.

I kissed him back, not so gently, and then pulled away enough to say, "We have to get up. I think they have other plans for this table."

He appeared confused as he looked around the room. "Oh, my God," he said. "How long have I been sleeping?"

"Only a few hours," I said. "But unless you want to be found buck naked by your surgery team, you had better get dressed."

As he pushed himself up and off of me, he asked, "Are you all right? I didn't mean to fall asleep on top of you."

"I'm fine. And I wouldn't have wanted you to sleep anywhere else."

While Peter dressed quickly, I took a little longer. I was having trouble moving because my left arm and both legs were asleep. By the time the orderlies arrived to prep the surgery we were both dressed and hopefully not looking too guilty.

I asked Peter if I could assist him with his operation, and when he said yes, I was almost as happy as I had been when I found him. It had been a dream of mine since I had met him in medical school that we would work together someday. Actually, we did four consecutive operations before we got a break, and I was exhausted by the time we finished.

When we were done in the surgery, Peter led me to the Doctor's quarters to let me get some sleep. They were only another section of the sewer, but there were several empty cots and a stove for heat. I was asleep within seconds after I hit the hard canvas of the cot.

When I awoke, Peter brought me some black bread and a slice of cheese to eat.

"Sorry it can't be more," he said. "But black bread is almost the only food we have here besides horse meat. And knowing how you feel about animals, I didn't think you would want any of that."

"Peter! That is so thoughtful. I didn't realize that you knew me so well," I said.

"I know you well enough to know that you are thinking you will stay here with me," he said.

"You need the help, and I'm a very good nurse. I'm in good health and..."

"Save it. I know all the arguments. I've thought of them all myself. But the fact is that you can't stay here."

"I won't leave without you," I said. "The army can't spare enough men to drag me back to the airfield, so there is nothing you can do."

Looking solemn, he said, "I knew you would say that, so I have made...arrangements."

"What sort of arrangements?" I asked.

"Doctors have been included in the specialties that are authorized to leave the cauldron. Very few are willing to leave the wounded, but we *are* allowed. If it is the only way to get you to go, I'll leave with you."

"You will? That's wonderful," I said as I leapt into his arms. But deep down inside, a part of me was disappointed that Peter would leave his patients...even for me.

There were several seriously wounded patients ready to be transported to the airfield. They needed a physician to travel with them, so Peter and I were soon on our way through the ruins of Stalingrad once again. We traveled through the relatively safe-occupied zones. Even so, there were many dangers to be faced.

Once, as our little group threaded its way along the paths cleared in the rubble, an explosion knocked me to the ground. When I got to my feet, I could see the man who had been leading us leaning against a piece of wall. He had no legs or arms anymore. By the time I could scramble forward to him, the light of life was already fading from his eyes. I couldn't even hold his hand as he died before me. I don't know if it was a mine or a stray shell that killed him.

Later, as we entered the ruined suburbs to meet one of the few remaining motor lorries, the man beside Peter dropped to the ground, dead from a sniper's bullet in his brain. It was then that I began to fear that my presence could cost Peter his life, since he wouldn't have been exposing himself to the dangers of the city if it weren't for me.

I realized that it was too late to worry about that as we boarded the lorry for the ride to Pitomik. Bodies littered the roadside as we moved slowly through the snow drifts. With a light snow falling, I tried to see if the discouraged soldier that I had talked to on my way into the city had actually sat where he was till he froze. I didn't know exactly where I had been at the time, so I couldn't tell if any of the frozen forms along the road were his or not. Maybe it didn't matter. I could feel the despair seeping into me even though I was getting out. How terrible it must be to know there was no escape.

We got to the airfield in time to catch the last plane of the day as it loaded wounded, and those lucky few with passes to freedom. I helped lift our wounded into the side door of the Junkers and then turned to Peter.

"I guess we're next," I said.

"I'm sorry, Anna," said Peter

My heart stopped as I awaited an explanation.

"I'm not going with you. I can't leave my patients. You understand, don't you?"

"No I don't!" I shouted, even though I knew perfectly well what he meant. "Why did you risk your life to come all the way to the field if you weren't going to leave?"

"It was the only way to get you here," he said.

"Well, your little plan won't work. I'm not leaving without you," I said.

As we had been talking, he had been rummaging around in his doctor's bag. Now he stood and held his arms out to me, saying, "Oh, Anna..."

I rushed to enfold myself in his embrace. But instead, he grabbed one of my hands and spun me around. Wrapping his arms around me from behind he said, "I'm sorry it has to be this way. Just remember that I love you."

Before I could ask what he meant, his free hand came up and over my mouth. There was a rag in his hand and I smelled the sickeningly sweet odor of chloroform. I began to struggle frantically, but he clamped the rag over my mouth until I was forced to breath in the fumes.

As my world began to turn dark, I could feel him kissing my ear.

When I awoke, I was laying in the center isle of the transport plane. I could tell from the feel of the motion that we were airborne. I was on my way back to the world, like it or not.

CHAPTER VIII

Death wish

I thought that I would be facing severe discipline on my arrival back at the hospital. I feared that I might even be discharged and sent home. I needn't have worried, however. Everything was still in such chaos that I hadn't even been missed, except by a few friends, such as Julius.

Part of the problem was that the Romanian Army had virtually ceased to exist. If the battle of Stalingrad was a disaster for the Germans, it was a catastrophe for Romania. The Germans only lost one of many armies. With the destruction of the Romanian 3rd and 4th armies, Romania had lost almost all of its fighting forces. While there were still two armies in the home country, one was a training army, while the other was stationed on the western border to keep an eye on our so-called ally, the Hungarians. Neither of these armies represented much of a fighting force since almost all the better equipment and most experienced soldiers had been with our armies on the Russian front.

The few remaining units of those armies were now integrated with the German army for the duration of the crisis. And a crisis it was. Having destroyed both the Italian and Romanian armies, the Russians were pressing hard against the surviving units of Army Group B, in an all-out effort to capture the key city of Rostov. That city's location at the eastern tip of the Sea of Azov was the key to the supply routes to the Caucasus, where Army Group A was now strung across hundreds of kilometers of steppe and mountain. Army Group A had been sent into the Caucasus to capture the oil fields that fed the Russian war machine, but just like our army at Stalingrad, they had been stretched too thin to accomplish their goal. Now they were running for their lives as they tried to withdraw through Rostov before the Russians could close that escape route and create a "Super Stalingrad."

All through January we treated the wounded at our hospital just behind the front, while our soldiers fought valiantly to hold the door open for Army Group A. Any thought of relieving our forces trapped in Stalingrad had been abandoned. On the fourteenth of January the airfield at Pitomik was lost to the Russians. The only remaining place to fly supplies into the cauldron was the small field at Gumrak. Also on the fourteenth, the Russians opened their third offensive of the winter. This time their armies fell upon the Hungarian divisions holding the Don River line farther to the north. As they had with us and the Italians, their well-equipped divisions rolled over the ill-prepared Hungarians and once again began to roll up our left flank. It began to look as though we may be pushed all the way back to our start line of the previous spring.

On the twenty-third of January, our troops in the Stalingrad pocket lost their last direct link to the outside world when Gumrak fell to the advancing Russians. Now, only supplies dropped by parachute could be flown in, and no one else would be coming out. At the beginning of February, while we struggled to keep our patients from freezing in the 40-degree below-zero temperature, the end came for our men in Stalingrad.

We first heard it from the Russian propaganda broadcast, but no one would believe it. Days later, the official broadcast from Berlin confirmed that the last resistance at Stalingrad had ceased. The broadcast praised the defenders and pledged to avenge them. The Fuhrer himself spoke of a period of mourning for the valiant warriors and how we would not take another step back. His senseless ranting went on and on. All I knew was that Peter was gone, and I might never know whether he was dead or a prisoner. I wasn't even sure which was worse.

I became very depressed and wouldn't communicate with the other hospital personnel except to carry out my duties. I still spent any spare time I had visiting with the wounded, but I doubt that I was able to cheer them up much. I don't think I even cared who was winning the war at that time. Of course, I had no way of knowing that Hitler and Von Manstein were locked in a battle of wills, with Hitler demanding no more withdrawals while Von Manstein insisted on being allowed to maneuver to meet the onrushing hordes.

In the end, Von Manstein won the argument, and the resulting battle was a resounding victory for the Germans. But first it required the further withdrawal of our front. It was this withdrawal that was very nearly the end of me.

By the third week of February, it had been more than six weeks since I had been with Peter, and you would think that a nurse would be able to tell if she were pregnant by that time. But these were not ordinary times. With the long hours, poor diet, foul weather, and the stress of dealing with death on a daily basis, it was impossible to know if my missed period was the result of pregnancy or just an erratic schedule. I was still wondering if I was carrying Peter's child when another stressful situation developed.

Since Maria's death, I had resisted all attempts to move another nurse into my tent. One advantage of my solitude was that I could read my mail from home without someone else looking over my shoulder. I was off duty, reading one of those letters, when one of the new nursing aides peeked in and said, "You have a handsome visitor here to see you." Then she actually *giggled!*

I had just read about some of my mother's cousins who had been deported from our reoccupied territories for no other reason than that they were Jewish and was in no mood to have visitors. Unfortunately, she disappeared from the tent before I could tell her.

A second later, the tent flap opened again to reveal Major Roider. "Hans, it's good to see you," I lied. Actually, my tolerance for dedicated Nazis had been completely exhausted, but I was still too civil to tell him so.

Uninvited, he entered the tent and said, "My division is stationed nearby, and when I heard that there were Romanian medical people at the field hospital, I just had to come and see if you were here. You look beautiful, as always."

"Hrumph," I snorted. "I'm overworked, underweight, and if these bags under my eyes were any bigger, I could be used as a pack animal."

"The war has been tough on everyone," he said. "But you are still a sight for sore eyes."

He walked over to where I was sitting on my cot and sat beside me. "I'm not going to be in the area very long. Soon we will be counter-attacking the Russian spearheads. Then we'll give those Bolsheviks what they deserve."

Several smart comments crossed my mind, but I held my silence.

"I was hoping that we could pick up where we left off, during my short stay here," he said.

"Pick up where we left off?" I said. "Where did we leave off, Hans?"

Putting one arm around my waist and his other hand on my knee, he said "I thought we were very close, Anna."

When I tried to pull away, he held me in place while his hand clamped down painfully on my leg, so I said, "I thought I had made myself perfectly clear on the beach at Yalta. I am engaged and I don't play around."

"You mean your doctor? I know that he was in Stalingrad at the end. You don't need to consider yourself engaged anymore. No one will be coming back from there, even after we win this war."

I was enraged that this man would think that just because Peter might not ever return to me that I would automatically fall into his arms. I tried to slap him, but he caught my wrist.

"You bastard!

"Do you think that I would lay with you under any circumstances? Go find yourself a good fascist Fraulein to screw."

He was pushing me down onto the cot as he said, "I don't want a Fraulein. I want you. And I am going to have you. Don't try calling for help, I happen to know that all your friends are busy elsewhere."

I wouldn't have given him the pleasure of hearing me scream. I knew just how to get him off me. It wasn't smart, but I was past caring. As he was pressing me into the surface of the cot with his face only inches from mine, I said. "I am surprised, *Herr Major,* that you would risk being caught having sex with a sub-human."

"What are you talking about my little minx?"

I was turning my head to the side to avoid his attempts to force a kiss on me. From that awkward position I struggled to say, "Your own Reich Minister Himmler has said that we Jews are only animals, no more than sheep or goats. Do you want to risk caught fucking a sheep?"

He drew back slightly and asked, "What do you mean?"

"I am telling you that I am a Jew. Only half-Jew actually, but that is just the same to you supermen, isn't it?"

He had pulled back from me completely as I continued. "I've never practiced my Judaism, but that makes no difference. Judaism is a genetic trait, not a religion. Didn't you know that? It's taught in all the schools."

I should have shut up at this point, but I was really angry. "Don't you want to fuck me now?" Holding my hands out to him I continued, "We could have such wonderful half-human children. Maybe they would let you live in the ghetto with me."

His face contorted through more emotions than I had ever believed possible. But mostly I saw disgust and rage. I thought he was going to hit me, but instead he left without saying a word.

I laughed at his retreating back. That wasn't very smart either.

Two weeks later, with a steady flow of wounded soldiers coming into the hospital, I had forgotten all about my little run-in with Hans. Unfortunately, he had not.

I was feeding a soldier who had no arms when Julius entered the ward. "We are moving again," he said.

"Oh, where to this time?" I asked.

"I don't know," he answered. "Somewhere west of Rostov, I think. Von Manstein has ordered a withdrawal. It's about time, too. The Russians are past Kharkov and moving south towards the sea. If they are successful, we will all be cut off. I don't know why we have waited as long as we have."

"What's the matter? Don't you trust the Field Marshal?" I chided. "You have always believed in him before."

"He hadn't lost Stalingrad before," said Julius. Then, remembering who he was talking to, he quickly added, "God, I'm sorry! I didn't mean to remind you..."

"Don't worry. I'm dealing with it.

"So, when do we leave?"

"As soon as Major Roider says, I guess."

"Major Roider? What does he have to do with it? I thought his unit would have left this area weeks ago."

"No, what's left of his 22nd Division is coordinating the withdrawal for this area. I hear that he was furious when his division didn't get sent to attack the Russians along with the 48th Corps."

"I bet," I said. "Now clear out while I pack my dainty under-things."

He thought that was funny and was laughing heartily as he left. I wished I could share his good humor, but I had a bad feeling about having Hans in control of our medical unit.

It was the middle of the night when we loaded our lorries and wagons once again. It seems that it is best to leave unannounced when pulling back from a hostile force that might be sitting only a few hundred meters away. At least this time our withdrawal would be a carefully planned operation rather than a confused rout.

My gear was all loaded and I was just climbing into the back of a 3-ton lorry when a messenger called my name. When I answered, he said that I was to report to Major Roider's headquarters before leaving. Feeling a bit nervous, I grabbed my medical bag and followed the man. He led me to a log and earth bunker, where we entered to find the major behind a desk.

"Anna, come in." To the corporal, he said, "You may go."

I must have looked very nervous, because Hans quickly said, "Don't worry Anna. I just wanted you to know that there are no hard feelings on my part. I can't understand your faithfulness to a man who is not here, but I will respect it. Also, I want to tell you that I'll not tell anyone your secret."

"I... I don't know what to say. Frankly, I'm surprised to hear you talk like this."

"I'm not a *monster*, Anna. And I may have some information for you about Peter..."

Just then, the field telephone on his desk rang, and he went to pick it up.

My thoughts were racing. Information about Peter? What could it be? There have been rumors for weeks about individuals walking back from Stalingrad. But that is hundreds of kilometers through the snow and cold. Could he have communicated by radio? I was dying to know, and there sat the major talking on the phone!

He hung up the receiver and said, "I'm sorry Anna, I have to take care of a situation with the loading of the column. I'll be right back."

Before I could protest, he was through the single door and gone. Like the fool that I am, I sat there waiting for his return. Thoughts of Peter, and his possible escape ran endlessly through my mind. It must have been twenty minutes before I began to wonder what might be wrong. After another twenty minutes, I got up and went to the door, intending to look outside for Hans.

The door wouldn't budge. It was barred from the outside! The bunker was designed for protection from shelling and bombing, not for fighting, so it had no openings to the outside other than the doorway. I returned to my seat to wait. *Surely Hans will be back in a few moments. He left his briefcase and papers on the desk.*

When nothing happened after another half hour, I got up and went to the desk. Looking through his papers, I realized that they were all blank. I quickly grabbed the receiver of the field telephone and cranked the handle. I heard nothing, not even the ringing of another unit at the end of the line. The phone was disconnected. I ran back to the door and threw all my weight against it, but it didn't budge.

I returned to the desk and smashed the chair over it. Then I used one of the chair legs to dig into the earth below the door. It took another half an hour to dig a large enough hole to crawl under the door.

When I emerged into the night, everything was totally silent. I ran to the spot where we had been loading our lorries, but everyone was gone. They had left without me. *How could they have done this?* Then I realized that it would have been easy for Major Roider to have told them that I was going to ride with him as I had in the past. No one would question the operation's commander.

But why is he doing this? To get even with me of course, but what does he hope to gain? So I have to walk to our new positions. They have to be somewhere west of here. But what if they are too far for me to reach before the Russians realize that our troops have gone?

That's it! He is leaving me here to be captured by the enemy!

Medical bag in hand, I set off at a fast walk in what I hoped was the proper direction. The Russians may capture me, but they were at least going to have to catch me first.

It was only a little past dawn when they caught up to me. I heard the approach of armored vehicles from behind, so I left the road I'd been following and moved into the wooded hills. My progress was slow there due to the deep and drifted snow. The temperatures had risen almost to freezing by this time, but the snow was still piled into drifts all along my path. Without snowshoes or skis, I was making very little progress, so it wasn't surprising that I soon had to look for a hiding place.

I came across a small burned-out village that sat off the main road and began to look for cover. There didn't seem to be any villagers around, and I knew that the enemy troops would search the buildings first, so I tipped over an empty watering trough and crawled under it.

Moments later I heard soldiers going through the buildings. The crashing and banging of the search didn't last for long, and soon all was quiet once again. Looking from under my trough, I could see Russian soldiers sitting in a group, cooking up a meal around a small fire. I was lying in wet snow, and hoped that they would move on quickly, before my clothes became soaked. That hope was for naught, as groups of soldiers came and went all day long.

Finally, just before dark, I saw my chance to get away. There were no troops in sight, and I couldn't hear anyone around, so I crawled out of my hiding place and began to stagger on half frozen legs towards the woods once again. My luck had run out, however. Before I had gone more than a few meters, I heard a shout from behind me. I changed my direction of flight and ran behind a shed. I tried to circle the small wooden building and continue my run for the trees, but I ran straight into a soldier coming from the opposite direction.

I turned quickly and tried to run back in the direction from which I had come, but a hand grabbed the back of my field-jacket and lifted me off the ground. The soldier who had grabbed me was stocky and almost as short as I am. He laughed loudly as my feet flailed ineffectively in the air. After a few seconds he became tired of this form of entertainment and tossed me sideways into the wall of the shed.

My shoulder slammed painfully into the wooden structure, and I slid to the ground in a heap. Other soldiers had gathered around me, so with nowhere to go, I just remained huddled against the wall. When none of them even bothered to point his weapon at me I realized that I had lost my hat and that my long hair had given me away as being a woman.

With much shouting and laughing, more Russians gathered around me until there must have been about a dozen of them. At last, one of them who seemed to be the leader, stepped forward and spoke to me in

Russian. I could only understand an occasional word, but I thought that he was asking me if I was German.

I stood up and pointed at my uniform and the hat that I had lost that lay beside me. I repeated the Russian word for "Romanian" over and over. Finally, he got the idea. But when he did, he spat on the ground and said something that sounded very derogatory.

He began questioning me again. In a combination of Russian and halting German, he seemed to be trying to ask what my job was. I was trying to think of the Russian word for nurse or doctor when he laughed and made some very rude gestures that showed that he thought I was one of the prostitutes that will be found following any army.

I shook my head frantically. Then I picked my medical bag from the ground and pointed to the cross embossed in the leather. "Nurse, nurse," I kept repeating.

He shook his head, and then he repeated his crude gestures.

He turned from me and spoke to the gathered soldiers. With much laughing and talking, they seemed to be working out some sort of organization. Then he turned back to me and indicated that I should enter the hut. I was so scared that I was ready to soil myself, but I clutched my bag and went through the door. This must have been almost the only structure in the village that was still mostly intact. Even the door still hung on its lopsided hinges. I hoped that I was to be held here as a prisoner until I was turned over to the proper authorities. But that wasn't to be, and I knew it.

Instead of leaving and barring the door behind him he followed me into the dirty one-room building. There was no furniture, and the floor was covered with straw, as if it had been used to house animals. I could see piles of animal dung scattered about in the straw. The Russian, who must have been the equivalent of a sergeant from the way his men listened to him, said something to me and spun me around to face him.

When I didn't respond to his words, he made the rude gestures at his crotch again and indicated that I should remove my clothes.

Violently, I shook my head and repeated that I was a nurse, not a *joy-girl*.

He didn't care. Stepping towards me, he grabbed the front of my coat and began to tear at the buttons.

I pulled away and held up my medical bag. It was time to play my last card. I opened the bag and held it out to him. Then I tried to tell him that there were drugs in the bag, drugs that would make him happy. Better than Vodka!

Either he didn't understand or didn't care because he just slapped the bag out of my hands. When it hit the wall, I saw my tools and the morphine capsules fly all over the dirty floor.

I was still looking at my equipment scattered over the floor when he grabbed me and ripped my jacket open. I moved away again, but now I was out of room, as I backed against the wall of the shed. He began ripping at my shirt, so I kicked him in the groin. I had heard that this would disable a man. Whoever had told me that had been lying. He just became enraged and pushed me to the floor, where he began unfastening my belt. I grabbed his hands to stop him, and he pulled my opened jacket down from my shoulders and over my elbows. Now I was on my back and my hands were trapped behind me.

I tried to pull my arms free of the coat sleeves, but he laid his weight on me so that I couldn't un-pin my hands. Then, keeping his weight on top of me, he began to pull my trousers down my legs. The trousers, along with my underpants, he left wrapped around my ankles while he began to unbutton his fly.

I was now naked from waist to ankles and as soon as he had his penis exposed, he began trying to push himself into me. I frantically kicked upwards with my knees together. I must have hurt him because he growled in anger and raised his right hand to deliver a back-handed blow to my face. The last thing I saw was a huge, gold ring coming at my right eye. Then my world exploded in a constellation of stars and pain.

I must have been unconscious for a few seconds, for when I regained my senses, he was in me and pumping in and out like a pig in heat. I hardly noticed his rutting on me since all I could feel was pain. The entire right side of my head felt like it was on fire and my eye had already swollen shut. My legs were bowed painfully between my ankles and my hips with him pounding up and down on them. All this pain, along with my arms being pinned under the two of us, distracted me from the discomfort of being entered without any preparation.

He didn't try to kiss me, thank God. Maybe the blood running down my cheek turned him off. He was done quickly and pushed himself up by pressing on my stomach. That almost caused me to vomit. While he grinned down at his work, I lay still and prayed that he would just go away.

He walked to the door, and I began to think of how to untangle my arms from under me. But before I could begin to roll over, another one of the soldiers entered the shed as the first left.

I froze. So that was how it was going to be. Of all the nurses' nightmares, this was the worst. And it was happening to me.

The second Russian strolled over to me with a big smile on his face. Bending down, he pulled my pants from around my ankles. But when I began to sit up, he pushed me back down and knelt between my legs. Then he began to undo his belt and fly.

All this time I was repeating, "No, no." Sometimes I even remembered to say it in Russian.

When he was ready, he began to lean forward onto me. When his face came close to mine, I lunged forward and hit him on the cheek with my forehead. I must have made him mad also. He reached forward and wrapped his fingers around my neck and began to squeeze.

I didn't know that strangling could hurt that much. At first, it was just my neck that hurt, but soon the blood-pressure in my head made my brain feel as if it were going to explode. For a few seconds I thought that being strangled was for the best. I would be dead, and I wouldn't care what they did to me. But soon, my body began demanding oxygen. Then it was screaming for oxygen. And finally, begging for oxygen. I would have begged the beast that was rutting on me for air, except that I couldn't make a sound. I would have done anything he wanted for one more breath. *So much for dying nobly.*

Then, miraculously, he removed his hand from my throat and I could breathe. As I drew my first ragged breaths and savored the feel of air entering my lungs, he savored the feel of entering me...over and over.

By the time that the third man entered the shed, I had decided not to resist anymore. I couldn't stop them anyway, and when they were done, they would probably kill me. And if they didn't, I would.

I had intended to lie completely still and not respond to him at all, but when he tried to kiss my mouth, it was too much. I rolled my head frantically from side to side, so he gave up. Instead, he tore the rest of my shirt off and took out his frustrations on my breasts. He bit my nipples hard enough to draw blood, but I'd be *damned* if I was going to cry out. I just bit my tongue instead.

I was concentrating on separating my mind from my body when the fourth man entered. I thought I was being very successful with my mind control when I felt nothing. But finally, I tried to open my eyes and see what was going on. Only my left eye would open, and that one only a little. I saw a very young and seemingly frightened Russian soldier standing just inside the door. He looked absolutely shocked to see me. Apparently, everyone was going to get a turn with me whether they wanted to or not. Finally, he moved to my side and knelt down.

Okay, I thought. Here it comes.

But he just reached down and lifted me by the shoulders to pull the jacket off my wrists. Then he laid my completely numb arms beside me as he lowered me back onto the dirty straw. Even though I was now completely naked except for my boots, I felt that he had done me a great favor. After a few moments, he left, and the next man came in.

I returned to separating mind and body as this one did his thing with me. But it seems that many men want their women to show some reaction to being fucked. When some of them got no reaction from me, they would either bite me somewhere that was particularly sensitive or simply hit me. Despite my best efforts not to, I usually rewarded their attentions with a groan or whimper. You see, for someone who had never even been paddled as a child, this abuse came as quite a shock.

I don't know how long this went on, or how many men used me. I do remember wishing at one point that Maria was there. Not because she could have prevented this from happening, but because she was prettier than me and most of these beasts would have used her instead of me. Then I almost died of shame for having such a thought. I promised myself that I would apologize to Maria as soon as I saw her.

But what if we go to different places? Maria was a good person and would surely be in heaven. I must be a bad person or God wouldn't have let this happen, would he?

I was aware that several more of the soldiers who came into the shed did not touch me. Not everyone gave in to the animal within. Then, somewhere in my delirium, I became aware that I was alone. Were they done with me? Had I served my purpose? I had always tried to give the soldiers everything they needed. I had bandaged cuts, sewn up wounds, and dumped bedpans for our soldiers. Was that my purpose in life? To be used by these creatures? When they needed to empty their bladder they used a toilet. When they needed to empty their cum, they used me... I was a human toilet.

I could hear them talking outside the shed. I was able to make out the words "kill" and "whore," and anger flared in my breast for a second. *They use me like this and then call me a whore! The bastards!*

The door opened and I raised my head from the floor to look at my executioner. With my feet towards the door, I had no choice but to look across my nakedness. I was shocked to see how many bruises and bite marks were on my breasts and arms. Apparently, I had supplied a great deal of entertainment other than sex for these pigs. *No matter. My salvation is here.*

It was the young soldier who first refused to use me. They must have figured it out and this was his punishment.

When he raised a pistol and aimed it at my head, he had tears in his eyes. I tried to reassure him with a weak smile, though God knows what it must have looked like on my ruined face.

The report of the pistol seemed extremely loud in the confined space, and I was surprised that I was alive to hear it. Then I realized that I had not been shot. The young soldier had aimed the bullet into the straw beside my head. I was wondering if it was an accident when he put his finger to his lips to indicate that I should remain quiet. Bending over me, he laid my field jacket over my naked, shivering body, covering me from thighs to shoulders. Then he turned and left, closing the dilapidated door behind him.

Again I was angry. How dare he leave me in this condition! Did he think he was doing me a favor? I should cry out. That would bring the others running and they could finish the job. But then he would be found out. What would they do to him? Laugh at him? Punish him? Shoot him for disobeying orders?

I heard more talking from outside. Angry voices were being raised. His little deception hadn't fooled anyone, and they were coming back to finish the job. Just as the door was being pushed open once again, I heard a familiar swishing sound. The explosion that followed less than a second later confirmed my thought. We were on the receiving end of a mortar barrage. One explosion followed another as the Russians ran to the woods for cover.

So I'm not to be shot after all. But that is all right. The mortars will end my suffering. All I need do is lay here and wait.

I passed out and awoke some time later to find myself not only alive, but alone.

I was shivering uncontrollably. Even though the shed broke the wind, it was still below freezing inside, and I was still naked under the jacket. I considered throwing off the jacket and just lying there until I froze to death. Hadn't that soldier at Stalingrad said that death by freezing was painless? But I had a better way.

I got up...and promptly fell back down. My legs didn't want to support my weight. I looked down to find that the inside of my thighs was covered with bruises while my genitals were bleeding and bruised also. I struggled to my feet and had the sudden need to empty my bladder. Hobbling over to a corner of the room, I squatted down and released the pressure. I cried out when I let go. The bruising and abrasions on my genitals had left me extremely raw.

Blood and semen ran down my legs now that I was upright, so I picked up the remains of my underclothes and tried to wipe myself clean. I gagged and would have vomited except that I had nothing in my stomach. I couldn't stand this. I had to end it.

Desperately, I searched through the rotting straw for the contents of my medical bag. The Russians hadn't been interested in it, but I knew that it contained several morphine ampoules. I also knew that three ampoules could end my suffering permanently. I needed three of them. I found a small examination mirror and couldn't resist looking at myself. Both my eyes were blackened, with the right eye swollen completely shut. A long irregular cut ran up my right cheek and across the eye where it continued through my eyebrow and halfway up my forehead. It had bled freely and left my face and neck covered with my own blood. My nose had also bled from both nostrils, and it looked a little out of place to me. My lips were cut and swollen to twice their normal size, while my neck had the black and blue imprints of a man's hands going all the way around it.

It took quite a while to find three unbroken ampoules, during which time I became so cold that, even though I intended to die within minutes, I had to put on those clothes that were still wearable. That is when I realized that someone had stolen my boots.

What would one of those bastards want with my small boots! For a moment, I was angrier about the boots than the rape. Then I laughed at the absurdity of it all. Actually, it wasn't as much a laugh as a hoarse cackle. My own voice scared me; it was so different after the pressure that had been put on my vocal cords.

I found that my shirt and underwear were ruined, and all the buttons were torn from my field jacket. I put the jacket and pants on to cover my nudity as much as to keep warm. I didn't want my dead body to be leered over by the next group of soldiers that passed this way.

At last, with the three unbroken ampoules in my hand, I prepared to inject myself with them. As I was breaking the seal on the first, I realized that I didn't want to die in this miserable shed, so I went outside into what turned out to be the first light of dawn.

I was pressing the first needle into my arm when I heard a scraping sound coming from around the corner of the shed. Also, I thought that I could hear a low moaning coming from the same direction. I moved to the corner and looked around. There, lying only a few meters away was a Russian soldier. He had dragged himself to the side of the shed to lie against the rough wooden siding. His path over the snow was plainly visible as it was marked with his blood every centimeter of the way.

I walked over and looked down at him. Shrapnel from a mortar shell had laid his abdomen open. His intestines lay stretched out behind him where he had crawled through the dirty snow. Delirious with pain, he didn't even know that I was standing next to him.

I would like to be able to say that I recognized him as one of the men who had used me the night before. Perhaps then I would have been able to leave him to the very slow, agonizing death that a wound like his had condemned him. But, except for the first few, I had not looked at any of them. So, I couldn't say if he was one or not.

In the end, it made no difference. I could no more walk away from his need than I could undo the ordeal I had just been through. There was no way I could save his life with a wound like that. But I had the means to relieve his suffering right in the palm of my hand. One ampoule would not be enough for his condition. And while three would put him out of his misery…that was not an option for one sworn to heal.

I knelt beside him and injected two of the ampoules into his leg muscle. He still didn't know that I was there, and now I had only one dose of morphine left. It was enough to let me forget my problems for a while. I might even freeze to death before I regained my senses. As I was thinking what to do, I could feel the warm, sticky flow of blood resume on my inner thighs. I was hemorrhaging. Suddenly I remembered that I might be carrying Peter's baby.

How could I think of dying when another life might depend on me? I roused from my lethargy and returned to the shed. The role of sterile gauze from my bag had been stomped into a pile of dung, making it completely unusable. From the straw-covered floor I retrieved a scrap of my former shirt and tore a section from the cleanest part I could find. I folded it into a pad and found my dressing tape amongst the litter on the floor. I almost passed out from the pain as I taped the makeshift pad tightly against my bruised and abraded vagina, but at least it would slow the bleeding for a while.

Now I had to get to our lines while I could still walk. I went back outside and sat beside the Russian soldier. He was semi-conscious and no longer in pain. I removed his boots and put them on. He wouldn't need them anymore. They were far too big for me, but I filled the empty space with straw I had brought from the shed.

I figured that our lines were to the west. They couldn't be too far away either. Since those had been mortars firing at the Russians, and small ones at that, they couldn't have been more than three or four thousand meters from here. I set off into the woods, determined to reach our lines, or at least force the enemy to shoot me if they wanted to stop me.

This area had many wooded hills, and I was soon winded. Never really a strong person, I'd gotten little rest, and no food for two days. I found myself plowing through chest high snow drifts and frequently sliding down snow-covered slopes. As I walked, my mind ran on and on over what had happened.

I hate those Russians.

But how can I hate Russians when my father's family is Russian?

I hate men, then.

But my father and brother are men.

I hate all soldiers.

But if all soldiers are beasts, then what have I been doing for the last year and a half. Have I been patching up all those young boys to go out and rape Russian women? I've always known that soldiers on both sides were capable of this kind of behavior.

As I became more and more tired, my mind ran in tighter and tighter circles. I wasn't really watching where I was going, so I was startled when I came upon a trench in the middle of the woods. Standing on a dirt mound beside the trench, I was shocked into immobility as I gazed down at the most horrible sight I could ever have imagined.

Filling the bottom of the trench were the bodies of several dozen civilians, frozen into grotesque positions. That they were civilians, there could be no doubt from their clothes and the fact that there were men, women, and children, all piled on top of each other. They appeared to have all been shot in the back and allowed to fall into this freshly dug trench.

But who had killed them? Had our troops shot them as spies as they withdrew from this zone, or had the Russian troops killed them for collaborating with us?

I was staring in frozen horror at the bodies when I heard voices from the woods behind me. There were no trees near the trench, and I didn't have the strength to run, so with nowhere else to go, I dropped into the trench and lay with the bodies there. My clothes were ragged and dirty enough to blend in with the poor clothing of the civilians. All I had to do was not move... and keep from retching.

As I lay there listening to the voices as they drew nearer, I found myself looking into the unseeing eyes of a young girl. She had not died quickly. Her face was distorted in pain and her hands were clinched tightly into fists where they were tied behind her back. Had she been humiliated like me before her final end? I prayed not.

Then the voices were right above me. From my position I couldn't see who they were, and I didn't want to know. Suddenly, a shot rang out and I felt a body drop on top of me. When I felt the flow of warm blood running over my back and arms it was all I could do to keep from screaming. I think I did whimper a little as the unseen victim kicked a couple of times, shaking the entire pile of corpses.

I held still until I heard the assassins leave and then I threw up all the bile in my stomach. I had to push the still-limp body of a young man off me before I could climb out of the trench. But first, I had to check for a pulse on this latest victim. I couldn't bring myself to look at his face as I felt his neck. He was dead, of course, so I scrambled into the forest once again.

My body continued to walk to the west, while my mind went on a journey of its own.

I am really lucky, I thought. Those soldiers at the shed had intended for me to be added to that trench. They hadn't even been that hard to satisfy. All they had wanted was a simple fuck. Nothing fancy. I knew that some men liked to take their women as they would a boy... or worse. Those soldiers that had used me were probably simple farmers before the war. Hard working family men. They might have wives and sweethearts. They were probably sorry after they raped me and would have felt bad about killing me too. They might even have shed a tear as they dropped my lifeless body into that trench.

I think I was even laughing out loud when I fell over the tree root. I had no idea where I was. I got up and told myself that if I could make it to the top of the next hill, I would take a rest.

On hands and knees, I climbed the steep wooded slope. With no buttons on my jacket, the snow forced its way in and against my chest and belly. It felt soothing on my still-bleeding wounds. At the top of the hill, I dragged myself upright by clinging to the side of a tree. As I looked around, I wondered where everyone was. I was just about to comment to myself on the lack of soldiers on these so-called front lines when a bullet hit the tree trunk beside my head. I looked stupidly at the hole in the rough bark while my mind tried to tell me something.

Oh yes, I am supposed to get down, said a voice from the back of my brain. My legs cooperated marvelously, and collapsed, starting me rolling down the front slope of the hill I had just climbed. A large rock broke my down-hill roll, and several ribs too, I think. I just lay there a moment, savoring the new pain to add to my list.

Seconds later, a soldier's helmeted head appeared over my rock.

In German, he said, "Who goes there?"

I giggled and said, "You are supposed to say that before you shoot, silly."

Unfortunately, I must have forgotten to speak German, so he didn't get the joke.

In my confused state, I couldn't seem to remember my German, but the tattered remains of my uniform and the ID discs around my neck were sufficient to get me through the lines. I soon found myself delivered to my own medical unit for repairs.

My fatigue-induced delirium had begun to fade by the time Julius found me lying on a stretcher awaiting my turn in the surgery. The shocked look on his face worried me more than all my aches and pains.

"Do I look that bad Julius?" I croaked.

"Anna? Is that you?" he said.

Oh God, I am that bad!

For once, Julius had failed me. He could have at least smiled and lied to me. Instead, he just stood there and looked stricken as the orderlies carried my stretcher into the operating theater. My ankles were being strapped into make-shift gynecology stirrups even before the anesthetic began to take effect. And then I slept.

I have no idea how long I was out, but when I awoke, I was in a small tent by myself. That stood to reason since a field hospital didn't get too many female patients. I was wondering if I was ever going to get anything to eat when a nurse, I didn't recognize bustled in.

"How are we today," she began.

I hate that "we," shit. "I don't know. Why don't you tell *us?*"

My sarcasm was wasted, however, as she said, "Well, the doctor says that you are going to be fine. Most of your injuries are minor and your face can be fixed at a good hospital."

My hand went instinctively to my cheek where I found the entire right side of my head covered in bandages. Only now did I realize that I was still seeing out of only one eye.

"Don't worry," she said. "Your eye wasn't damaged, and you'll be able to see with it as soon as the bandages are off."

Julius walked in just then and I said to him, "Hey, the nurse says I'll have a hell of a dueling scar to go with my war stories."

He didn't laugh. He didn't even crack a smile, and I began to feel worried again.

The nurse prattled on. "I'm sorry about the baby, but the doctor said that you'll be able to try again."

My vision began to tunnel onto Julius's angry face as he turned towards the nurse. Before he could say anything though, a terrible screaming began to fill the tent.

The baby? Does she mean Peter's baby? I was pregnant then? But I'm not pregnant now? Those bastards tore it from me?

Tell that woman to quit screaming. Doesn't she know that I lost my baby?

I want to yell at someone, but I can't because I can't be heard over that damned screaming.

Tell that woman to shut up! I can't tell her myself because....it's me!

Why is Julius holding my arms down?

I have to go find my baby! Did they put my baby in the pile with the amputated body parts? I have to go get him. He'll be lonely there with nothing but arms and legs for company.

What is she doing with that needle? I don't need to sleep. I just need to scream!

CHAPTER IX

No going home

The next thing I remember clearly was the face of a very old woman. Looking at her profile, as she sat quietly in a chair, my attention was drawn to her temple where the throb of her pulse caused the vein to move under her translucent skin. A beam of sunshine from the window illuminated her features, showing every crease and flaw in her skin. Many wrinkles and age spots covered her face, while her hair was mostly gray with a few wisps of black in it. Her scalp was plainly visible through the thin strands of her hair. She had heavy brows and a large nose above a receding chin. Watery eyes of an indeterminate color stared out from loose folds of skin, sunken into deep sockets.

For some reason, I found her fascinating, even though she was sitting quite still. But she *was* doing something. She was being fed. As my awareness of my surroundings expanded, I saw that a nurse was sitting in front of the old woman, trying to feed her from a bowl of Mamaluga, the ever-present cornmeal porridge so familiar to all Romanians. The homely smell was making my mouth water.

The nurse's expression was set in a scowl, as she tried repeatedly to get the old woman to open her mouth and take the spoonful of porridge. However, she wasn't cooperating, and most of the porridge was running down her chin where it dripped into her lap, unnoticed.

After a while the nurse said, "Fine, Elsa. Just starve then!" She plopped the bowl down on the stand beside the chair and stalked away.

As my eyes followed the nurse's retreating back, I realized that we were in a ward with many patients sitting quietly in chairs or lying in their beds. *This isn't our field unit*, I realized. *I must be in a regular hospital, and I shouldn't be sitting around being idle. Why can't I remember what I'm supposed to be doing?*

Rising from my chair, I moved to the one vacated by the other nurse and picked up the bowl of porridge. Looking deeply into the old woman's eyes, I could now see that they were a faded gray in color. For a few moments, I just stared into those vacant eyes, trying to see some flicker of intelligence. When I felt that I could see a faint glimmer of recognition, I leaned forward and placed my lips against her ear.

With the feel of the tiny hairs on her ear brushing my lips, I whispered, "Elsa, I have seen people willing to kill for less food than is in this bowl. If you really wish to die, keep your mouth closed, and you'll get your wish." Then, looking her in the eye again, I held the spoon before her mouth. After a brief pause, she opened her mouth and even moved her head forward slightly to take the food.

I was just spooning the last of the porridge into the woman's mouth when someone approached me from behind. A familiar voice said, "Anna? Anna, what are you doing?"

"My job," I answered, turning to face the short, rather heavy nurse that stood there. The face was familiar, but my mind seemed to be working through a fog as I struggled to remember. Finally, it came to me.

"Girta. You're Girta! But what are you doing this close to the front? You're supposed to be back in Bucharest."

With a worried look on her face she said, "I *am* in Bucharest. And so are you. Don't you remember? You have been here for four months."

"I'm in Bucharest? I've been here for four months? I don't remember being assigned here," I said.

"You weren't assigned here. You were sent here as a patient. You *are* a patient."

I looked down at myself for the first time and realized that I was barefoot and wearing a hospital gown.

I looked back at Girta and said, "I've been here for four months? How did I get here?"

"You were sent back by train, after your... um, trouble."

"Trouble? Oh, yes. I remember now. I was... And then I lost my... I think I remember traveling and being moved from place to place."

"You were completely... unresponsive. You were brought in on a stretcher and were bedridden for two months before we even got you to sit up.

Actually, it was Miss Lovinescu who kept you here. The administration wanted to send you to an institution, but she wouldn't hear of it. She said you would recover, and she didn't want you to be locked away somewhere when you came out of it."

"Where is Miss. Lovinescu now?" I asked.

"She works the trauma ward on the first floor," said Girta. "You may remember that I don't do well when faced with blood and knives, so I work here in the... psychiatric ward."

"So I'm a patient in the psych ward," I mused. Then I looked under my gown.

"Oh my God. I'm wearing diapers! Was I that bad?"

"I'm afraid so," said Girta. "But don't worry, I didn't mind changing you."

"Oh, God," I repeated. "Can I get some underwear? I can take care of myself now, I promise."

"Sure," said Girta. "Come with me."

We started down the hall towards the supply closet, but I was soon out of breath and my legs became wobbly. By the time we reached the closet, I had to sit on the floor with my back against the wall to rest.

"Don't worry," said Girta. "You haven't moved under your own power in months. I've exercised your legs and arms as much as I could, but you know how much good *that* does. You'll have to take it slowly for a while."

Girta had to show me which bed was mine so that I could return to it and put on my undergarments and a pair of hospital slippers. Girta was in a hurry to tell Miss Lovinescu of my improvement, so after she hurried away, I began to exercise by walking the center aisle of the ward. It was a women's ward, of course, and all the beds were occupied. Most of the patients sat or lay quietly looking into space but seeing nothing. Some wandered the hall muttering to themselves, while a few just cried constantly.

When I reached the end of the hall, I could see out a barred window that overlooked the city from the fourth floor of the hospital. It was summer outside, and the city was beautiful. Trees and flowers were in full bloom, and the park just beyond the hospital grounds was covered with lush green grass. It seemed truly odd to look at such a pleasant summer scene since the last thing I remember was the cold and snow of the Russian winter. It was as if I had just blinked my eyes for a second and the whole world had changed.

Not only did the change of scenery and seasons seem odd, but after a moment I realized that there were no sandbags, bomb craters, or gun emplacements in sight anywhere. That seemed more than odd, it seemed like a miracle. My legs were so weak that soon I had to return to my bed to rest.

That is where I was when Miss Lovinescu found me. I saw her tall, willowy figure approaching up the hall. As I watched her coming towards me, I realized that she was not nearly such a forbidding figure as I had remembered. What I had always considered her stern and intimidating face seemed not only younger than I remembered, but actually quite attractive for a woman of her age. Her presence seemed to have a positive influence on my spirits. Somehow, with her around, I felt that everything would be all right.

I was probably grinning like a fool when she finally reached my bed.

"Well, you certainly are looking better," she said. "At least you aren't drooling all over yourself anymore."

"Did I ever drool on myself?" I asked, smiling.

"No," she admitted as she began to crack a smile of her own. "But those fools in administration would have put you in with the real crazies, and then you might have."

"Girta told me that you fought to keep me at the hospital. Thank you, I don't know what I would have done if I had come to my senses in one of those places."

"You would have had a hell of a time getting released from an institution once you were in there," she said. "And I need all the nurses I can get."

"Then you'll let me work here?"

"Let you? My dear, I wouldn't have you work anywhere else. I understand that you became a hell of a nurse before... before you were sent home."

I didn't want to go there, so I said, "Well, I certainly got a lot of practice. And you seem to need help. Why is the ward so full? I don't remember ever seeing this many patients in the psychiatric ward when I was training here."

"It's the war," she answered. "The psychological pressures on everyone are intense. Many of these women have lost men in the war. Some can't deal with the stress of the bombings, though thank the Lord, Bucharest has been spared so far."

Then, in a softer voice she added, "And some had men at Stalingrad, and don't know if they are widows or not."

When my mind flashed back to the snow-covered ruins filled with starving men, my face must have shown some of the torment that I felt because she quickly added, "I didn't mean to upset you, Anna."

"It's all right," I said. "I remember everything that happened...everything. But it is like all my memories are wrapped in cotton. I can't really feel them anymore.

"So... when do I start work?"

"Not until you are stronger. Girta told me how weak you are, so take it easy and build up your strength."

And I did take it easy. The next day, I began by helping to feed the other patients. I didn't have the strength to change bedclothes, but I sat and talked to those who needed someone to listen. Soon I was helping with distributing medications and washing those who couldn't take care of themselves.

Less than a week after her first visit, Miss Lovinescu came to me again.

I was watching a patient as she swallowed her medicine, to be sure that she didn't try to tongue her pills when Miss Lovinescu came up to me.

"Well, since you are going to work anyway, I might as well assign you to a regular duty station," she said. "But first, you will need an apartment to stay in. I have contacted the Army Medical Corps and gotten them to assign you a flat. They help veterans when they muster out."

"But I am not a veteran," I protested. "You know that we were only auxiliaries for the army."

"That is true. But I have some influence with them and prevailed upon their better nature to help you out. You can move in anytime. And it's only a short bus ride from the hospital."

"That's great. Thank you. I'll move in today. I think my living here on the ward is confusing some of the patients when I act like one of the nurses."

"I have decided to transfer you to the convalescent ward. Most of the patients there are wounded soldiers, and you should be able to relate to them better than most, due to your background."

For a second, I wondered if I could face soldiers...any soldiers, again. Miss Lovinescu must have read the indecision on my face because she asked, "Will there be any problem for you to work with the men?"

"Um...no, I don't think so," I said.

"Well, you don't have to worry about your new assignment right away," she said. "One of the stipulations I have for you to continue working here is that you go home for a few days before beginning your new assignment."

"Home? I don't know. My parents haven't come to see me. Maybe they would be uncomfortable around me. I mean...you know...with everything that has happened."

"That is the first really stupid thing I've heard you say. Of course, your parents want to see you. Didn't you know that they were here right after you arrived from the front?"

"You mean while I was a... vegetable? Oh, God! That must have been terrible for them."

"It was," said Miss Lovinescu. "Your mother couldn't stop crying. That's why you must go home before you start work here, to show them how much better you are."

Two days later I was a nervous wreck as my train pulled into the station at Ploesti. I strained to see my family on the platform while the train rolled to a stop. Seeing no one I recognized from the window, I climbed down the iron steps of the car with my one small bag in hand. Even that small bag was almost empty since I had nothing with me at the hospital. My clothes were all borrowed from other nurses for this trip.

I wasn't thinking of my clothes, however, as I searched the faces in the crowd. I was beginning to wonder if anyone was going to meet me when I saw a familiar face approaching through the crowd. It was Emil, my eleven-year-old brother. I raced to him, and we embraced each other enthusiastically.

"Emil," I said. "How you've grown! You're almost as tall as me now."

"That's not saying much, sister," he quipped.

"Well, you're still a wise guy I see. Where are mama and papa?"

"Father is at work, as usual. They hardly ever let him come home anymore since the Germans are in such a hurry to take our oil. And Mother is at home waiting for you."

"Why didn't she come to the station with you?" I asked.

Emil wouldn't look at me in the face as he said, "She hardly ever leaves the house anymore. It's too dangerous."

"What do you mean, too dangerous? Why can't she leave the house?"

My little brother began leading me down the platform as he whispered into my ear. "It's the 'Special Echelon' people... the Jew hunters. Whenever you are on the street, you are liable to have your papers inspected. If you are a Jew, you can be arrested on the spot for no reason, so mother stays at home as much as possible."

"But everyone knows that mama is Jewish. That's no secret."

"Sure, but no one in our neighborhood cares. On the street, you never know who you will run into. It's probably only father's position of importance to the refinery that keeps mother from being deported to the camps in the Ukraine."

"But I thought they only deported Jews living in Transnistria, the territory we took back from the Russians."

"You *have* been out of it, sis. Even Dr. Wilhelm Fieldman was deported to Moghilev, out on the frontier, last month."

"Dr. Fieldman? My God, he has had tremendous influence with the government throughout this whole war. If they have deported him, no one is safe."

"There is a rumor that Antonescu has signed a deal with Hitler to send all Romania's Jews to Germany as slave labor," said Emil.

"Slave labor my ass, Emil. I've seen what they do to Jews in the occupied territories. They call them spies and kill them all. Funny how only Jews are spies, huh?"

"Don't tell any of this to mom...mother. She is worried enough already."

By the time we had walked to our small house on the outskirts of Ploesti, I had determined to say nothing to mother that would upset her. But as soon as I got the chance to tell my father everything, I would. That way, I was sure that he would do everything in his power to keep mother safe.

I would like to say that my time at home was wonderful, but the truth is, I felt awkward and out of place the whole time. I found myself unable to sit still for any length of time, while every time I closed my eyes, my mind would turn to scenes from the past. When I wasn't reliving the war in my mind, I would find myself thinking of how much there was to do at the hospital and how I was slacking off while there were so many people in need of help.

I'm afraid that I alienated Emil when I wouldn't tell him all about the war. Even with it in my mind constantly, I couldn't bring myself to talk about it. If I had tried to explain it I am sure that I would have broken down and made a complete fool of myself.

After a while, Emil quit asking about the war. A little while later, I noticed that he seemed to be avoiding me. Shortly before I was to return to Bucharest, I asked my father if Emil was angry with me.

"No," he said. "I think he is a little afraid of you."

"But why should he be afraid of me?" I asked.

"It's your eyes..."

"My eye? You mean the scar across my right eye? Does it make me that ugly?"

"No, no," said my father. "You're still as beautiful as ever. It's the look in your eyes. You have what we soldiers call the thousand-yard stare."

"What do you mean?"

"It's the way a person looks *through* other people, when they have seen too much. Too much pain, too much suffering, too much death...too much war. It's as if a part of you has died along with your friends."

"I'm sorry that I scare Emil, but I just can't 'turn it off.'"

"I know. But you are a strong person. Someday, God willing, you will be able to forget the ones you have lost and return fully to the living."

"I'm going to talk to Emil right now," I said. I found him in the back yard, kicking a Soccer Ball against the side of the house.

215

"Can we talk a minute?" I asked.

"Sure, Sis," he said as he continued kicking the ball, and not looking in my direction.

"Papa says that I make you nervous. Is he right?"

"Oh, you know Poppa. He always…"

"Tell me the truth," I interrupted. "I'll understand."

He stopped kicking the ball and was silent for such a long time that I began to think he wasn't going to answer. Finally, he said, "You seem so different that sometimes I don't think you are really my sister."

"I seem different, in what way?" I asked.

"You're so…quiet. And you sit so still, staring at nothing. You used to talk all the time. I couldn't get you to shut up." He warmed to his subject as he continued. "You were always telling me what was good for me and how I should act. You know, being bossy."

"I smiled and said, "I guess I found out that I didn't know everything.

"What's it really like?" he asked eagerly. "You know…being in the war?"

"It's terrible," I said. "It's also very sad."

"Sad? What do you mean?"

"I mean there is so much suffering and death. So many people are killed or injured, just to settle some dispute that they don't even understand."

"But it's exciting too, isn't it?"

"I don't know if you would call it exciting. Most of the time it is just boring. Then, every now and then, it's scary as hell. And I'm not on the front lines. I can only imagine what it's like for the soldiers in the trenches.

"I want to be a soldier," announced Emil. "I want to fight for my country and do great things."

"You're crazy if you think being a soldier is fun. And as for fighting for your country, *why?* Your country doesn't give a shit for you, you're a Jew."

"I am not a Jew! Mother is, but I'm not!" he said hotly.

"As far as Romania is concerned, you're a Jew. The best you can hope for is to keep your background a secret. Even if you weren't, why would you want to be a soldier? At the least, you get bossed around all day. At the worst, you get killed…No I take that back, getting killed isn't the worst that can happen by a long shot. I've seen too many 'worst cases' sent home to be cared for by grieving families."

"You don't understand," he persisted. "A man has to stand up and be counted or he isn't a man."

"You're only 11 years old. You're not a man yet, thank God. With any luck at all this war will be over long before you're old enough to get in it," I said.

"That's what I'm afraid of," he said.

"Don't be afraid of missing the war. Be afraid that it will find you," I said.

"What do you mean?"

"I mean that the way things are going, the war may be coming to us. The Russians have been pushing the Germans back for some time now, and you know Romania is in the middle. Even worse, are the bombings by the English and Americans. I can't believe that they will leave us alone much longer." Unfortunately, I was more right than I knew.

"Enough of this serious talk," I said. "Let's pass the ball back and forth."

"Aw, Sis, you play soccer like a girl," he teased.

"It beats playing with the wall," I said.

"The wall is better than you!"

I chased him all the way around the house, but I couldn't catch him.

Before I left, I made Papa promise to redouble his efforts to protect Mama. It was an empty gesture, but what else could I do?

Two days later, as I was taking my leave of momma to return to the train, she pressed a small, tightly wrapped package into my hand.

"What is this?" I asked.

"It's 100,000 lei. I want you to take it to Dr. Chirila. Do you know him?"

"Yes, certainly I know him. He is one of the top administrators at the hospital. Why should I take this money to him? And where did you get this much money with all the new taxes that they are imposing on Jews?"

"The money is from our neighbors plus what little we can spare," said Momma. "Dr. Chirila is funneling money and supplies to the Jews at Mogilev, and the other camps in the Ukraine. It helps them pay bribes to the officials there. That money is keeping many people alive who would otherwise be sent to the death camps."

"But Dr. Chirila is not a Jew," I said. "Why is he helping us."

"You can thank God that he isn't a Jew. If he was, he wouldn't be able to help. You don't think that all gentiles are against us, do you?"

"It certainly seems like it sometimes," I said. And then I thought of Miss Lovinescu, and Julius, and my other friends who had kept my secret at no small risk to themselves.

Later, at the train station, I was waiting the last few moments before boarding. I was alone since father had been required to work and Emil, who had walked me to the station, had made an excuse to leave as quickly as possible. I told myself that his remoteness didn't bother me, but it did. I was clutching my small bag tightly, not only because it contained the clothes I needed in the city, but also because it contained the money that my momma had given me.

Just as the train was entering the station, an officious-looking little weasel of a man came up to me and asked to see my papers.

"And you are?" I asked.

"I am with the Special Echelon. It is my duty to weed-out any undesirables from our country. Now let me see your papers."

I handed my papers over to him. They identified me as a nurse who worked at the Bucharest Hospital. They also specified my religion to be the same as my father's, Romanian Orthodox.

He studied them briefly, and then handed them back.

"Now I need to see in your bag," he said.

Somehow, I managed to look down on him, even though he was taller, and said, "No."

"What?" He said in some little shock.

"I said no. If you read my papers, you saw that I have just returned from duty with the army at Stalingrad. I didn't return home from that hell to have some glorified clerks go through my underwear on a train platform."

I then pushed past him and climbed the steps onto the railcar. The whole time I was boarding and finding a seat, my heart was pounding against my ribs as I waited for a hand to grab my shoulder. When nothing happened, I glanced out the window to see the little man harassing another traveler.

As soon as I returned to my duties at the hospital, I asked Miss Lovinescu to arrange for me to talk to Dr. Chirila.

"What do you want to talk to the administrator about?" she asked.

"It is a personal matter," I said.

"This personal matter wouldn't have anything to do with money changing hands, would it?"

When I stared at her, open-mouthed and looking stupid, she continued. "Let's see...you just came back from the country, where you spent time with your Jewish mother and her friends. Your papers list you as a non-Jew, so you can travel in relative safety. And now you want to see Dr. Chirila, a noted Jew sympathizer.

My guess is that you have a large sum of money hidden somewhere on your foolish person and you can't wait to give it to the good Doctor. Am I right?"

"Yes," I said meekly.

"Hand it over," she said, holding out her hand.

"But it is relief money for those who need it," I protested.

"And that is just where it is going," she said. "I'll give it to the doctor, and you will stay as far away from him as possible. He is skating on thin ice. Everyone except the authorities knows what he is doing. If he gets arrested, anyone who has come into contact with him will be investigated, and your background can't stand a close look.

Now give me the money and get back to work. This won't be the first time I have given him 'donations' for his favorite charity."

The funny thing is, I never even once doubted that Ms. Lovinescu would deliver the money to Dr. Chirila, and I have every confidence that she did just that.

I began to settle into the hospital's routine over the next several weeks. Once I started working with the soldiers, I found that I could relate to them as human beings, and not as potential rapists as I had feared. I even returned to my habit of visiting the men on my off-duty hours. Increasingly, however, I found myself wondering how I could raise more money to send to the displaced Jews in Ukraine.

I even considered stealing drugs from the hospital to either send directly or sell for money. I rejected that idea because the hospital didn't have enough for the patients we had, let alone supporting my 'fundraising'. My salary was far too small to allow a useful contribution. I knew that as much as 90% of the money raised was consumed in paying bribes just to get the rest of it to those who needed it so desperately.

One night, as I peered from the blackout-darkened, third-floor window of my flat, I saw something that gave me an idea. A man approached a woman on the corner of my block. After a few moments of conversation, the two of them disappeared around the corner, arm in arm. I'm pretty naive, but even *I* could recognize a prostitute when I saw one.

After closing the blackout curtain, I turned on the light in my bedroom and looked at myself in the mirror. The face that looked back at me seemed to be that of a stranger. Though I was still only 20 years old, I thought my appearance was that of someone much older. At least my long coma had given me plenty of rest, so that the bags under my eyes and the lines around my mouth had receded almost to invisibility. My skin was still very pale as always, but the scar that ran up my right cheek and across my eye into my right eyebrow had faded somewhat.

I thought that with some makeup on my cheek I could cover the scar pretty well, while an eyebrow pencil would fill in the gap in my eyebrow. My eyes were still my best feature, and being still young, I thought that I could make a fair amount of money as a prostitute.

After all, there was no reason not to. I was a ruined woman anyway. My honor had been taken from me, along with any reason I'd ever had to worry about it. And even though the doctors said that I could still have children, I had no desire to have any now that Peter was gone. It would be easy for me to get drugs at the hospital that would prevent an unwanted pregnancy, and besides, there were people who were dying for lack of food and medicine that I could buy with my body. I went so far as to put on my best dress and make myself up, even trimming my hair. But when I reached for the doorknob to leave my flat, I couldn't make my hand work.

Dropping onto my bed, I cried because I couldn't do what was needed to help my people. When I finished crying, I promised myself that I would find another way to get more money. Little did I know that I would soon have a need for that extra money in my own life. I was about to become the head of a household. That particular nightmare began with the roar of engines passing low over the hospital late in August of 1943.

I was on the third-floor balcony of the hospital, watching a group of convalescent soldiers as they took the late morning sun, when I heard a familiar sound. It was as unpleasant as it was familiar. Beginning from the south of the city, it drew nearer by the second. It was the banging of anti-aircraft guns firing into the clear blue sky. As the firing drew nearer and louder the air-raid sirens began their ominous wailing. Several of the soldiers became obviously agitated. Inside myself I felt the same fear and dread. Even as my bowels felt they would loosen and disgrace me I knew that it was my duty to care for the men in my charge. I had to get them back into the building before anything threatening could develop. The administrators were thinking of bad weather when they had assigned me to watch the men, but an air-raid was more dangerous than any storm they might have had in mind. Even if no bombs came in our direction, I knew that the falling shrapnel from the exploding anti-aircraft shells would be a great danger.

I herded the men, many of whom were amputees, into the patio doors at the rear of the balcony. They were almost all inside before I could hear the drone of aircraft engines approaching. The sound of numerous engines began to reverberate from the walls of the surrounding buildings, making it sound as though the enemy were closing in from all directions. *The planes must be flying at very low altitude for them to be so loud*, I thought. The last patient, a man who had had both arms blown off by a bomb, was running about the balcony in panic. He was dangerously close to the edge when I caught up with him and threw my arms around his chest. I had to push furiously to move the panicked man in the direction of the door. Just short of my goal, the two of us stumbled to the floor and I found myself looking up just as the biggest airplane I have ever seen roared into view over the roof of the hospital. It had four engines on the long tapering wings, with white stars with blue bars painted on them. It seemed to clear the hospital by only a few meters. The Americans had sent their great long-range bombers to strike at us again. As I struggled to drag the panicked man through the doors, I was aware that there seemed to be no explosions of bombs following in the wake of the giant planes. For a second I was thankful that they had chosen not to bomb the city, then I realized that they were headed north, directly towards my home of Ploesti. Standing in the doorway watching the air armada that seemed to consist of hundreds of aircraft disappear in the distance, I was consumed with the most horrible feeling of dread that I have ever felt.

My parent's home was on the outskirts of Ploesti, well away from the refineries that would be the bomber's targets. But I had seen the large numbers of anti-aircraft guns ringing the town when I had been home, and I knew that the German troops that manned those guns had been prepared for aircraft to come from any direction. Why the Americans had over flown Bucharest, I couldn't guess. It had certainly given their approach away and given the gunners at Ploesti plenty of warning.

Ploesti is almost 40 kilometers from Bucharest, but I was sure that I could hear the gunfire and the bombs exploding. In less than half an hour I, and everyone else in the capital city, could see the towering columns of black smoke rising from the Northern horizon.

I went immediately to Miss Lovinescu and begged for permission to go home.

"There is no way you will be able to get north right away," she said. "No doubt the roads and rail lines will be clogged with official traffic for quite some time."

"But I just know that something terrible has happened." I said.

"I'm sure that your family will be fine, but if you are that worried, I promise to get you on the first lorry that the hospital sends north. They'll certainly be sending for emergency supplies if the damage is as bad as you fear."

That is how I came to be arriving at Ploesti, the day after the raid, on the back of a supply lorry. There had been no telephone communication with the bombed area, of course. All the lines were down and there was no electric power in the city either. When the main road brought my transport as close as it would to my home, I banged on the top of the cab and had the driver let me off. My house was shielded from the road by a small, wooded area and some other homes, so I had to walk about a half kilometer to get within sight of it.

When I finally got there, I just dropped to my knees and buried my head between my hands. My home was gone...completely gone. Only a black patch of smoking rubble greeted my eyes. *Please God, please...let them have been somewhere else when it happened.* But I knew that it had happened on Sunday morning, the one day that my father had always tried to spend at home with mama. When I thought that I had cried myself out, I got up and stumbled to the wreckage. I had to blink the tears from my eyes several times before I was sure that I was seeing what I thought I was. Right before me was a huge aircraft engine. When I looked to my left, I could see the remains of the nose of an aircraft. When I looked to my right, I saw a path of burn marks and debris stretching for a hundred meters leading up to my house.

I couldn't bring myself to look through the rubble, so I knelt down beside the ruined engine and leaned my head on the still warm metal. I don't know how long I was there before I heard someone calling my name.

"Anna. Anna is it you?" I heard from behind me.

It was Emil's voice! I scrambled up and turned around. Emil was running towards me from the direction of the road!

"Emil!" I screamed and ran to him faster than I believed possible. We collided so hard that we fell to the ground, but I didn't let go for a second. "Are you all right?" I asked. "Where are Mama and Papa?"

Emil's eyes filled with tears as I pulled him up to a kneeling position and he said, "They were in the house when the plane crashed into it." Then his voice broke, and he couldn't continue.

"They are gone, then?" I asked.

He nodded "yes" and buried his head in my shoulder, crying uncontrollably.

I rocked him for some time, until he pulled away and said, through his sobs, "I was at my friend's house when the raid came. His parents wouldn't let me go outside until it was over. When I got here there was a burning plane sitting on our house. The soldiers found mama and papa's bodies last night and took them to the morgue."

The next several days went by in a haze. Those relatives that lived nearby helped with the funeral arrangements. To protect her relatives, we couldn't draw attention to mama's religion, so we kept everything very quiet. The funeral was held in the dining room at Aunt Serran's house in Ploesti.

As I stood before the two closed pine coffins I wondered if what remained of my parents were really in them. Many times, we sent boxes of sand home to the families of dead soldiers when we couldn't find enough of the remains to fill a teacup, let alone a coffin. Of course, that only applied to the family wealthy enough to afford to have their loved one's remains sent home. Most of our boy's graves were somewhere on the empty Russian Steppes.

Emil wasn't there yet and I was feeling completely alone standing in the crowded room when I saw Uncle Stephen approaching. He lived in Focsani with his wife and two daughters. A big man with a round, bland face, he used his size as he seized my arm and led me into the next room, saying, "We need to talk."

I was a little put off by his imperious tone, but he was my uncle, so I went with him willingly.

"Don't worry Anna. We'll take care of Emil from now on," he said.

"You will?" I asked. "How will you raise him?"

"We are well-off enough to take care of one more," he answered.

"No, I mean in what religion will you raise him?"

"Christian of course, you wouldn't want him raised a Jew, would you? That would only be asking for trouble."

"Mother and father always showed us both ways and let us choose our own path."

"What path have you chosen?" he asked.

"Neither" I answered. "I seriously doubt that there is a God."

Sounding as though he thought lightning would strike any second, Uncle Stephan almost screamed, "You shouldn't say that Anna!"

"Why not? After what I've seen, it's better to think there is no God than to think there is. If there is a God, I would have to think that He has a very warped sense of humor. You should try to tell a young man that he will have to live out his life with no face or listen to another's last breath whistle out through the hole in his chest.

"WOULD A GOOD AND MERCIFUL GOD SIT STILL WHILE A CHILD IS BEING BLOWN TO PIECES BY A LANDMINE? Would He watch quietly while a woman is…?" I realized I was yelling loud enough to be heard in the next room where the mourners were still waiting for the funeral to begin, so I lowered my voice and said, "Anyway, you know what I mean. I think that if there really is a God, He must have lost interest in us and gone somewhere else. He wouldn't be able to stomach watching us."

"If your parents had given you a better religious upbringing, you could have better handled the terrible things you have seen," he said.

His pious attack on my parents angered me, but I replied calmly, "You mean if my parents had forced me into one mold or another, I would have had some handy platitudes ready for any emergency? Thanks, but no thanks."

"Your experiences at the front have unbalanced you," he said coldly. "Tomorrow we will take Emil with us when we return home. And I don't think you should have any contact with him for a while. Sooner or later, your attitude will bring you to the attention of the authorities and you will be disposed of like any other Jew. I don't want you bringing notice to your younger brother when you do."

Believe it or not, I wasn't angered by Uncle Stephan's words. I realized he was doing what he thought best for Emil. Logically, he made sense. But I wasn't interested in being logical. I didn't want to lose my brother any more than I had wanted to lose my parents. Besides, there was something else. I could see it in my uncle's eyes. It took a moment for me to recognize it, but there it was. Fear! Uncle Stephan was afraid.

I had seen the look often enough. As a matter of fact, I saw it every time I told a soldier that he was well enough to go back to the front. It was the kind of fear a man had when he was afraid to do what he had to but even more afraid to admit his fear. So the soldier would return to the front just as Uncle Stephan would take Emil into his house even though it could bring the wrath of the Black Shirts down on him if Emil's secret got out.

I decided to let Emil make the choice, and there was nothing Uncle Stephen could do about it. He might be bigger than me, but he wasn't stronger.

We buried Mama and Papa together in a small ceremony at the local church. The pastor was a good man and willing to keep Mama's secret to protect the family, while her family had to remain in hiding. Behind the church, I quietly said the Kadesh for mama and a prayer for papa. I'm not sure if there is a God, but I am sure that if there is, He won't let a small thing like religion keep them apart in His kingdom.

After the funeral, while my uncle explained to the other relatives about how he would raise Emil, I drew Emil into the next room and asked him who he wanted to live with.

"I want to stay with you," he said.

"Even if you have to live in the big city?"

"Yes."

"Even if we won't have very much money on my salary?"

"Yes."

"Even if your sister is crazy and scares you?"

"I don't think you're crazy." Emil said. "And you don't scare me...much."

"I'm glad I don't scare you," I said. "But I *am* crazy, which just helps me fit in. Your bags are packed, aren't they?"

"Sure, they're upstairs," said Emil.

"Then get them, and we'll leave now."

Pointing to the crowd of adults arguing in the next room, Emil asked, "But what about them?"

"They will still be arguing when our train is pulling into Bucharest."

"But won't they just try to bring me back?"

"They might try, but they won't succeed," I answered.

Emil smiled and went to get his bags.

So that is how I came to have my own family, after all. Miss Lovinesqu was a real help in getting us settled in the city. Emil had to be registered for school, so I needed his birth certificate and other papers. When I contacted our relatives for them, I had no problem dealing with them. Apparently, Papa's side of the family decided that they were well rid of him. Of course, mama's relatives couldn't take him because that would just have put him in the same danger that they all faced. Also, I suspect, they were all secretly glad to be out of the position of feeding one more mouth.

My flat was only one room, so Emil had to sleep on the sofa. He even insisted on stringing up a line to hang a sheet on, to give us each some privacy. I thought that was very sweet of him to think that I could worry about privacy anymore.

I found that I had to take some time from my visiting with the patients to spend with Emil in the evenings. With radios banned, and newspapers tightly controlled, our entertainment consisted of talking or reading books. One evening, about a week after his coming to live with me, he mentioned something that really caught my attention.

"I wonder what happened to the pilot of the plane that landed on our house?" he said.

"I imagine that he died in the crash," I answered.

"Oh no, I saw them carry him from the wreckage. He was burned pretty bad, but he was definitely alive when they carried him to the ambulance."

"The pilot lived?" I was shocked that anyone could have lived through a crash such as that. *So the man who killed my parents is alive. They died and he walked away. I wonder where they take wounded prisoners. I bet I can find out.* Suddenly I had another reason besides Emil to live for. I was going to find the man who had murdered my parents.

A little judicious inquiring with the army liaison office, followed by some discreet questioning of the hospital staff, disclosed that a prison not far from Bucharest was the only one with adequate facilities to care for seriously wounded prisoners of war. A call to the prison medical facility, in the name of the Red Cross, revealed the name of the only prisoner that had been pulled from a crashed aircraft. His name was Joseph Todd. How typical of an American to be named Joe. He must be some hot-shot fly-boy. A fun-loving rake that chased women and bombed civilians from a safe distance, I'll bet he never gave a thought to how many lives he was destroying. Now all I had to do was to find a reason to visit the prison hospital.

If I ever doubted that God had a sense of humor, my doubt was put to rest a few days after my discovery of the pilot's identity. I had been puzzling over how to get into the prison for a couple of days when the word spread through our hospital that King Michael himself was to visit the prisoners. The King was going to check on the treatment of the captured men. He would be checking on the wounded prisoners as well.

I don't think that my feet even touched the floor once as I flew to Miss Lovinescus' office. As head nurse for the hospital, I was sure that she would be allowed to pick which members of the nursing staff would go on the mission.

Arriving at her office, I took a moment to catch my breath and collect my thoughts before I knocked on her door. When she told me to enter, I got straight to the point. "I hear that the hospital is sending a mission to the prison to check on the prisoners of war. I would like to be with that group."

"Well, I guess I was right," she said. "I didn't think this would stay a secret for long. I was only informed this morning. It must be all over the hospital already."

"It is," I said. "May I go?"

"Why do you want to go?"

I had been expecting this question and had been trying to come up with a plausible answer. "I want to meet these Americans. I've heard so much about them that I need to see them for myself."

"You *need* to see them? That sounds as if it is very important to you. Why?"

"Well...as you know, my parents were killed in the Ploesti bombing, and I am very curious about what kind of people have come from so far away to fight against us." I hoped that this sounded reasonable.

"But that's just the point," said Miss Lovinescu. "You just lost both your parents, and you haven't been out of the...ward, that long yourself."

"You can say psychiatric ward, Miss Lovinescu. I'm not ashamed to admit that my mind was in worse shape than my body when they brought me back from Stalingrad. But I'm better now, and I have the most experience dealing with soldiers of all your nurses."

"That is true," she admitted. "But the Americans were responsible for your parent's deaths. Can you deal with that?"

"Miss Lovinescu, since I returned from the front, and recovered my wits here at the hospital, I have... How can I say this? My emotions...No, my feelings have been turned off, in a way. As an example, let me say that when I found that my parents were dead, I felt loss and grief. I cried and prayed for them, but in a way, their deaths didn't really touch me. Not here in my soul," I said, touching my heart. "I don't know if it is a good thing or not, but I don't think anything can hurt me anymore. Does any of this make sense to you?"

"Yes, in a sad way, it does," she said.

"So, do I go or not?"

"It is just as you said. You are my most experienced nurse with the soldiers, and no one seems to empathize with them as well as you do. Yes, you can go. The King himself is going to the prison to talk to the prisoners. He intends to see that they are getting proper treatment. Are you excited to be traveling with the King?"

"Oh, yes. Yes, I am," I lied. I didn't care about the King or meeting the Americans. I just wanted justice for my dead parents. I felt guilty lying to the person who had done so much for me, but I was going to find this Joseph Todd. I would see what this man who killed innocent people from thousands of meters in the sky was like. Maybe I could make him pay for what he had done.

The medical staff involved in the Red Cross prisoner evaluation mission gathered in front of the hospital at 0500 the next morning. We boarded a bus and were soon on our way out of the city. It was a short ride, but to me it seemed to take an eternity. All the way to the prison I wondered what I should do when I found the man who had murdered my parents. I know that in time of war you are not supposed to call it murder, but my parents were just as dead no matter whether you called it the fortunes of war, fate, or anything else.

Suddenly we were there, and everyone was filing off the bus to the accompaniment of much talking and speculation about what the Americans would be like. I stayed close to Miss Lovinescu as we were processed through security and our papers were checked. Once into the prison grounds we proceeded directly to the medical wards. As we entered the ancient building, I noticed the King going into the prison section of the compound surrounded by his entourage of courtiers and interpreters. He had arrived at the same time as the rest of us, but in a small convoy of autos belonging to the royal family.

Once into the prison hospital I made my way to the burn ward as quickly as I could without seeming to neglect my duty to inspect the condition of the other prisoner patients. I was the first of our group to enter the burn ward and I immediately began checking the medical chart at the foot of each bed. There were two rows of beds in the ward and Joseph Todd was in the last bed, farthest from the door.

I looked down on the killer and was surprised to see that he didn't look like the dashing flyer type at all. He appeared to be a middle-aged man of average height, with thinning hair already beginning to turn gray at the temples. It was hard to say just what he would look like under normal circumstances. His face was bruised, and both his eyes were still swollen almost closed even now, two weeks after the raid. The chart said that his most serious injuries were under the bandages that wrapped his torso and arms. He was suffering from second and third degree burns over 40-percent of his body, and his prognosis was still in doubt.

So the killer of innocents might still die from his wounds. Would that be justice? Should he be helped on his way to paying for his sins? Do I hate this man enough to do what I should.

"Well, are you going to check him, or just look at him all day?" Miss Lovinesqus' comment, delivered from just behind me, startled me out of my revere.

"This man's chart says that he is due for a scraping," I answered. "I'll do it. That should allow me to determine the quality of care he has been getting."

"I know that periodic scrapings of the burn tissue are needed to prevent infection, but that is a very time-consuming procedure. Are you sure that you want to spend that much time on one patient?"

"The quality of his care should be a good indicator of the care received by all the prisoners. The time spent should be worth it," I said.

"It is also a very delicate and painful operation. What do you need?"

"I have everything I need in my medical bag except morphine. Can you have the dispensary send me some along with a syringe?"

"All right but be careful with the morphine. We have a very limited supply, and you know how delicately you must balance the dose," said Miss Lovinescu.

"I know. Too much morphine will kill him, and too little will kill him also, through shock," I said.

As Miss Lovinescu left, I thought to myself, This is perfect. The slightest miscalculation on my part will kill him, and no one could blame me. The risk involved is probably why no one has done this yet even though it is plainly called for on his chart.

When the orderly brought the morphine, he said, "I have a full bottle here. How much do you want?"

"Just leave the bottle," I said. "I'll have to balance the dose against the pain as I go."

I took the bottle from the tray and inverted it. Pushing the needle into the seal, I withdrew a syringe full and tapped the side of the syringe to force out any air bubbles that might be trapped in the liquid.

"That is quite a large dose, isn't it, nurse," asked the orderly.

"I'll be careful with it," I said.

"I'm sure you will take good care of our hero," said the orderly.

"Hero?"

"Yes. I understand that he is considered quite the hero amongst the other prisoners."

"Why?"

"Well, the raid was flown at very low altitude..."

"I know. I was in the hospital when they almost took the roof off. So what?"

"It means that when one of their bombers was hit by our flack, they had to climb to a high enough altitude to be able to bail out. This pilot's plane was too badly damaged to climb, so he crash-landed it and saved two of his crew, besides himself."

"So, two for two, I wonder if it was worth it?"

"What do you mean?" he asked.

"Nothing. Don't you have other duties besides gossiping to do?"

He said, "Yes, nurse," and hurried from the ward.

So, you're a hero and a murderer, I thought as I began to cut the bandages away from his arms where they hung in traction. Joseph Todd mumbled something in English and turned his pain-filled eyes to me as I disturbed his rest.

I bent down close to his face and looked deeply into his eyes. "So, hero...do I look familiar to you? Many people say that I look just like my mother. She was the woman that you crushed under your great bomber. Did you see her? Did you know that she was there? Do you even care?"

He didn't answer me, of course. I really didn't expect him to understand Romanian, so I returned to cutting the bandages from him. When his burns were fully exposed, I prepared to inject his first dose of morphine.

A length of clear tubing ran from the intravenous bag filled with glucose solution to a needle inserted into an artery in his leg. The bright sunlight streaming through the window made the clear tubing glitter like an icicle, making me think of the Russian front. I remembered how desperately I had searched for enough morphine to end my own life in that filthy, freezing-cold shed. Perhaps Joseph Todd would rather be dead than endure his pain. As I inserted the needle into the port in the tubing and placed my thumb on the plunger, I knew that this man's life was now balanced on the pressure of my fingers. I squeezed and then began the scraping.

From time to time, when his moans became screams, I would inject a little more morphine. By the time I was done I was sweating freely, and Joseph Todd was still alive. I don't know why I hadn't killed him, but I do know that I wasn't as disgusted with myself as I thought I should be. I was applying antiseptic cream prior to replacing his bandages when I looked up to find two figures standing in the door to the ward. Miss Lovinescu and King Michael were watching me.

Well, that is not so surprising. The King wanted to see everything concerning the prisoners. Rumor has it that the King is interceding directly on the prisoner's behalf to see that Antonesque lives up to the Geneva Conventions.

Funny, the Iron Guard forced his father to abdicate so that they could have a young, controllable monarch on the throne. It seems that they got more of a man in the boy than they expected. But he is so young. Why he is only 20...the same as me!"

They were coming my way, so I rose and bowed politely to my King.

"Hello, Anna," he said.

"Your Majesty, I am honored," I said as I kept my eyes on his shiny boots. But I had already had a good look at the young King's face. He was quite handsome with his wavy black hair and noble nose. His mouth had particularly sensuous lips. In some ways he reminded me of Peter.

"No, Anna. I am the honored one," he said.

Keeping my eyes lowered, I could only say, "Your Majesty?"

"I am honored to have subjects as brave and capable as you."

"I am only a nurse, Your Majesty. I simply try to do my duty."

"You are modest also. Do you think that I have not heard of you? Miss Lovinescu speaks very highly of you."

"If you are referring to my escape from the Russians," I said. "That was merely self-preservation."

"That was an amazing feat also. But I am talking about today, about you and this man."

"I... I'm afraid I don't understand, Your Majesty."

"Oh, Anna," he said. "Please don't underestimate your King. When I heard how hard you worked to get on this team, so soon after your loss, I did some investigating of my own."

I was startled into looking the King directly in the face as he continued. "Did you think you could track down the American who landed his plane on your home and I could not?"

"Yet you allowed me to come on this mission," I said.

"Miss Lovinescu persuaded me that we owed you a chance to face him...and yourself."

"But you let me treat him. I could have killed him at any time."

"No, you couldn't have. We just had to let you learn that for yourself," said the King.

My emotions seemed to sort themselves out even as I spoke. "You're right. I couldn't find it in my heart to hate a man who was doing his duty as he saw it. He only tried to save his crew in a terrible situation." Still looking the King in the eye, I said, "I realized that he is not the enemy. This war is the enemy! It is destroying us!" By now, I was shouting at the King, but I didn't care. Something had to be done.

The King glanced over his shoulder to be sure that we were the only ones within listening distance and then whispered to me. "I tell you this in the strictest confidence because I know that you are someone who can keep a secret and be trusted. There are many of us who feel as you do. We are investigating several...options, to get our county out of this mess. When the time comes, we may all have to do our part to end this madness."

On the bus for the ride back to the city, I sat amidst the chatter of the medical staff but listened to none of it. My mind was going over and over what the King had said. Plans to get us out of the war? The Germans will never stand still for that. Any attempt to leave the Axis coalition will end in a fight with the German army, and they are everywhere throughout our country. How can we get rid of them?

Well, I know one thing. If it comes to a fight against the Germans, Emil and I are keeping our heads down. I've had enough. We will stay in our flat and keep out of it.

I should have known better.

CHAPTER X

Of friends and enemies

For a while it looked like my life might actually return to normal, whatever that might be. I worked days at the hospital and spent my evenings either visiting with the wounded or at my flat with Emil. He was enrolled in school and seemed to be settling down to his studies.

The war with Russia dragged on and things were not going well. The great German summer offensive at Kursk had failed, and everywhere the Axis armies were withdrawing to the West. Raids by enemy bomber fleets were becoming a regular occurrence over our country and the people were becoming dissatisfied with Antonesque's government. We were not aware of it at the time, but the specter of losing the war persuaded the Romanian government to cancel its plans to deport its "Old Kingdom" Jews to the German concentration camps. It seems that Antonesque had come to worry, rather belatedly, about what the world would say of his persecution of the Jews. The government even relented and allowed the repatriation of Dr. Fieldman. Sometime later, other Jews were quietly returned from exile on the frontier.

My curiosity about the Americans had been piqued by our mission to the prison, so I persuaded Miss Lovinescu to appoint me the official liaison person to the prison hospital. In that capacity, I frequently visited the injured prisoners. My main interest in visiting them was to learn to speak English the way I had learned German, by talking to the soldiers. I was also interested in learning more about what kind of a person Joseph Todd was.

I found that he was not as old as his prematurely balding head indicated. Actually, he was still attending the university, as a dental student, when he enlisted with the American Army Air Corps. He had "washed out," as he put it, from fighter school, but had gone on to earn his wings as a bomber pilot. He wasn't married, but he had a girlfriend that he hoped would be waiting for him when he got home.

At one point, while we were learning each other's language from our halting conversations, he slipped up and mentioned that he had flown from Africa on his bombing raid to Ploesti. It was supposed to be a military secret, and he begged me to tell no one of the mission's origin. I agreed to keep silent. After all, it made no difference to me where he had come from.

Once he had given his secret away to me, he went on to tell me about the African desert. He talked all about the heat of the day and the cold of the nights, and how the sand and fleas got into everything. But I was more interested in his stories of his home in Akron, in the state of Ohio. He said the countryside was beautiful, but the town smelled of rubber from the tire factories.

I told him of how pretty it was around Ploesti, and how bad it smelled from all the refineries. That was a mistake.

The day came when I arrived at the burn ward to find Mr. Todd silent, with his back turned to me. "Are you in pain?" I asked. There was no answer, so I moved to the other side of the bed to face him.

There were tears in his eyes as he tried to turn away from me again. I grabbed his shoulder and stopped him. "There is something wrong," I said. "Tell me. Maybe I can help."

"How can you stand to be near me?" he said as his tears began to flow in earnest.

"What do you mean?"

"When you talked of Ploesti with such familiarity, I got suspicious. I asked the staff here who you were...you never would talk of your past. They told me about your family."

"It was stupid of them to tell you---"

"I tricked one of the orderlies. I convinced him that you had told me your big secret, so he gave me the details.

Why are you here? To see what kind of monsters we are? To get some kind of revenge?"

"Yes, that is exactly why I came here...originally. But I found that you and the other prisoners are just people, like us. I really wanted to hate you, but I can't. Maybe it's a character flaw."

He smiled through his tears for a second, and then said, "But how can you stand to look at me? My God, I killed your family."

"You did your duty, just like I am."

"But you are saving lives, not taking them."

"Am I? Where do all the soldiers go after I treat them? They go back to the war, to kill...or worse. So, am I doing good or evil? I don't know."

Once I had opened up, I found myself telling him my whole story. He is the one who suggested that I write my story down and send it to the West, so that those people far from the war could see what it was really like for those of us caught in the middle.

On my very next visit to the prison hospital, Joseph Todd was gone. I knew that the Gestapo had been putting pressure on the government to turn all enemy prisoners over to them, so I rushed to the administration office to see where he had been sent. I was assured that he had been transferred to the general prison population now that he was well enough, and that none of our prisoners were being turned over to the Gestapo.

By now, we were on the receiving end of a steady stream of bombing raids by the Americans, now flying from bases in occupied Italy, so I had no shortage of Americans on whom to practice my English. At home, things were changing also, though I didn't notice it at first.

I blame myself for not paying enough attention to Emil. I thought that he was doing rather well adapting to big city life. Then I began to notice that he was coming home later and later after school. Also, his manner of speaking began to change. He started using phrases that I had heard on the eastern front. Things like, "power of the

proletariat," and "workers' paradise."

I knew that there were many underground cells of the communist party, as well as others, working to overthrow the government. I suspected that Emil was mixed up with one of them. One evening, when he came in several hours after school had dismissed, I confronted him.

"Why are you so late?" I asked.

"I was busy," he said.

"Busy doing what?"

"None of your business," he said in a surly tone.

"It is my business. If I am to raise you, I need to know---"

"You're my sister, not my mother!"

"Same thing, in this case," I said. "You're hanging out with a communist party group, aren't you?"

"So what? It's my life, isn't it?"

"It'll be the end of your life if anyone finds out. You already have one strike against you. You're half Jew. You can't afford to draw attention to yourself and have people looking into your past.

"Mr. Ceausescu says that the Party is the only way out for Romania---"

"You mean your that rabble rouser, Nicolae Ceausescu?"

"No, he's in prison. His brother, Marin is the leader of our communist youth group now. He says that we will overthrow the government and kick the Germans out of Romania!"

"Who will? Him and the thirteen-year-olds of Bucharest? Ha! Give me a break."

"You're only a woman. What do you know about anything?"

I lost it.

"You ungrateful Chauvinist Pig! What do I know? I've been shot at, bombed, shelled, beaten, and raped! My fiancée is either dead or in Siberia. I've seen my best friends shamed, injured, and killed! I've crawled through mud, snow, and blood! I've shoveled shit and body parts from here to Stalingrad and back! And they were *my* parents that were killed in that air raid too, you know! You have no idea of what you are getting yourself into!"

Emil ran from the flat and I was immediately sorry for shouting at him like that, but it had all just poured out. I hadn't been able to stop. Then I realized that I had never before told him that I had been raped. I wondered what he thought of me now.

It was several hours after dark, and I was sitting in the flat with no lights on, when Emil returned. He didn't see me sitting in the dark as he entered.

"I'm sorry, Emil," I said. "I shouldn't have taken out my frustrations on you."

He didn't answer for quite some time, and in the dark, I couldn't see his face. Finally, he said in a voice hardly more than a whisper, "You never told me that you were raped. Was it the Russians who captured you?"

"Yes."

"Why didn't you tell me?"

"Would it have helped anything to bother you with my problems? Besides, I was... ashamed."

Even in the dark, I could tell from the quaver in his voice that he was holding back tears as he continued. "I'll quit the Young Communists."

"Why? It's not because of my rape, is it?"

"Of course, it is. The Russians are communists. I won't have anything to do with people who could do something like that."

"Don't be silly. It wasn't communists who raped me. It wasn't Russians either. It was *men* who raped me. Must I now hate all men...even you? Or will you quit being a man?

If you quit the communists, do it because it's dangerous, or because you can't believe in what they tell you. Don't do it because of what happened to me."

"All right, I won't quit. But how can you go on?"

"Do I have a choice? There are injured who need help. I'm good at helping people, so I do what I can. And then there is you. I'll tell you another secret of mine. I thought of ending it all. But I'm glad that I didn't because that would have left you all alone, and I couldn't allow that, could I?"

Emil didn't say anything else, but he came to me in the dark and hugged me. That night I cried myself to sleep. Emil stayed with his communist youth, and I kept on praying that he would never be found out.

Throughout the winter of 1943 things continued to go badly for our forces. In the spring of 1944, things got worse. The Soviet armies

245

pushed westward relentlessly. By summer they were nearing the border of Transnistria. Soon we would lose everything we had gained. The Iron Guard continued to parade in the streets of Bucharest. I know because one of them chased me down in the street and kicked me because I had the temerity to cross the road ahead of their goose-stepping band of ruffians. But while they continued to intimidate the populous, their base of power in the government was shrinking.

Finally, in late August of 1944, it happened. Despite his claim of planning for Romania's exit from the Axis, I think that King Michael just got fed up and acted with no real plan in mind. Or maybe his plan was so simple that it seemed like no plan. At any rate he simply invited Antonesque to dinner, and with the help of only two loyal officers, arrested him and stuffed him in a closet. Then they proceeded to arrest the rest of his government. By the next day the Romanian army was battling to throw the Germans out of their positions throughout the country.

Unfortunately, in Bucharest, there were nearly as many German military personnel as Romanian. Even worse, once the Germans found out that their units in Bucharest were surrounded, they had large numbers of reinforcements to send from Ploesti, whose defense had been handed over to the Germans almost completely.

With the army's forces stretched to the breaking point, Ceausescu and his young communists saw their opportunity to make a name for themselves with whoever wound up in charge after the fighting.

An early morning knock on the door awakened me, but Emil was already at the door when I got there. I saw another young boy running back down the hall as Emil closed the door.

"I have to go! I am needed," he said, as he rushed to get dressed.

"Where are you going?" I asked.

"To my Young Communists cell, The whole city is in revolt against the Germans. We need every man to stop the soldiers coming down from Ploesti."

I wanted to scream, "You are a boy, not a man!" But I knew that would be the wrong thing to say. Instead, I said, "All right. I'll go with you."

"Don't be silly you're just... I mean you can't go. There will be fighting."

"That is why I must go with you," I said. "I can help."

"You wouldn't hurt a flea; how could you help"

"No, but do you know how to stop a tank with your bare hands?"

"Do you have a way?" he asked with a little awe in his voice.

"I know at least a half dozen ways," I said. "Now, I thought you were in a hurry."

That is how I found myself facing Mr. Ceausescu and his band of babies in a basement room under the school. As soon as we entered the dimly lit storeroom Emil tried to distance himself from me. It was understandable, considering the harassment he was being subjected to by his friends.

"What's the matter, Emil? Wouldn't your sister let you out on your own?"

"Hey, Emil! Are you going to hide behind your sister's skirt?"

Emil, red-faced and silent, went directly to a seat as far from me as possible and sat hunched down with his eyes on the floor. I ignored the chatter and walked directly to the front of the room where Mr. Ceausescu was standing. Rather short, with small dark eyes peering out from behind his spectacles, he didn't look very much like a revolutionary leader, but then, I suppose no one ever does.

Getting directly to the point, I said, "I would like to help you."

247

"Well...Emil tells me that you are a nurse, so I suppose that we may be in need of your services before this is all over," he said.

"I'll be glad to help medically if necessary, of course. But that is not what I had in mind. I can help you plan your defense and show these boys how to stop the German tanks."

That brought on a new round of laughter and silly remarks from the school- children-cum soldiers.

Turning to his unruly followers, Mr. Ceausescu motioned for quiet and said, "Now now boys, let me speak to this young woman."

He turned back to me and said in his best, father-knows-best voice, "My dear, we have been preparing for this moment for some time. I think we can handle this ourselves."

"Oh?" I said as I turned to the table behind him and lifted the bottle of petrol that sat there. It was corked, with a cloth "fuse" running under the cork and into the bottle. "And what do you call this?"

"It's a fire-bomb, for blowing up the German tanks," he explained in a tone that clearly showed that he thought me a complete idiot.

"Forgot something, didn't you?" I said.

Looking at the bottle, he said, "Bottle, petrol, and fuse. It's all there. Perhaps you would be better off spending your time making babies for the Homeland."

I chose to ignore that rather bizarre remark, and said, "Soap."

"Excuse me. Did you say soap?"

"Yes, I did. Powdered soap would be best." He looked at me blankly, so I continued. "The Germans and Finns call these Molotov Cocktails. If you put powdered detergent into the petrol, it causes it to become like gelatin."

It was obvious that he still didn't get the point. "If you throw one of these at a tank without the detergent in it the petrol will probably run off of it before it can do any harm. If you make it sticky, it will stay on the vehicle long enough to set something on fire."

"And how do you know this, young lady?"

"Tank fighting school. The Germans teach many ways to destroy a tank."

"You went to tank fighting school? He sounded very skeptical.

"Don't be silly," I said. "I'm a nurse. I don't fight tanks. But I did listen to the soldiers who went through it, and I have a nearly perfect memory. I can show you many ways to defeat an armored vehicle."

"Well, I don't know..." he began.

Do you know that if you are within 3 meters of the side or rear of a tank, you are virtually invisible to anyone inside it?"

"Really? Um...perhaps we could use some of your advice," he said. He turned to the boys, who had been following our conversation, and called for attention. "Boys, boys. I think that Emil's sister has some valuable information to share with us."

With that, he indicated that I should speak to the "Class".

"The first thing is to separate the tanks from their supporting infantry," I said. "Only a foolish tank commander will attack without infantry support, and the Germans aren't fools."

"How do we do that?" asked one of the boys in the front row.

I was glad to see that they were willing to listen to me. "By bringing the infantry under heavy fire just as they pass through chokepoints. That is, places where their path is restricted by either natural or man-made obstacles.

"Once you have stripped them of their infantry you have to force them to 'button up', by that, I mean to make the tank commander pull his head back into the tank. And close the hatch. That way they can only see what is visible through the view ports, and that is very little."

Emil was sitting up a lot straighter now that he could see that his sister knew what she was talking about. I was happy to help his standing with his friends. I just wished that my information didn't have to get some of them killed.

"Just remember," I said. "The tankmen hate fighting in a city because it is so easy for them to become stopped. And a stopped tank is a tank that you can kill.

"Now, let me tell you some of the ways that you can stop a tank..." They were listening to me intently now, but I wondered how well my "text-book" instructions, delivered from memory, would work against real tanks.

"Emil, I need you to go back to our flat and get those ugly brown dinner plates from the cupboard---"

"Why?" he interrupted.

"Because we need them for anti-tank mines," I said.

"How can you make a mine out of a dinner plate?" asked Mr. Ceausescu.

"Simply by turning it upside-down in the street," I answered.

"What!? That won't blow up a tank!"

I think he was beginning to doubt my sanity...again, so I explained. "It doesn't have to blow up the tank. It only has to stop it, so *you* can blow it up. And believe me, dinner plates turned upside down in a roadway look just like what they call a 'hastily laid minefield' to a tank driver looking through a view slit. Of course, the Germans know this trick, but only a fool or a very brave man would drive over something that *might* be a mine. When the driver hesitates is when you run up to it and use your fire-bombs.

"Now you need to learn about cluster grenades and shot-traps..."

Two hours later our rag-tag band, carrying an unlikely assortment of equipment, commandeered a milk-wagon and several taxies to take us to the northern edge of the city. We heard scattered firing coming from several directions as we drove north on Balesqu Boulevard. The Germans had maintained numerous offices and missions throughout the city. It was these scattered outposts that the units of the Romanian Home Army were trying to rout out before the Nazis could rescue them with troops sent south from Ploesti.

We crossed Dacia Boulevard and headed for the Ploesti to Bucharest Road. When we reached the outskirts of the city, we found a battalion of the Home Army in place, ready to stop the Germans from entering the city. They had light and heavy weapons, plus several anti-tank guns. It wasn't a very formidable force, but they certainly didn't need a bunch of untrained children to help them, and they said so in no uncertain terms. I, for one, was glad to be told to go home and leave the fighting to the professionals. Unfortunately, Mr. Ceausescu wasn't to be put off so easily. He pestered the officer in charge until he the poor man would have done anything to get us out of his way.

"Look," he said. "There is a secondary road coming down from Ploesti. It passes through Buftea and enters Bucharest a couple kilometers to the west of here. I don't think that the Germans know of that route, but I sent one gun and a squad of soldiers there to keep an eye on it. Maybe they could use your support if any Nazis come their way."

Mr. Ceausescu's eyes lit up as the prospect of taking part in our *glorious* revolution improved. I wasn't quite as happy as I asked the Lieutenant,

"You only sent one gun and a handful of men? That won't stop anything."

"Like I said, I don't think the Germans know of that route."

"And if you are wrong, the fascists will be coming from your rear before you have any warning," I said. He only shrugged, so I turned to Mr. Ceausescu. "We had better get over there."

The taxies had disappeared back into the city, so we loaded our equipment into the commandeered milk-wagon and walked the two kilometers to the other road. When we got there, we found the anti-tank gun set up in the middle of a short, steel-girder bridge that spanned a stream feeding into the Dambovita River.

Mr. Ceausescu and I walked onto the bridge and approached a sergeant who stood beside the gun. "Who is in charge here?" asked Mr. Ceausescu.

"I am," answered the sergeant. "What are you civilians doing here?"

"Your battalion commander sent us to help you," said Mr. Ceausescu, stretching the truth a little.

As the sergeant digested that bit of news, I asked, "What kind of a position is this? You have no cover, not even a sandbag. The German tanks will drive right over you."

"Who the hell are you? Get off my bridge before I throw you in the river!"

Now it was my turn to exaggerate just a little. "I fought with the Third Army at Stalingrad. And I know that this gun is a German 50mm PAK38. It is a decent little gun and can handle any of the light tanks that the Germans may send. But it would be completely useless against the frontal armor of a Panzer 3 or 4, and I happen to know that the enemy have several of those very models at Ploesti. If they come this way...you're dead."

Some of the wind seemed to be out of the sergeant's sails as he said, "Look, until this morning I was a cook. Now I am supposed to defend Bucharest from the Germans. If you have any experience in combat, I'm willing to listen to your suggestions."

"Fine," I said. "Then I suggest that you get off of this bridge. You have the right idea of defending this river crossing, but you are going about it wrong. Your little gun needs a side shot to penetrate a tank. Why don't you pull your gun back into that side street just south of the bridge and wait for the enemy to stop in the middle of that intersection?"

"But why would they stop there?" he asked.

"You just leave that up to me and these, uh...Young Communists."

The army men had no transport for their gun, so they had to manhandle it back into the side street. While they were busy with that, I turned to Emil and said, "Get the plates out of the wagon. Then turn them upside down in the street, just south of the intersection. See how the level of the roadway drops just as you come off the bridge. The tanks won't see the plates until the last minute. When they stop, the gun will have a perfect target."

"But what about the infantry that will be with the tanks? You said that the Germans won't come without infantry," said the sergeant.

"They won't," I said. That's why our boys and the rest of the army squad will have to keep the bridge under constant rifle and machine-gun fire. Then the Germans will have to use the tanks to force their way across the bridge."

Turning to Mr. Ceausescu, I continued, "You need to get some of the boys up into the girders over the bridge's roadway. The Germans will lead the way for the tanks with a light armored vehicle if they have one. Give each boy several petrol-bombs and tell them to use them on the first vehicles to cross the bridge. Then we have to do something with those four-story buildings that line the road."

We continued making our preparations throughout the morning. That included warning the residents of the buildings in the area of the impending battle. Most of them were smart enough to leave. By mid-afternoon we were as ready as we were ever likely to be. At last, I sat down atop one of the tall apartment buildings with my back against the brick parapet that surrounded the roof. I wanted to sleep, but first I had one more thing to do. As I sat there, I prayed as I had never prayed before. I prayed that the Germans wouldn't come this way. I prayed that they would just leave and never come back. I prayed that we would be allowed to quit this miserable war and have peace in Romania. I guess I prayed for too much because it was the unmistakable steel-on-steel squealing of tracked vehicles that awoke me from the troubled sleep I had fallen into.

As expected, when I looked across the stream from my rooftop perch, I saw dismounted German infantry rushing up the street towards the far side of the bridge. Some of the children got excited and began firing far sooner than I had told them to. Ordinarily, this would have caused the enemy to go to ground and get under cover. Instead, the Germans picked up their pace and rushed for the bridge even faster. They were obviously trying to take the bridge "on the bounce" as they liked to call it, before the defenders could react. This told me that this crossing was very important to them. It might even be their main point of attack, what the Germans called the "Schwerpunkt".

The scattered rifle fire picked up in intensity, but the enemy kept on coming. Then the two ZB30 light machine-guns that our army friends had with them joined in the firing and the Germans began to falter. At first, they began to take momentary cover wherever possible and then rush forward as soon as they had an opportunity. But, as their casualties began to mount, they began staying under cover longer. Finally, they were making no progress at all.

With his infantry pinned down, the German commander had no choice but to send his armor across the bridge in the hope that we had nothing strong enough to stop them. The first vehicle to come into sight was an armored car. It was an obsolete SDKFZ 222, four wheeled cars with an open-topped turret. The open top made it an easier target for our petrol bombs, but the automatic 20mm cannon that it carried could cause a lot of casualties among our lightly armed fighters. We had to stop this car before it crossed the bridge.

When it began to move up the road, I signaled to the two boys hidden in the overhead girders to light their fuses. The small, armored car was capable of moving very fast and I was afraid that the bomb throwers might not be able to light their fuses quickly enough. Indeed, I could see one of the boys struggling to light his match as the enemy vehicle accelerated onto the bridge. The first boy threw one of his bombs too soon and it exploded like giant flower in the center of the bridge.

The car's machine-gun began firing up into the girders as the vehicle ran through the burning petrol. The second boy got his bombs lit just as the armored car passed under him. In his excitement, he dropped both bombs together. The first struck the wire netting that protected the top of the turret. It bounced into the street before it exploded. The second bomb had more luck. It struck the edge of the turret top and scattered its burning contents both into the turret and over the engine deck. The results were immediate. The gun crew threw open the covering screen and jumped, burning, onto the roadway. While they scrambled over the side of the bridge and into the water, their driver wasn't so lucky. Trapped in the front of the hull when the burning fuel spread over him, he turned the car sharply to the right where it crashed into the steel girders at the side of the bridge. I was glad that I was too far away to hear the screams that I knew would be coming from that inferno.

The boys in the girders had been instructed to keep under cover and crawl to the side of the bridge once they had dropped their bombs. One of them did this successfully and jumped into the river. The one who had hit the armored car got excited and stood up. In seconds he was struck by several bullets from the enemy on the far bank. I could tell from the way his limp body hit the hard surface of the bridge that he was dead before he landed.

I turned around and slid down with my back against the parapet. Leaning forward, with my head between my legs, I threw up. Emil, who I had insisted stay with me as a runner, looked at me. I expected him to say something about my weakness, but he just looked as if he wanted to be sick also. When I next peered over the parapet, I could see the burning armored car wedged into the bridge-side girders. It was partially blocking the roadway and the Germans seemed to be holding back while they decided what to do.

Emil and I hurried down from the roof of the apartment building into the side street where the army had set up their gun. Running up to the sergeant, I said, "They will send a tank next. It's the only way they can clear the bridge under fire. Have your sights set on the crossroads at the bottom of the bridge. They should stop when they see our 'mines'. You'll have a side shot, so you should be able to destroy any tank they can send over."

The sergeant looked worried, so I added, "As soon as you get a penetration, get your men to wheel this gun out of the street and under cover. If the Germans have mortars with them, they will try to knock out your gun as soon as you give away your position."

With the sounds of small-arms fire in the background, and with the occasional tracer round ricocheting along the street, the sergeant's voice had a slight waver in it as he asked, "Is this the way they did it at Stalingrad?"

"Sure thing," I said. "But at Stalingrad this would be a slow day." That brought a weak smile and I hurried off to the basement of the building across from the bridge.

In the basement we had several teams of the younger boys. They had light rope strung across each of the streets with another team of boys on the other end of each rope. The ropes had a cluster of six hand grenades tied in the center. The boys were supposed to use the ropes to maneuver the grenade cluster under the tracks of any passing tanks in order to disable the enemy long enough for the boys on the roof to drop petrol bombs on them. I was instructing the boys on how to pull the fuse-cord when the unmistakable sound of a heavy engine came from the bridge.

I turned to Emil and said, "Run up to the roof and tell the boys there to fire at the tank's commander. We have to be sure that he is inside the tank when they get close enough to see the plates. We don't want them to get a good look, or they won't stop." As Emil ran up the steps, I tried to get a view of the bridge approaches from the basement window. It was too narrow and low for me to see anything in the direction of the bridge, so I hurried up to the main floor. The doors to the building were recessed into small alcoves, so I moved into one of the doorways to get a view of the street. The brick walls would protect me from anything but a shot coming directly from the street, and I hoped that the Germans wouldn't get that far.

The screech of metal on metal came from the bridge, so I peered around the corner of my doorway to see a heavy tank pushing the burning armored car through the bridge girders and into the river. The sparks of small arms fire hitting the tank showed that the boys on the roof were doing their job. The tank commander had lowered himself into the armored vehicle and closed the turret hatch behind him.

With the armored car out of the way, the German tank began to move forward once again. As it came over the slight rise at the foot of the bridge, they must have seen our plates in the road. The armored monster lurched to a stop. I could just imagine the confused argument going on inside the vehicle. I couldn't see the army's anti-tank gun from where I was, but I knew that they had a perfect shot. To myself I was saying, "Shoot, shoot!" But as the seconds dragged on, nothing happened.

At last, just as the tank began to advance once again, I heard the crack of the high-velocity gun. A shower of sparks erupted from the side of the turret as the cannon shell deflected from the sloped armor. It hadn't penetrated! The tank stopped once again, and the turret began to swing in the direction of the anti-tank gun. I prayed that the gun crew hadn't panicked and run off. A second later a second shell slammed into the side of the Panzer. It hit the hull just over the road wheels, where it punched a small hole through the armor.

Nothing happened for a second. Then I heard a small, muffled explosion. I was just wondering if that was all the effect that the small shell was going to have when the vehicle dissolved in a violent explosion that tore it completely apart.

No sooner had my hearing returned to normal from the explosion, than I heard the approach of the next armored vehicle. I ran back to the basement to warn the boys who waited there. "There is another tank coming. Be ready to get your grenades under the tracks. I am going up onto the roof." As I started back up the steps, a boy of about ten years of age stopped me.

"I can't get the cap off the end of my grenade," he said.

I took the wooden stick-like handle of the grenade and twisted the screw-on cap from the base. Pulling the string-loop from the base, I said, "Tie your string to this loop and don't pull it until a German tank is just about to run over it. Once you pull the string, you'll have 4 seconds to get under cover before it goes off." When he nodded his head and ran back to his friends by the basement window, I started up the steps again. It was then that the absurdity of the situation really hit me. I had just handed an armed grenade to a ten-year-old boy. All I could do was shake my head as I continued my climb.

A second panzer was just coming off the bridge as I arrived on the roof. Emil and I signaled the boys on the rooftops to get their bombs ready as the armored beast worked its way around the burning hulk of its predecessor. It was spraying machine-gun fire into the storefronts as it rumbled up the street. Firebombs rained down at the enemy machine, but by keeping to the center of the pavement and making frequent changes in speed and direction, the skillful driver avoided all the missiles directed at him.

Suddenly an explosion came from under the monster, and it slued to the side. The young boys in the basement had succeeded in getting their grenade cluster under the tracks. The panzer came to rest with its front end partially buried into the storefront directly below us. Instantly it was engulfed in a flurry of petrol bombs that set it on fire from end to end.

I raced from the roof and back down the steps to the ground floor. Emil called after me, but I didn't have time to explain. As I ran through the shattered store into which the enemy panzer had crashed, the flames were already beginning to spread to the building. I wasn't worried about the building, however. I knew that there were escape hatches below the driver's position. If anyone had survived the fire, they would have to get out of the vehicle through those hatches since the entire upper surface of the vehicle was in flames.

By the time I arrived the bottom hatch had been opened and a soldier was rolling on the floor, trying to extinguish his burning uniform. I grabbed a curtain from the window and jumped on top of him. When the terrified man began fighting me, I yelled at him in German, "Stop fighting me! I'm trying to save you!" His flailing about decreased and I managed to get the curtain wrapped all the way around him, extinguishing the flames at last.

"Is there anyone else alive in there?" I asked, but he was already going into shock and couldn't answer me. Looking at the hatch that he had so recently crawled from, I could see nothing but red-hot flames licking from the edges. No one could survive that, and the ammunition would soon be exploding, so I began dragging the burned man to the rear of the shop. He was a big man, and I wasn't making very good progress. I was beginning to wonder if we would be able to get away in time when Emil came running in and began pulling on me.

"Grab his other arm," I yelled. Between the two of us we managed to get out of the now burning shop before the tank's ammunition began to explode.

"Why did you do that?" yelled Emil.

"I had to see if there was anyone that could be saved," I said.

"But he's a German!"

"A life is a life," I said. "It doesn't matter what nationality."

Emil just looked disgusted, so I sent him back to the rooftop while I treated our prisoner's wounds. After I had turned him over to two armed boys, I found that I had received some slight burns on my hands and arms. My hair was singed quite a bit also. "Oh well," I thought. "I've just about ruined my skirt and blouse too. Lucky we don't have to stand inspection in this army."

I was out of breath as I stumbled onto the roof and dropped down beside Emil again. Between my gasps I asked, "What's coming now?"

"I don't know what you call it, but it has a big gun on it," answered Emil.

I peered over the parapet to see an open-topped self-propelled gun just coming off the bridge. "That gun is big enough to knock down these buildings with a few well-placed shots," I said. "But the good news is that it has no overhead armor. We have to get some boys with petrol bombs on the roofs above it."

The gun had two armed infantrymen crammed into the fighting compartment along with the regular crew. It stopped just off the bridge and well away from any of our petrol bombers. From its secure position it began to fire on the building across the street from us. The first muzzle-blast was followed almost immediately by the detonation of the shell. A large section of the building's lower floor erupted into the street in the form of shattered glass and brick.

"They are trying to destroy the building by blowing out the first floor and letting it fall in on itself," I said, just as the second explosion rocked us.

"It's too far from the rooftops to reach with a bomb!" yelled Emil. I could see that he was right. Several of the deadly "Fire blossoms" were burning in the street where petrol bombs had been thrown at the gun but hadn't reached their target.

"With those infantry on board, we can't ask the boys to rush it either. We need to get that anti-tank gun into a position to shoot at it," I said. We ran back down to the street level and up the side street to where the army's gun had been. There was nothing in sight. As we stood looking up and down the street, the sergeant emerged from the archway to a cinema house and waved to us. We ran to him and began to explain the situation to him.

"We need you to bring your gun up this street to get a shot at that self-propelled gun. It's blowing the hell out of the buildings and we can't reach it with the firebombs," explained Emil.

"I can't do that," said the sergeant. "If we poke our nose around that corner, they will put a shell down our throat before we can get our sights set."

"You aren't afraid to take a chance, are you?" asked Emil.

"Why you little---," began the sergeant."

"We need a distraction!" I interrupted. "Emil, you help the sergeant and his crew to move the gun quickly. I'll go to the other side of the street and arrange something to draw their attention. As soon as they are focused on us, roll the gun out and take your shot...and made it good."

I circled the block and came to the contested roadway a good two hundred meters from the bridge. The heavy German gun was methodically pulverizing the first floor of an apartment building. I could see the entire structure shaking with each explosion. I gathered my skirt above my knees and sprinted across the open space. I was halfway across before they even saw me, and I was safely through an open doorway as bullets began to spatter the pavement behind me. Two of the older boys ran up to me and asked what we were going to do now.

"We have to get to the street on the east side of that gun. Then we will try to rush it," I answered.

"Rush it?" they said in unison.

"We won't get anywhere close to it," continued one of them.

"I'm glad to see that even kids as young as you can recognize a dumb move when you hear one," I said. "We only need to make them think we are trying to attack them from that side so that the army can use their gun to knock them out.

"But first, I am going to get out of this damned skirt before it kills me."

The boys were kind enough to scrounge up a pair of pants for me from one of the flats in the building. They then looked in the other direction while I changed, though they snickered the whole time.

We gathered about a dozen of the boys and were soon ready to start moving towards the enemy gun. "We only need to draw their attention in this direction, so I don't want to see any of you taking any extra chances trying to get close enough to hit them with a petrol bomb. When they start shooting at us, take cover and stay there," I said. "Now give me a bomb to carry."

"I thought that you weren't going to try to hurt anyone yourself," said one of the older boys.

"I'm not. But they don't know that. Like I said, we only need to draw their attention."

With that, we ran into the street and began charging towards the enemy. They were so intent on their mission of destruction that, for a while, I thought that they might not see us until we were actually close enough to throw our bombs. Then I would have had to decide if I could actually take a life. In the end, I didn't have to make that decision. If they were slow to notice us, they were certainly not slow to begin shooting at us. In seconds, the air was alive with the whine and crack of bullets aimed in our direction.

"Get under cover!" I yelled. Then I dropped down behind a telegraph pole. I soon realized that the pole provided poor cover, even for a small person like me, so I sprinted to a doorway a few meters away. As I dove headfirst into the opening I was followed closely by chips of concrete from the sidewalk, thrown up by a line of submachine-gun bullets. Crawling back to the edge of the doorway, I tried to locate the rest of my group. Some of the boys were behind an auto, while several others were in doorways like mine.

"Move from cover to cover to keep their attention on us," I called as I scrambled to the next doorway.

Bullets caromed off the wall above my head as I tried to see what the Germans were doing. The concrete dust stung my eyes, preventing me from getting a look at the enemy gun. I could only hope that our army was taking advantage of our diversion to get into position. Minutes seemed like hours as we scrambled about, drawing fire whenever we showed ourselves.

I was wondering if the army was ever going to fire their damned gun when an explosion rocked the entire street. I raised my head above the culvert pipe that I was lying behind to find that the German gun had been blown apart. Flames licked high into the air from the hull, and I could see no movement anywhere around the gun's former position.

Quickly gathering the boys around me, I found that the only injuries we had taken were two boys with minor scratches. Once these were tended to, I returned to Emil's position on the rooftop.

"Anything else coming over the bridge?" I asked as I slid to a stop behind the parapet.

"No," said Emil. "It sure is quiet over there now."

"It's almost sunset," I said. "They'll probably wait until after dark and then try to infiltrate across the bridge...and over the river if they can find any boats."

"How can we stop that?" asked Emil.

"God help me, I don't know. We can't ask these kids to stand up to experienced soldiers in a face-to-face firefight. Let's find Mr. Ceausescu and get him to have the army squad occupy the bridge after dark. At least they have some chance against the Germans."

We found Mr. Ceausescu with some of the boys on another rooftop and together we went in search of the sergeant. He was with his gun, back in the cinema courtyard. He wasn't too happy with our idea but couldn't think of anything better. Just as he was getting ready to call his men together, we heard the sound of approaching lorries. And this time they were on our side of the bridge and approaching from behind us.

"Everyone get under cover," yelled the sergeant.

We had just scattered to various doorways and windows along the narrow roadway when the first lorry pulled into view. It was a German Opel, but that didn't mean anything since our army used any vehicle it could get its hands on. We waited, looking out from our hiding places as the vehicle pulled even with us. The uniforms of the troops in the back of the lorry were Romanian! We jumped happily from our cover and nearly scared the unfortunate troops to death. At least we stopped them before they drove right into the Germans' field of fire.

It was the unit that we had talked to earlier in the day. It turned out that they had repulsed a German attempt to enter Bucharest along the main road and had not been disturbed for the rest of the day. When they heard of the fight going on at our bridge, they had sent this company of men to help us out. As far as I was concerned, they were none too soon.

I kept my mouth shut while the sergeant and Mr. Ceausescu explained the situation to the newcomers. There was no sense in pressing my luck with my "military advisor" role. Besides, Mr. Ceausescu seemed to have a pretty good grasp of military operations for a simple teacher. Once the new troops had been informed of the need to occupy the bridge during the coming night, they thanked us for our efforts and politely informed us that we were no longer needed.

I expected Mr. Ceausescu to be somewhat put out at having the army replace us in our "moment of glory." But he didn't seem upset at all as we rounded up our street fighters and loaded our equipment onto our faithful milk wagon. As we started off, I tactfully pointed out to Mr.

Ceausescu that we were on the wrong road to return to the school from which we had started, seemingly a lifetime ago.

"Oh, we are not returning to the school," he said. "I have been informed that there is a small detachment of German troops holding out at the railway station a short distance south of here. We are going to drive them out of the city."

Damn...I had just begun to think that this Ceausescu guy was not crazy after all. And now this!

'What kind of help will we have from the army this time?" I asked.

"I don't know," he replied. "Let's go there and find out."

I had a bad feeling about the whole idea, and like most veterans, I had learned to trust my instincts. But I went along. What else could I do? I knew that Emil would never abandon his friends, no matter what Ceausescu led them into.

My instincts were right. When we arrived at the railway station, we found that there were only two Romanian soldiers there to keep an eye on the Germans...and they were over-age reserves. At least they were a wealth of knowledge.

"There are a dozen Germans in the station," said the first reserve. They were waiting for the arrival of two replacement panzers by rail when the...trouble, started. The rail system is shut down now, so they have no transportation out of here."

"You seem to know a lot about them," I said. "How do you know so much?"

"We were working with them when all this started. I told them that we would look for a way to get them out, and never went back."

"You say they are panzer troopers," I said. "Are they armed?'

266

"Oh yes, they're armed all right. Besides their personal weapons, they had two of those machine-guns that can be used either in a vehicle or on the ground."

"You mean MG-42's," I said.

"Yes, and plenty of ammunition. They were supposed to install them in the panzers when they arrived since they were going to drive them directly to the front."

"Great! A dozen heavily armed troops. They may not be trained primarily as infantry, but you can bet that they are all veterans. There is no way we will be able to force them out of that building."

"I have thirty-five young men under my command. We will attack and wipe them out," said Mr. Ceausescu.

"You have thirty-five *boys*...left," I said. "If you attack those seasoned troops, you'll get all your boys killed for nothing. Then you will be the commander of nothing." That seemed to give him pause, so I took advantage of his moment of indecision to take charge of the situation.

To the reservist, I said, "Do you know to which unit the Germans belong?"

"They are from the 22nd Panzer Division," he answered.

"Perfect!" I said. "I knew many of the men in that unit. Who is the officer in charge?"

"A Colonel Roider, I believe."

The world seemed to lurch under my feet as I said, "Oh my God!"

"You seem to recognize the name," said Mr. Ceausescu. "Is he a friend of yours? If he is, maybe you can talk him into surrendering."

I knew that under the soot and grime that covered my face, my complexion must have gone from pale to pure white as I felt the blood drain to my feet. "I know him, all right," I said. "But he is no friend.

He's the one who arraigned for me to be a guest of the Russians for a short while. I guess you could call him my best enemy."

"Too bad," said Mr. Ceausescu. "I had hoped that you could have helped to avoid bloodshed by getting him to surrender."

"He would never have surrendered, even for his best friend, if he has one. But maybe we can still take advantage of this situation. I may hate him, but I know how he thinks."

"What do you have in mind?"

"First, let me ask you a question." I said. "If you get all your followers killed trying to take that station, what will you have left?"

"Nothing, I suppose," he said.

"That's right. With no followers you have no power base. No power base means no say in the administration that will follow the revolution. You will truly have nothing."

"So what are you proposing? You already said that this Colonel Roider wouldn't surrender for his best friend."

"True, but he would listen to his worst enemy if that enemy could save his troops for him. I'll go to him with a proposition that will save his men while giving you possession of the station and control of the rail line.

Mr. Ceausescu and I spent the night working out the details of my plan and making sure that our little rag-tag band made enough noise for a battalion of His Majesty's finest troops. By dawn I found myself getting ready to go out to meet my old friend Hans. *The same friend who had arranged for my capture by the Russians. The same friend who had almost raped me, only to decide that I was not even a human being simply because my mother happened to be a Jew.* My blood ran cold in my veins, and it must have shown.

"You're shivering," said Emil.

"I guess I'm cold," I answered.

"Take my sweater," said Emil as he pulled the bulky brown sweater over his head. "Mr. Ceausescu says that it came from England. The British dropped it to the Yugoslav partisans. The Germans took it from a prisoner, and we took it from them.

"Thanks," I said. "The Englanders sure know how to make their wool into a great sweater. Too bad they can't make a decent tank."

Emil laughed at my joke, but then became serious again. "You're doing this because of me, aren't you? You're afraid I'll get killed if we attack the Germans."

"I'm doing this for all of you. I couldn't stand to see any of the boys get killed if I could have prevented it." I had the sweater on now and coupled with the baggy pants we had found in the apartment building, my scorched hair and dirt-covered face, I must have made quite a sight.

Emil said, "You look like a homeless displaced person."

"I guess I am, when you think about it. Maybe we all are till this is over."

Emil didn't say anything more, but he wouldn't let go of my hand. Finally, I had to pry him lose and go in search of Mr. Ceausescu. When I found him I said, "I'm ready. Wish me luck."

"I hope you succeed," he said.

What a strange man, I thought. He hopes I succeed, but not a word about my living through this. He probably thinks that if I'm not pregnant, I'm not worth anything.

I had tied a dirty white rag to the end of a broken broomstick. I raised this above the stone wall that I lay behind. When no shots came my way, I slowly stood up, put my hands together on top of my head and began to approach the station building. The little patch of ground ahead of me looked as wide as the Russian Steppes. With every step the hair on the back of my neck stood up at the thought of all the weapons that must be aiming at my head. Finally, I reached the station platform and halted just short of it.

'I have an offer to deliver to your commander," I yelled out in German. "I can get you all out of this situation alive and free if you will listen to me."

For more seconds than I care to remember, nothing happened. Then, just as I was ready to call out again, the door swung open. No one was visible, but the invitation was unmistakable.

I climbed onto the platform and crossed to the open doorway. The bright morning sunshine made it impossible for me to see anything in the darkness ahead of me. All I could do was plunge into the blackness. Once inside, with my hands still above my head, my eyes began to adjust to the gloom of the building's interior. The first thing my watering eyes could see was the shapes of men outlined against the glare of sunlight where it filtered through the shuttered windows. The shapes were wearing the black berets and tunics of the armored corps, and all their eyes were on me, though no one said anything. I heard the stamp of jackboots on the stairs to my left and turned my head just enough to see the officer descending from the second story of the station.

"Anna!" he began. "When I saw you approaching our position, I thought I was hallucinating. You should be dead."

"You should know," I said. "You're the one that left me for the Russians." His smile was much too smug, so I felt that I had to take him down a peg. "You knew that I was half Jew. What you didn't count on is that I am half Russian also. After my visit with my old countrymen, I prevailed on them to let me go."

His smile didn't waver as I had hoped. Instead, he said, "Really? I had heard that they brought you home in a strait jacket."

His self-satisfied attitude infuriated me, so I lashed out. "That was because I am a crazy person. But at least I'm not crazy enough to get myself trapped with a handful of men in a hostile city with no way out.

His smile faltered some as he said, "Who said we have no way out? A relief force from Ploesti is on the way here now."

"*Was* on the way here," I corrected him. We stopped them at the river."

"You're lying," said Hans. But his voice carried no conviction in it, and I knew why.

"I saw a military radio antenna on the roof when I came in here. If you have a radio, you know that I am telling the truth.

You wouldn't be trying to lie to these 'old hares', would you?" I had deliberately used the German trooper's slang term for veterans of the eastern front in order to let them know that I was one of them.

I saw the faces of the men turn towards Hans as the last trace of his smile disappeared from his face. "It doesn't matter what you rabble do! Soon our army will retake Bucharest and all you traitors will be hanging from the light posts!"

I raised my voice so that I could be heard by all present. "Save me your superman rhetoric. Even your own high command has realized that you can no longer win this war. Why do you think they tried to assassinate 'Grofaz.'" Once again, I was trying to make myself seem closer to the troops by using the enlisted men's own derogatory acronym for Hitler. It had come from the Nazi party's ill-conceived attempt to promote Der Fuhrer as "The Greatest Military Leader of all Time".

While I saw a few stifled smiles amongst the men, I could also see that I had driven Hans, a faithful Nazi, to the breaking point. He clinched his right hand into a fist as if to hit me. When he hesitated, I took advantage of his indecision. I smiled slightly and stuck my chin out a little. "Go ahead," I said. "And then you can start on your men. They all know that I only tell the truth."

He began to draw his fist back, so I quickly added, "But first you had better check the basement."

"What do you mean?" he asked with a bewildered expression on his face. "It's a trick. I checked the basement when we first occupied this building. There is no way in except from this room."

"No way except this room and the storm drain that runs under this station," I said.

"I checked that too. No one could get in that way. It is full of water."

"Water and petrol. Right now, our men are dumping a whole lorry full of petrol into that sewer. In a few moments they will float a bomb down the drain and set this building aflame."

Actually, there was no lorry full of petrol in the whole city, but the Germans didn't know that. I was playing on every tanker's fear of fire when I had told Mr. Ceausescu to pour five litters of petrol into the drain. I hoped that it would be enough to create a basement full of ominous smelling fumes.

Colonel Roider dispatched a man to check the basement. While we waited for his report, I noticed a familiar face standing behind the colonel.

Looking past the Colonel's shoulder I said, "Lutz, my old friend. Are you still working for this pompous ass?"

Lutz didn't say anything, but he did smile just a little.

I think Colonel Roider was about to say something to me, but he was interrupted by the return of the trooper he had sent to the basement. He whispered into the colonel's ear too quietly for me to hear him, but the look of fear on his face told me that the fumes in the basement must have been quite satisfactory.

Hans said nothing about the basement. Instead, he changed the subject. "Why are you here, Anna?"

Raising my voice once again, saying, "Just like I said, I am here to get you and your men out of here without any bloodshed. I have talked the local commander into letting you leave under a flag of truce. You can take your weapons and ammunition with you. You are to follow the street due North until you get to the river. Once you cross the river you will be in German-controlled territory."

"You expect me to lead my men out of a good defensive position and into the street where your murderous traitors can shoot us down? You were right about one thing. You *are* a crazy person."

Loudly, I said, "If you stay here this building will be your funeral pyre. If you leave, I can guarantee your safety."

"How can you do that?" asked Hans.

"You will have a hostage to take with you...me."

Colonel Roiders' voice dripped sarcasm as he said, "And you do this to help out your old comrades? I am touched, Anna."

"You know that I have always tried to save lives, Hans. In this case, however, it is the lives of my own countrymen that I have in mind. If you stay here, they will wipe you out. But in doing so, they will pay a terrible price. We both know that. If you leave quietly everyone can come out of this situation a winner." I knew that even though Hans was a bigoted monster, he was also an excellent commander. In a way, he even had a warped sense of honor. That is why, when I had confessed my Jewish heritage to him, he had not turned me over to the Nazi Jew hunters. I had counted on that at the time, although I had not expected him to take personal revenge on me.

So now I awaited his decision. Many lives depended on whether he would do the practical thing and withdraw or the Nazi thing and fight to the death. I let out the breath that I hadn't known that I had been holding when he ordered his men to saddle up and get ready to move out. Within minutes I was once again holding my white flag high as I lead Hans and his men out of the station.

As arraigned, no one was in sight, although I knew that dozens of weapons were aimed at us as we emerged. I was acutely aware that the first shot, or even loud noise I heard, would be the last thing I would ever hear.

****

So here I was, with Colonel Roider holding me by one arm while his other hand, held the muzzle of his Luger pistol against the base of my skull. In this manor the colonel and I walked boldly up the center of the street while his troops rushed from cover to cover along the edge of the roadway.

In this uncomfortable manner we walked the 2 kilometers to the bridge over the river. It was the same bridge that we had defended the day before. The army troops had been advised of our coming and were nowhere in sight as we approached the first of the burned-out panzers.

"Your band of children did this?" asked Colonel Roider.

"The army helped," I said.

"But how could you..."

"Your tank killing school was very thorough, and I have a good memory."

"You'll pay for this," he said in a voice choked with rage.

"I'm sure that my soul will," I agreed.

When we reached the bridge, Hans sent his troops across ahead of us. That left only Hans, Lutz, and me standing on the bridge when Hans spun me around to face him.

"You know that I cannot send you back to your murderous friends, don't you," he said.

"I know. I knew that when I came to you," I answered.

"Then why didn't you send someone else?"

"Because someone else would not have been able to convince you to leave. I told you that I wanted to save lives, and I did. But I had one life in particular in mind. My little brother would have been one of those boys that attacked you. He would have been carrying a rifle taller than he was, and he would have died so very bravely. I couldn't allow that, could I?

Besides, if there is anything I have learned from this war, it is that dying is far from the worst that can happen."

As he raised the Luger to point at my forehead, he said, "Because you have served the cause so well in the past, I will grant you a quick death. You have---"

"Are you going to shoot me, or talk me to death," I interrupted. I hadn't really meant to be flippant. I was just tired of waiting for it to happen.

The Colonel's eyes opened wide, and I thought that I had shocked him for a second. Then his eyes seemed to lose focus and his mouth formed a silent "Oh." A hand reached from behind him and swept his gun hand away from me. My eyes traveled down the front of his uniform, and I was surprised to see the hilt of a bayonet protruding from his sternum. As my mind automatically noted the precise angle of the killing stroke and appreciated the precision of the thrust through the heart while avoiding the ribcage, my eyes traveled to the man behind him.

Lutz lowered the body gently to the pavement and removed his bayonet. I must have had an accusing look on my face when he looked up at me. He said, "I had to do it. He was going to kill you. You, who have never done anything but help us. We even called you our little angel of mercy behind your back. You understand that I had to do it, don't you?"

"Yes," I said. He was right, of course. But somehow, I felt... cheated. What a foolish reaction! I had a brother to look after, and a whole country to help heal.

"Lutz?" I said.

"Yes?"

"Didn't you once tell me that you were from Bavaria?"

"Yes, I am."

"I think that you should try to go home. Germany is finished, and there is no reason for good men like you to give your lives for nothing."

"That is a good idea," he said with a smile. "I'll have to think about that."

"Good-by Lutz," I said. Then I turned and walked back down the street, past the burning panzers where the smoke filled my nose and made my eyes water.

****

So, now I sit here on the highest balcony of the grandest hotel in all of Bucharest. It is badly shot up and deserted except for us "freedom fighters," but from the comfortable lounge chair we have dragged outside, I can see all the way to the east side of the city. That is where the squat green shapes of the Russian tanks can be seen nosing cautiously down the boulevards. They are meeting with no resistance, for we are now an ally, and we welcome them as friends and equals.

Will our new allies welcome us with open arms? As I have said before, I am a fool. But I am not *that* big a fool. We have invaded their country and killed their people, and no matter what justification we felt we had in the beginning, the Russians are not going to forgive or forget for a long time.

Am I worried for myself? Not much. There isn't much left for them to take from me except Emil, and he is a leader in the Young Communists. He should do well.

I am sad for my country though. As your very astute western politician Winston Churchill has said, it is as if an iron curtain is descending over all of Eastern Europe. It's just a shame that my country is going to be on the wrong side of that curtain. I don't think that you will be hearing from us for a while. But don't forget us. We'll still be here. We'll be doing what we have always done when we fell under the heel of the invader's boot.

We will learn what they have to teach us. We'll take the best and make it a part of us and let the rest pass from us as surely as the invader himself will someday pass... they always do. And when this iron curtain rises, we will be ready to take our rightful place on the world's stage once again.

Let's hope that by then we will have learned our lesson about pride, greed, and "Great Leaders."